CAT LOVE

UNDERSTANDING THE NEEDS AND NATURE OF YOUR CAT

BY PAM JOHNSON

A Storey Publishing Book

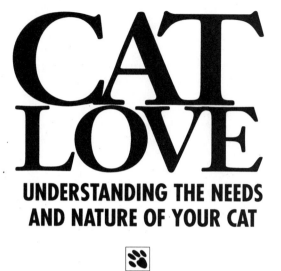
STOREY

Storey Communications, Inc.
Schoolhouse Road
Pownal, VT 05261

PLEASE NOTE

It is our intention to give you sufficient knowledge and instruction to maintain your cat's health and general well-being. The author and Storey Communications, though, cannot be responsible for any illness or reaction that may result from the consumption of any food or food supplement that may result from the advice in this book, or from employing the cat health care advice, contained herein. If there are any indications or symptoms that give you concern, seek veterinary advice promptly.

Cover design by Leslie Noyes
Front cover photograph by Grace Davies
Designed and produced by Leslie Noyes
Edited by Constance L. Oxley
Typesetting by Arcata Graphics
Printed in the United States by Crest Litho

Second printing, August 1990

Library of Congress Catalog Card Number: 89-46016

International Standard Book Number: 0-88266-594-4 (pb)

Library of Congress Cataloging-in-Publication Data

Johnson, Pam, 1954-
    Cat love : Understanding the needs and nature of your cat / by Pamela Johnson.
    p.   cm.
    "A Storey Publishing book."
    ISBN 0-88266-594-4 (pbk.)
    1. Cats.   2. Cats—Health   I. Title.
SF447.J633   1990
636.8—dc20

                                                          89-46016
                                                          CIP

For Lucy, the cat who trained me
and for Joe

CONTENTS

PREFACE

As a child, I grew up with dogs as pets — loving, devoted, affectionate, attentive dogs. My best friend owned a cat — a moody, stubborn, unaffectionate, aloof, boring cat. Every time I went up to the cat with nothing but the best intentions I was either ignored, given a "Don't bother me" look, or issued a warning smack by an unfriendly paw. Boy, did I grow to dislike that cat! And, being the uninformed eight-year-old that I was, I thought ALL cats were like that. I would go home, be greeted by my wonderful pup, and thank my lucky stars that my parents chose to give me a dog instead of a cat!

Who would've thought (certainly not me) that years later, while walking down the street one winter afternoon, I would fall for two little kittens in need of a home. I remember thinking "What have I gotten myself into?" Afterall, kittens are CATS!! Oh, but they were so adorable. Well, home they came and much to my surprise, those two kittens became sweet, playful, affectionate, devoted CATS. CATS!

Because my only experience had been with dogs, I treated my cats the same way — with lots of love, affection, and proper training. For instance, I had heard that cats won't greet you at the door the way dogs will. Nonsense! I wanted my cats to do it, so whenever I walked in the door I called to them and made a big fuss over them. It didn't take long for them to start running for the door before I even got the key in the lock.

I learned that it's the *owner* who makes the difference in a cat's personality. Now that I think back on my childhood friend's behavior, I remember she never did pay much attention to her cat other than to feed him and change his litter. Animals need more than the "basics" of food and shelter. They need a commitment of love and caring. The affection I give my cats comes back to me a hundred times over.

Whenever cat-owning friends would come to visit, they'd remark on how friendly and affectionate my cats seemed. I also got compliments on their glossy coats and apparent good health. My friends wanted to know how I did it because their cats would hide when company came, were finicky eaters, or had dull, dry hair that shed like crazy. I told them that because I was so obsessed with the health and welfare of my cats I read everything I could get my hands on, researched cat food, pestered veterinarians, and did a lot of trial and error. I kept all kinds of records, noting what worked and what didn't.

When my friends asked for my help with their cats, I jumped at the opportunity to share what I'd learned. I began by helping them change their cats' diets over to a higher quality food, and lecturing them — sometimes this was greeted with less enthusiasm than I would've liked, but that didn't stop me — on the importance of regular grooming. As I watched my friends having success with their cats in terms of behavior, nutrition, and grooming, I decided it was maybe time to make a change and go into business doing what I loved most. I now spend my days as a groomer and consultant, surrounded by these beautiful, intelligent, mysterious, and ever-fascinating creatures and consider it a high compliment when people call me "The Cat Lady."

I've come across so many well-meaning but misinformed owners who are operating under inaccurate beliefs about cat care. After years of successful results with nutrition, grooming, and behavior, I finally sat down and wrote this book in order to share what I've learned with as many cat owners as possible. I've tried to make this book clear, easy to read, and informative. I hope what stands out most though is the deep love and respect I have for these wonderful animals.

As you undoubtedly know, but I must stress anyway — this or any book can never take the place of the personal attention of your veterinarian. My hope is that you'll use the information in this book to help you become alert to potential dangers, solve problems, try new ideas, and make your cat's life a happy and very healthy one.

Pam Johnson

1

BEFORE YOU GET A CAT

IS A CAT RIGHT FOR YOU?

The sight of a cute little ball of fur is irresistible to just about everybody, but the decision to get a cat should never be made impulsively. Owning a pet requires a commitment on your part to provide for all of your cat's needs. Here are some issues to consider before you go out looking for a cat:

■ Cats don't have to be walked like dogs, but you will have to keep a litter box in your home and change the litter regularly. Cats are very clean pets, but if you have a problem with scooping out fecal waste each day or cleaning the litter box (believe me, it's easy), then you might not be comfortable with a cat.

■ Owning a cat (or any pet) requires an ongoing financial investment. In addition to the initial costs of food bowls, a litter box, scratching post, carrying case, and toys, there are the ongoing costs of food, veterinary examinations, yearly vaccinations, and any surgery or medications your cat may need. Think about if you can really afford to own a pet.

■ Look around and make sure you have enough room to keep a cat. Although they certainly require less space than a German Shepherd, make sure the cat would have enough room to play and get exercise without being cramped. Don't forget that you will have to find a spot to set the litter box.

■ Do you have enough time to devote to a cat? If you have a job that keeps you away from home for so long each day, then a cat is going to live a very lonely life. Sure, you don't have to worry about rushing home to walk him the way you would with a dog, but what about his emotional needs? Pets get lonely just like people. If your job takes you out of town often and you would have to constantly put the cat in a kennel or have a neighbor come over to care for him, then you should maybe reconsider and not get a cat until your life is more settled.

■ If you want to give a kitten to someone as a gift, make sure they know about it in advance and *really want* to take on that responsibility. Giving pets to children to "teach them responsibility" is fine as long as the children are old enough to handle the job and you have taught them in advance what is expected. You should constantly monitor the situation because children can't be expected to know when a pet is sick or in need of medical care.

WHAT KIND OF CAT SHOULD YOU GET?

Purebred? Mixed breed? Do you want a longhair cat or a shorthair? Cats come in all shapes and sizes. There's the sleek Siamese or maybe you'd prefer the Persian with his cobby body. Some cats are quiet and reserved and some breeds are reknowned athletes. Do you like an alert, clever companion, or do you love a sweet affectionate cat whose favorite thing to do is sleep? Before running out to bring home a cat, learn more about all the different personalities. Start by reading chapter 16, "Breeds in Brief," to give you a general idea of how many choices there are.

If you are looking for a cat to love, care for, and provide you with companionship, then consider a mixed breed. Your local ASPCA and animal shelter are filled with cats in need of homes. You could provide a loving home for a cat who really needs one and who might otherwise end up being euthanized. Purebred cats sold by breeders and pet stores will almost always get a good home—the animal shelter kitten may not.

If you want a purebred cat, then I suggest you do some research before going out to buy. First of all, each breed has different physical characteristics and different temperaments. Think about the kind of characteristics you like in a cat. Do you love the longhaired Persians? If so, be prepared for the fact that a longhaired cat requires *daily* grooming to prevent tangles and mats. This daily grooming will have to be done for *the rest of the cat's life*. Do you have the time to make this kind of commitment? Another factor to take into consideration is what kind of temperament would be best for children. Some breeds are good with young children and some are really "one person" cats. There are also breeds who have sensitive physical features that might get injured more easily around children. The tail of the Japanese Bobtail is *very* sensitive and once injured, the cat will hesitate being touched again.

Don't get me wrong, I love purebred cats, but unless you are either planning to breed or show him, or unless you really love certain specific features, don't overlook the mixed breeds. In most cases, a mixed breed can be adopted for free or for a nominal amount of money. Purebreds are much more expensive. Now, while it's true that with a mixed breed you don't really know what you're getting healthwise—they can be tougher than some purebreds. Certain purebreds are more susceptible to some disorders. For instance, Persians are more inclined to respiratory problems.

One way to get an overall view of the many different breeds in person is to find out when a cat show is being held in your area and spend the day there, looking at all the cats and talking with their owners. The Cat Fanciers' Association can also supply you with specific breed and show standards, should you find a breed that appeals to you. See Appendix for address.

SHOULD YOU GET A KITTEN OR A CAT?
MALE OR FEMALE?

Take some time to figure out your needs. First, unless you're planning on breeding your cat, it doesn't matter whether you choose a male or female. Once neutered or spayed, both are equally affectionate and wonderful. If you're planning to breed your cat (something I don't recommend—you should probably leave that to the professional breeders), then you'll have to decide what you'd rather put up with: an unspayed female who will be restless, noisy, and downright annoying while in heat, or an unneutered male who will spray a very offensive-smelling urine as a territorial marker.

Now, the other question is, should you get a kitten or a cat? With an adult cat, the personality and habits have already been established. This is good because you can see exactly what to expect as far as those qualities go. An adult cat will also require less supervision. The only negatives to getting an adult cat are that you will not have had an opportunity to affect his personality while growing up. In other words, if he grew up in a home without affection, he may be less inclined to be affectionate to you; and if he has any bad habits, they will be harder to break. With a kitten, you get more of an opportunity to have an impact on his personality and temperament, *but* you also have to put up with an erratic schedule. Kittens require several meals a day, so you have to be sure you can provide the time and attention needed.

I have a friend whose home is decorated with many valuable collectibles and when she told me she wanted a kitten, I advised her to reconsider and think about getting an adult cat instead—since a kitten's playfulness can be accompanied by recklessness. She picked a beautiful four-year-old cat from the local humane shelter and they've been living happily among her valuables ever since.

If you already have a cat and want a second one, then I recommend getting a kitten because it may be less threatening to your current cat.

WHERE TO GET YOUR CAT

Before we get into that, I recommend that you select a veterinarian *before* selecting a cat. You don't want to go running around looking for the right vet after you already have the cat—it will be much smoother if he or she has been chosen in advance. In many cases, the vet can help you locate the cat you want. Read chapter 2 on how to select the right veterinarian.

Now, where should you go for a cat? If you're looking for a purebred, then I suggest you do your homework and find a reputable breeder. If you're going to spend the money for a purebred cat you will be much safer with a breeder. Not all breeders are reputable, so you will have to do good research. There are a few who inbreed cats which can result in lots of health problems. I suggest you ask your vet for recommendations and also friends who are owners of the particular breed you like. Publications such as *Cat Fancy* and *Cats* have listings of breeders in the back of their magazines. See Appendix for addresses. I suggest you first visit a few breeders to see the condition of the premises and how the cats are raised. Are they handled with love or are they kept locked up and secluded? Do you get a good feeling about a particular breeder or do you sense a high-pressure sales job?

If you want a mixed breed cat, then visit your local ASPCA or animal shelter. I guarantee you'll find a furry bundle of love waiting for you there.

And of course, because there are so many homeless cats wandering the streets, there's always the chance you may rescue your future companion from the side of the road, a parking lot, or even right on your front porch. I adopted Ethel, one of my cats, from the street years ago and we've been the best of friends ever since. Be sure the foundling cat does not have an owner before you keep him. Check local newspapers and public bulletin boards for lost cats.

CHOOSING A HEALTHY CAT

Of course you don't *have* to choose a healthy animal. You may prefer a weak or sick cat and try to nurse him back to health. If this is the case (I admire you), just make sure you're ready for the time and expense that will be involved—not to mention the heartbreak should your efforts be unsuccessful.

Whether you get your cat from a breeder, pet shop, or animal shelter, check him over thoroughly. Note the following:

1. Look in the cat's eyes. They should be clear and bright with no discharges.

2. The inside of the ears should be clean with no sign of infection or ear mites. Ear mites look like gritty black dirt in the ear.

3. Open the mouth and make sure the tongue and gums are nice and pink.

4. There should be no discharge from the nose and the cat shouldn't be sneezing.

5. The coat should be shiny—make sure there are no bald patches.

6. Check the skin for any sores or irritation.

7. The abdomen shouldn't be distended, which can indicate internal parasites.

8. Never adopt a kitten under eight weeks old.

If you are picking a kitten from a litter, observe the different personalities. Does one kitten constantly try to hide? Is one more playful and outgoing than the others? Healthy kittens should be fearless and curious.

Finally, no matter where you get your cat, the first thing you will need to do is have him examined and vaccinated by a vet (see chapter 2).

INDOOR OR OUTDOOR CAT?

Ah, yes, I do have very definite feelings on this subject. Cats should not be allowed to roam freely outdoors. Here are my reasons:

■ The risk of being hit by a car

■ The risk of getting into a fight with another animal

■ The risk of falling from a tree

■ The risk of accidental poisoning from chemicals, pesticides, rotting contents in outdoor trash cans, or *intentional* poisoning by a human

- The risk of indiscriminate mating

- The risk of being stolen

- The risk of getting lost

- The risk of being exposed to infectious disease

- The risk of internal or external parasite infestation

- The risk of aggravating allergies

The life of an outdoor cat can be shorter and more violent than the cat who is kept indoors. If you allow your unneutered male outside, he will undoubtedly end up in a fight with other males. When two males fight for the right to mate with a female, the battle can be very violent and can lead to serious injury or death. For an unspayed female, repeated matings can leave her weak, and in the case of violent matings, she can easily get injured. For more information on the importance of spaying and neutering your pet, see chapter 11.

If you want your cat to enjoy the outdoors, please do it under controlled circumstances. For instance, I know several people who have built enclosed "cat runs" for their pet on their patios or in their backyards. I advise that your cat never be left outside in these "cat runs" unsupervised, though. Some of the enclosures I've seen have been very elaborate with small cat trees inside for climbing and houses for hiding in. Make sure that you provide shade for your cat when he's in the enclosure on a hot day, and always have a water bowl nearby.

I also know people who walk their cats on a leash. If you do this, I advise you to get a harness instead of a collar so he can't slip out and get away. You will also have to give your cat time to adjust to being walked on a leash—this should be done indoors. Let him get used to wearing the harness a little at a time each day. Once he's accepted that, then try attaching the leash. Don't pull him or force him to go where you want— make this a positive experience for your cat. When you feel your cat is ready, then you can try walking him outside. *Only* do this if you have an enclosed backyard because a cat who isn't used to the outdoors may *panic* at the new surroundings. And, of course, realize that while outside, your cat is subject to fleas or ticks hopping on for a meal.

2

SELECTING A VETERINARIAN

SELECTING THE RIGHT VET

One of the very first things you'll need to do when you get a new pet is take her to the veterinarian for a physical examination and vaccinations. From that day on, you and your vet will work together to ensure the best possible health for your cat.

How do you go about finding a vet? I've found the best way is to ask friends and neighbors who own cats. Now I don't mean for you to accept the first recommendation you get—you should ask everybody you know in your area who owns a cat. Of course, eliminate people you feel do not take very good care of their cats.

Don't just ask what vet they go to, be *specific* with your questions. Ask how long they've been going to their vet. If they've recently switched vets, ask why. Find out what kind of medical treatment their cat has needed, if the cat has ever had surgery, or if she just gets her vaccinations and a checkup once a year. Keep notes on the recommended names until you find a vet you'd like to try. Be objective while listening to owners as they talk about their vet. If an owner raves about someone, find out *why*. Be careful when listening to owners who tell you that their cat died while under a particular vet's care. Don't disregard a possible vet unless you know the reason why the animal died. The animal may have had a fatal disease or was brought to the vet after the disease had progressed too far.

Other ways to find a veterinarian is to call your local veterinary medical association and they will provide you with some names. And, of course, you can also get names from the yellow pages. When you're collecting the names, something to consider is *location*. It's best to stick to a vet located close to your home in case emergency trips are needed.

There are some vets whose practices are limited to felines. If you think your cat may get very upset at seeing a big dog in the waiting room, then you might consider finding one of those vets.

When you've gotten a name (or names) that you find worth checking, you'll want to see the facilities. First call and inquire about services and fees. Ask about the equipment available and what arrangements are made should a cat need testing or treatment on any equipment the vet doesn't have. Inquire about office hours and find out if the vet has emergency hours. If not, the office should give you the name and location of the nearest animal hospital. If the closest hospital is too far from your home, make sure you choose a vet who does have emergency hours. If there *is* a hospital near you, know in advance exactly how to get there—don't wait for an emergency.

When you call to inquire about the vet's services, explain that you'd like to set up a time to come in and meet the vet and view the facilities. Don't be embarrassed by this request, it's perfectly acceptable and most vets are very willing to take a little time out of their schedule to meet you.

While touring the facilities, be aware of cleanliness and how well equipped it looks. Are the floors kept clean? Are the cages clean and in good condition? Are all messes cleaned up immediately? Notice if the sick animals are kept separate from the healthy ones. How does the equipment look? Does it seem well maintained?

During your visit, make sure you're able to meet the vet. If he or she is unwilling to take a minute to meet you (unless of course, something crucial has come up), then I suggest you start looking elsewhere. The veterinarian's staff should also be friendly, helpful, and knowledgeable.

YOUR CAT'S FIRST TRIP TO THE VET

When you take your cat for her first examination, bring any vaccination and health records from the place you bought or adopted her. Also bring a fresh stool sample with you so the vet can check for signs of internal parasites. Put the stool sample in a sealed container or plastic bag. One very important, but often neglected thing you should do is to prepare *in advance* any questions you might want to ask the vet about your new cat. Otherwise, you'll end up walking out of the office realizing you forgot to ask something.

On the first visit, the vet will do a physical examination and give the first series of vaccinations. During this first visit, watch how the vet handles your cat and make sure you're satisfied. Is the cat treated gently, and does it come across that the vet likes and respects animals?

THE VETERINARY EXAMINATION

Even if your cat looks perfectly healthy, she should get an examination, along with a series of vaccinations when you first get her. Your cat will also need an examination and booster vaccinations annually. So even if your cat never shows a single sign of illness, make sure she gets examined yearly. Whenever you take your cat for her yearly exam, always bring a fresh stool sample so the vet can do a parasite check.

During the examination the vet will check your cat's eyes and examine her teeth for tartar accumulation. The tongue and gums are examined to be sure they're healthy looking and pink in color, with no sign of inflammation. The ears are checked, looking for signs of redness, infection, or ear mites. Your vet will check the lymph nodes by feeling for any enlargements. The cat's rectal temperature is taken and a stethoscope is used to listen to the heart and lungs. The abdomen is palpated, feeling the bladder, spleen, intestines, liver, and kidneys for any changes in size or abnormalities. Your vet will look closely to check the condition of the skin and coat. The cat should also be weighed during each visit.

Should your vet come across anything that requires closer scrutiny, then further testing, such as blood tests, X-ray, urinalysis, electrocardiogram, monitoring, or medication will be advised. Make sure you understand what's involved and don't hesitate to ask questions.

VACCINATIONS

The first milk produced by the mother cat (called the colostrum) provides antibodies for newborn kittens. They must receive the colostrum within the first twenty-four hours of life. If the mother has been properly vaccinated, then the protection is passed to the kittens. The immunities provided protect the kittens until weaning time. After they're weaned though, the kittens will need their own vaccinations.

A kitten gets her first set of vaccinations when she's six to eight weeks old. The second set is given at twelve weeks and the third series at sixteen weeks. Booster vaccinations are due yearly. Based upon the requirements in your area, the types and schedule of vaccinations may vary.

Vaccinations are usually combined to minimize injections. The immunization for feline rhinotracheitis, calicivirus, and feline distemper are combined into one vaccine called "three-in-one" (for more on these diseases see chapter 13).

The vaccine for the feline leukemia virus is given in three injections several weeks apart, followed by a yearly booster. The cat should be tested for the disease first through a blood test because the vaccine won't help an already infected cat and she could then spread the disease to other cats. The feline leukemia vaccine is still controversial among some vets. There are those who doubt its effectiveness and safety. Talk to your vet about it. I feel it's an important vaccination that your cat should have, but if you do decide against it, you *must* do everything you can to keep your cat in optimal health to reduce her chances of getting this deadly disease, and never allow her outdoors.

The rabies vaccination is one that cats in certain areas are required to get. If you live in an area that does not require this vaccination but you allow your cat outdoors, ask your vet's advice about vaccinating against rabies anyway. The intramuscular vaccine is given into the leg which may cause your cat to limp temporarily.

In addition to the annual revaccination schedule, cats may need boosters before air travel, pregnancy, or entering a cat show. Consult your vet.

Some vaccinations can have temporary side effects. Most vets make you aware of any potential side effects, but if nothing is said, then don't be afraid to ask. The most common side effects are a temporary loss of appetite or sleeping more than usual for the remainder of the day. If your cat has *serious* side effects from a vaccination, then call your vet.

For further information on the diseases mentioned in this section refer to chapter 13.

YOUR CAT'S MEDICAL HISTORY

Keep your own record of vaccinations (dates and types of vaccinations), medical exams, illnesses, and medications prescribed. Make a note of when the next vaccination or exam is due. Vets usually send reminder cards, but by keeping your own records, it provides extra insurance in case the card doesn't get sent or is lost in the mail.

Many vets give out medical record booklets for their patients. This booklet provides space for immunization schedules, important exams, weight and growth charts, and medical history. This is an easy way for you to organize the medical information about your cat. This information is important to have with you should your cat need medical attention while you are traveling with her. Keep the book in a safe, convenient place and bring it along if you need to take your cat to an emergency hospital. If your veterinarian doesn't supply you with a medical record booklet, I think it's a good idea to suggest that he or she provide this service.

Always request a copy of your cat's medical file from your vet when you move or decide to change veterinarians. This is vital information for your new vet to have.

HEALTH INSURANCE

Medical expenses for your pet can be very expensive. There are medical insurance programs for pets, but they aren't available everywhere. If you're interested in finding out about available insurance in your state, ask you vet or call your local veterinary medical association. Be aware though, the coverage they provide is *limited* so make sure you read **all** the information very carefully.

3

DID YOU KNOW?

A FEW FELINE FACTS

■ Normal temperature ranges from 101.5°F.-102.5°F.

■ The heart averages around 120 beats per minute.

■ Respiratory rate averages 26 breaths per minute.

■ There are two feline blood types—A and B.

HOW CATS AGE

Cat's Age	Comparable Human Age
6 months	10 years
8 months	13 years
1 year	15 years
2 years	24 years
4 years	32 years
6 years	40 years
8 years	48 years
10 years	56 years
12 years	64 years
14 years	72 years
16 years	80 years
18 years	88 years
20 years	96 years
21 years	100 years

Cats are mammals belonging to the Carnivora order, which means "flesh-eating." They walk on the ball of their foot, with only the toes touching the ground—as opposed to other mammals who walk on the entire sole of their foot. Walking on the toes enables the cat to have more speed because there's less friction.

The flexible spine of the cat allows him to be both fast and agile, but it's the position of the shoulder blades on the sides of the chest that really provide speed. As fast as cats are, though, they are built for only short runs. A cat can outrun a dog but not over a long distance due to his small-size chest cavity. The heart and lungs don't have the capacity for distance.

You've heard the saying that cats always land on their feet? The truth behind this is that they do have an ability during a fall to right their bodies while in the air so they'll land on their feet. This doesn't mean that a cat can't get hurt though! A fall from a window or tree can be miscalculated by the cat and he may not have enough time to right himself, resulting in serious injury.

THE HUNTER

If you've ever watched a cat stalk prey, you know how fascinating this little hunter is. When a cat spots prey (whether it is a mouse, a toy, or even a bug), he slinks along the ground until he finds a spot for cover. He then freezes to observe the prey, waiting for the right time to ambush. I've seen my cats freeze like statues, watching a bug walk across the floor. Sometimes the only indication that a cat is excited while in this position is the slight twitching at the end of his tail. Patience is truly this hunter's best weapon.

SCENT GLANDS

Cats produce chemicals called "pheromones" which convey information about them to other animals. Scent glands are located on the forehead, lips, and around the anus. In your house, you may notice your cat rubbing his head on a piece of furniture or even on your leg. What he's doing is saying "This is MINE!"

The pheromones in urine are unfortunately not so subtle when a cat sprays to mark his territory. Unneutered males are very territorial and tend to establish their ownership by spraying this strong-smelling urine. This is one very good reason to have your cat neutered before the habit begins (see chapter 11). A cat's posture for spraying is different than the normal squat for urination. To spray, the cat turns his hindquarters toward the "target," raises his tail (which usually twitches), and sprays a stream of urine higher than he usually would when urinating. This urine is sprayed high so it's at a convenient level for another cat's nose to catch the scent. But, believe me, your nose doesn't have to be anywhere near the target to notice the smell!

For cats in the wild, the urine marking tells another cat who claimed this property and how long ago it was marked. The pheromones fade after awhile, so if the scent is old, a new cat may spray over it to establish that this is now his territory. If you allow your cat outdoors, you may notice that he goes around checking the area to make sure all his territorial claims are intact and haven't been violated. There are also scent glands around the cat's anus so he can mark his feces with his own scent. Scent marking also serves another purpose—it tells a cat in the wild if he's been in a particular place before and if so, how long ago.

Cats also use scents as a way of recognizing and communicating with each other. When two cats who are friends come across each other, they greet one another with a round of nose-to-nose and anal sniffing. In fact, your cat behaves this way with you by presenting his head for nose-to-nose sniffing, then maybe arching his back and turning his hindquarters toward you. Don't be insulted because he's just doing what is considered polite in cat circles.

THE EYES

In relation to the size of the head, a cat's eyes are large. The iris (the colored part) is also large in comparison to the sclera (the white part). On a cat you usually don't even see the sclera.

Set forward on the head, the cat's eyes provide binocular vision, which means both eyes see an image at the same time, as opposed to a rabbit, whose eyes are on either side of the head. Binocular vision allows the cat to have excellent depth perception.

Light enters the eye and passes through the pupil (the dark center). The lens focuses the light onto the retina, which is in the back of the eye. In bright light, the muscles in the iris contract, squeezing the pupil into a slit. These muscles are in a figure eight which is why the pupil becomes a vertical slit as opposed to the way our pupils contract to tiny dots. In low light, the muscles pull the pupil open to allow all available light to enter the eye. Excitement, anger, and certain drugs can also cause a cat's pupils to dilate. With certain drugs, the pupils can remain dilated regardless of the amount of light, so if your cat is on one of those drugs, make sure you protect him from bright light.

Many people think cats can see in total darkness, which is not true. They can't see in *total* darkness, but they can see in light so dim that we would consider it totally dark.

To make further use of all available light, cats have mirror-like cells in the back of the retina. This section of the eye is called the tapetum lucidum. These cells act like a mirror, reflecting light back into the eye that wasn't absorbed the first time. This allows the cat to use and amplify every bit of light. This is what gives that shining look to the eyes in photographs or oncoming headlights. This shining only occurs if sudden bright light hits the eyes when the cat is in the dark with dilated pupils. The tapetum lucidum is present in most nocturnal animals.

Cats have better peripheral vision than we do. When you see your cat "staring into space," what he's actually doing is using his total field vision. When he spots something move, he will then quickly focus in on it.

Cats have a third eyelid known as the nictitating membrane. This membrane is located at the inner corner of the eye and unfolds upward when needed. Usually, only a small portion of the nictitating membrane can be seen. You may be able to catch a glimpse of it when your cat is asleep if his eyes aren't fully closed. The purpose of this membrane is to provide extra protection for the eye. When a cat walks through a bushy area, he will keep the third eyelid unfolded to prevent scratches.

As sharp as an adult cat's eyes are, as a kitten he starts out with eyes that don't focus well and are light sensitive and very delicate. Kittens are born blind and with blue eyes. Eye color changes or deepens as a kitten gets older. It takes about three months for a kitten's eyes to be as good as those of an adult cat.

THE EARS

Because cats are also nocturnal hunters, hearing is as important as sight. The upper range of a cat's hearing is higher than a human's.

The cone-shaped flap of the ear is called the pinna. Its job is to collect the sound waves and funnel them down to the inner ear. Cats have many muscles in their pinnae which enable them to rotate their ears in a wide arc to locate sound waves. The comparable part on our ears is shaped like a cup handle and doesn't move. A cat can point one or both ears in the direction of the sound. There are fine hairs just inside the tip of each pinna and also a tuft of hair at the base to keep dust and particles out of the ear (cats still need your assistance with ear cleaning, though).

The position of your cat's ears can also give you an indication of what he's feeling. For instance, flattened ears indicate irritation and twitching ears usually mean anxiety. Ears pointed forward and slightly outward are the ears of a happy cat. When hunting, the ears are pricked forward. When a cat is about to do battle, the ears are flattened to prevent damage.

THE MOUTH

A cat has thirty teeth (twelve less than a dog). Kittens get temporary (or milk) teeth when they're about four weeks old. The permanent teeth start coming through at about five months and are usually all in by eight months. There are six incisors set in the center of both the upper and lower jaws. These teeth are used for pulling prey. Next in line come a pair of canine teeth. These teeth are shaped like daggers and are used to give that fatal bite to the prey's spinal cord. The premolars and molars are next—four on each side in the upper jaw and three on each side in the lower jaw. These teeth are used like scissors to cut and slice meat into bite-size chunks.

The cat's tongue is thin around the edges and thicker toward the center. By curling the edges inward, the cat creates a spoon for himself to drink liquids. The tongue is also covered with tiny backward-facing barbs—that's why his tongue feels "scratchy" when he licks you. These barbs are used to remove meat from bones and also loose hairs from the coat.

There is a special scent organ located in the roof of the mouth called the Jacobson's organ (or vomeronasal organ). This organ has ducts that lead into both the mouth and nose. Several other animals have this Jacobson's organ and they use it to "analyze" scents. As the cat inhales, he opens his mouth slightly, curls his upper lip, and picks up the odor onto his tongue—sometimes touching the tongue to the odorous object. The tongue then reaches up to the roof of the mouth with the collected odor and passes it to the Jacobson's organ. You'll see the cat raise his head with his mouth partially open and his lips pulled back, looking like he's grimacing at a bad odor. This "grimace" is called a flehmen reaction and is done more often by males reacting to urine or pheromones of females in heat, but can happen with other scents, too.

Cats also have scent glands on their lips which they use to mark objects as their territory. You'll see this when your cat is rubbing the sides of his mouth on a piece of furniture.

THE WHISKERS OR VIBRISSAE

The stiff hairs that stick out beyond the body are called the vibrissae, but are more commonly known as "whiskers" and are used as a sensory device. If an object makes an ever-so-slight contact with the tip of a whisker, a signal is sent to the sensitive nerve endings at the root. The message is then relayed to the brain. Cats have vibrissae on each side of the upper lip, above the eyes, far back on the cheeks, and on the back of the forelegs. The vibrissae on the upper lip are in four rows. The upper vibrissae extend beyond the head, and the cat can spread them to determine if an opening will accommodate his body. The vibrissae also help guide a cat as he walks in total darkness because they can detect the slightest changes in air currents around objects.

THE CLAWS

Cats have five toes on the forefeet and four on the hind feet. Running down each toe are three bones. The claw is attached to the middle bone by way of a tendon and a ligament. When the claws are in the retracted position, the bones have a humped look to them. When the claws are extended, the ligaments at the base of the claws stretch back, which puts the bones in a horizontal position. This unsheaths the claws.

The claws on the forelegs are sharper than the hind claws. Cats keep their claws in peak condition by removing the outer sheath when they scratch on a tree or a scratching post. The removal of the sheath allows the new growth to come through. To learn more about how important claws are to a cat, see chapter 6. In addition to conditioning their claws, cats use scratching as a visual way of marking territory. The sweat glands in the pads of the paws also leave a scent.

The hind claws of the cat are kept in shape by the cat chewing off the outer sheaths. These claws are not as sharp as the front ones because they get worn down from walking. The hind claws are also thicker and not as flexible. Cats don't use these claws to catch prey, but they are used when fighting a larger animal. By rolling on his back, the cat can then use the claws on all four feet to defend himself.

Because all of the claws point in one direction and the toes and muscles aren't as flexible as other natural tree climbers (like squirrels), cats have a heck of a time going *down* trees. Going up is a breeze, but many cats realize too late that the trip down is much harder. A cat will either sit and cry in the tree, waiting for rescue, or he'll muster up the courage and slowly creep down.

THE TAIL

The tail is a continuation of the cat's spine. It contributes somewhat to balance, but from what I see, it's more of a mood indicator. Unlike dogs, cats don't wag their tails when they're happy, but they will do other things. For instance, a tail held upright when standing or walking indicates confidence and happiness. When your cat flicks his upright tail at you, it's meant as a greeting. A tail that whips back and forth or thumps the ground means irritation or anger. When a cat is resting, an occasional twitching or sweeping motion of the tail is his way of saying he's relaxed but still alert. A frightened cat will puff out the hairs on his tail so it looks more than twice its size.

THE SKIN

A cat certainly seems to have more skin than he needs. The looseness of it helps him to escape from an attacker's grasp. The skin is also very sensitive, which is why you must use caution when it comes to flea preparations, shampoos, conditioners, etc.

THE VOICE

I've heard different theories on how cats purr. Here's the one most experts agree on: The purr is produced by the "false" vocal cords which are two folds located in the larynx, behind the actual vocal cords. If you listen carefully, you'll notice subtle differences in your cat's purr. For instance, when he's content his purr is loud and rough, but as he gets sleepy the purr gets softer and smoother. There's also the purr of anticipation, the kind you may hear from your cat as he watches you preparing his dinner. Some cats also purr when in trouble—maybe to calm an attacker, when the cat is weak or sick and unable to defend himself.

Your cat can also make a variety of sounds to be used for very specific purposes. One of these sounds is a kind of murmur which I call "the greeting." This is the sound your cat makes when you walk in the door from work or when he jumps on your lap and asks for affection.

Then there's "the call." This is the sound your cat makes when he wants something that he knows is due him. For example, he may be saying "You're late with my dinner!" This call can range from a worried plea ("Please hurry") to an all-out demand ("Get dinner now!"). Then there's the angry call—you might be very familiar with this call whenever you try to administer medicine.

When a cat is suddenly startled, he may make an involuntary short spitting sound. This is different from the deliberate sound issued as a warning. The warning spit is usually accompanied by flattened ears and a not so friendly facial expression.

A very unforgettable sound is "the mating call." The male emits a shrill wail or howl. If you've ever heard that sound of a male cat calling to a female, you know what I'm talking about.

4

HOME SAFE HOME

YOUR CAT'S NEW HOME

To own a cat you'll need to start out with certain basic supplies, such as a litter box (chapter 5), scratching post (chapter 6), food and food bowls (chapter 7), grooming supplies (chapter 9). Buying toys for your cat shouldn't be taken lightly either and the ones that are safe, as well as ones to watch out for, are discussed in chapter 8, along with suggestions on how you can use these toys to interact with your cat.

The only other equipment you may want to buy at this time may be a bed. You can buy any kind, ranging from an inexpensive one to a top-of-the-line model. Your cat will be just as happy though, if you lay a box on its side, lined with a towel. As for the location of the bed, you can try putting it on the floor, but you'll probably have more success if you elevate it. Cats feel more secure when they're up off the floor. My cat, Albert, rejected his bed until I put it on top of my filing cabinet. Floors can also be drafty, so placement of the bed is important.

THE FIRST NIGHT

When you first bring your kitten home, as tempting as it might be to let her run around the house, it's best to confine her. Have one room set up with the litter box, bed, scratching post, toys, food, and water. This is just so she can become accustomed to the new surroundings and to make sure she's trained to the litter box (if you train her, see chapter 5). Let the kitten hide if she wants—don't force her to come out and be sociable. Once she's gotten comfortable, she'll be out investigating the area. With a kitten, be prepared for the fact that she won't sleep through the night. You'll just be slipping off into dreamland and suddenly you'll hear her up to something.

CREATING A SAFE ENVIRONMENT

To the new kitten, your nice cozy home, decorated with lots of interesting things, is actually a dangerous jungle. Look at your home through the eyes of a small, inquisitive kitten, and you'll see some incredibly "innocent-looking" dangers.

SOME THINGS YOU WOULDN'T THINK OF AS DANGEROUS. Cats are attracted to shiny things, so that a pin or needle left on the table or sitting in an open sewing box is very tempting. Things like thumbtacks, rubber bands, buttons, pills, earrings, and other small items can easily get swallowed by your kitten. Keep all items such as these safely stored away and make sure every family member cooperates.

The backward-facing barbs on a cat's tongue make it almost impossible for her to spit something out. If she gets hold of string, yarn, thread, or a rubber band, there's only one direction for it to go—down! Keep these items put away. Use yarn or ribbon for a toy *only* when you are supervising the cat and take it away when playtime is over.

Many people roll up aluminum foil into a ball to use as a toy or allow the cat to play with the cellophane from cigarette packs. Cellophane turns glass-like inside the stomach and can cause internal hemorrhaging. Aluminum foil can cause intestinal blockage. The sight and sound of an aluminum foil ball skittering across the floor will almost always bring out the "kitten" in any cat, but only allow her to play with it while you are supervising. Take it away when playtime is over, and if she stops batting it around and starts chewing on it, find her another toy.

Don't leave plastic bags around or allow your cat to play with them because she could easily suffocate or choke.

Mothballs are very dangerous, and if your cat breathes the fumes, it can cause liver damage. Since cats love dark, out-of-the-way places like closets, make sure mothballs are *inside* sealed garment bags and put them in a closet that is off-limits to your cat. Before closing the door, always check to make sure the cat hasn't dashed into the closet.

This leads directly into another very important warning: You should always check before closing any door because it's so easy for a cat (especially a tiny kitten) to sneak in when you're not looking. Cats love cozy, dark spots and they're also very inquisitive, so do a double check before closing closets, drawers, cabinets, ovens, suitcases, dishwashers, refrigerators, washers, and dryers. I've heard of kittens getting into the clothes dryer because they're attracted to the warmth after you've dried clothes. *Always check before loading clothes into the dryer and before closing the door.*

All bags and boxes should be checked before tossing them out in the trash. I know someone who bought a new TV and when they went to throw out the box, they found one of their little kittens had somehow gotten inside. The box had pieces of Styrofoam in it and the kitten had crawled down underneath them. If the owner hadn't done a last minute check to make sure he'd removed the manual and warranty, that tiny kitten might have suffered a terrible fate.

Breakable items should be put where they can't get knocked over. Cats are usually very careful as they walk among objects, but should they be on the trail of a fly or involved in some serious play, they could accidentally knock something over, resulting in shattered glass on the floor.

The lid on your toilet should always be kept closed. Chances are a kitten wouldn't drown in that amount of water, but if she panicked, it could then lead to possible drowning. Leaving the lid closed will also prevent objects that are knocked off the shelf from falling into the bowl.

WINDOWS. They need to have *secure* screens if they are to be opened. Don't for a second assume that your kitten or cat knows how far down it is to the ground. She could easily slip while watching a bird or bug go by. When my cats see a bird go passed, they bolt for the window, which is why I have very sturdy screens. Without screens, a window that's open "just a little" can tempt a cat to squirm through.

ELECTRICAL CORDS. They pose a very dangerous risk to cats. Since kittens love to chew, these dangling cords can look very tempting. Make sure all wires are well insulated and that there are no signs of wear. Secure all electrical cords to baseboards. Reduce the temptation by not having anything dangling. If you catch your cat chewing on an electrical cord, make a sudden loud noise to scare her away, like a loud "NO!" and clap your hands. If your cat has been shocked by the electricity, the current must be shut off before you attempt first aid, which is covered in chapter 13. Don't touch the cat while she's touching the wire. If you don't actually catch your cat in the act, but you do see burns around her mouth, get her to the vet because that's an indication that she's been shocked. Check all electrical cords to find where she's been chewing.

Usually, as a kitten matures, she loses her fascination with electrical cords. If your cat refuses to stop, try using bitter apple (available at pet supply stores) on the cords. Some people use Tabasco sauce on electrical cords for cats who continue to chew. This may seem cruel to you, but it will probably only take one taste for your cat to get the message. I rubbed lemon on my electrical cords and that successfully kept my cats away from them.

In addition to the danger of electrical shock, dangling cords, when pulled by a cat, can cause the object attached to the other end, such as a lamp, iron, toaster, or hair dryer, to come crashing down on top of her.

HOUSEPLANTS. Cats love to nibble plants, but unfortunately, many houseplants are poisonous, such as the common philodendron and ivy. If you catch your cat nibbling on one, issue a strong "No!" or squirt the cat with a spray of water. For more specific information on houseplant dangers, with a list of some common poisonous plants and first aid, see chapter 13.

Grow a little wheat grass for your cat which will satisfy her need for nibbling greens. Wheat grass is safe and seems to provide digestive benefits. You can buy prepackaged grass kits (you supply the water), or you can grow your own from wheat berries (see chapter 7 for instructions).

If you supply high quality food for your cat, grow a batch of wheat grass, and are consistent in your training, your cat will soon learn that houseplants are off-limits. I recommend that you do without the very dangerous plants anyway, such as the "dumb cane" plant, and don't have plants in your cat's favorite window to reduce the temptation.

TRASH CANS. How many pet owners have come home, only to discover the kitchen trash can on its side and the contents spread all over the floor? Look at it from an animal's point of view. Here's this container filled with lots of enticing smells—chicken, meat, fish, and other goodies. It can be more than a cat's willpower can stand. Invest in a sturdy, covered trash can that cannot be easily tipped over, or keep it secured in a cabinet. The contents of a trash can hold many dangers: rotting meats, splintery bones, sharp objects, poisons, and more. If you know your cat is particularly attracted to a certain food, then you might be better off taking the waste right to the outside can after you have prepared that food. My cat, Ethel, is a chicken fanatic and every time I prepare some she's right at my feet, watching what goes into the trash. Even though my trash can has a cover, I still lift the trash bag out and remove it from the house.

Outdoor trash cans are a hazard if you allow your cat outside. Even if you keep your can closed tightly, your neighbors may not and your cat could get into something dangerous.

SMALL APPLIANCES. Cats can get burned from curling irons, electric rollers, hair dryers, toasters, irons, etc., if they are left to cool in an unsafe place. Make sure you don't leave the cords dangling or the hot appliance may topple over onto the poor cat. Be careful about where you put these items and keep your cat away from them while they are still warm.

POISONOUS CHEMICALS. Many substances that you wouldn't suspect are poisonous to cats. This subject is covered specifically in chapter 13, with instructions for first aid.

In general, keep all detergents, cosmetics, and chemicals in sealed containers, out of your cat's reach. Don't allow your cat in the garage or basement, where the most dangerous substances are kept. Keep poisonous substances in their original containers so you will have the correct antidote instructions on the label.

Be careful when using aerosol sprays such as deodorants, air deodorizers, window cleaners, oven cleaners, hair sprays, etc., so that the chemical doesn't spray onto the cat or get inhaled. Cats who suffer from asthma will benefit from your reducing or eliminating the use of aerosol sprays.

If you have a cockroach problem in your home, don't use roach sprays. Use the traps (they really do work!) and put them *in* cabinets, out of your cat's reach.

HOLIDAY DANGERS. The holidays are a time of love, joy, and celebration for people, but for cats it can be a very dangerous time. All the sparkling, dangling, jingly ornaments on a tree are enticing. A cat could knock one from the tree and break it, swallowing small pieces. Tinsel on trees is so tempting as it glitters and moves with just the slightest breeze. Don't use it if you have pets, not even on the top of the tree because strands so easily find their way off the tree and onto the floor. This is very dangerous for cats. The twinkling lights on trees can be attractive to a cat and she might chew on the wire.

The pine needles on trees are poisonous and so is the water in the base of the tree, so never allow your cat to drink it. It may be safer for your cat if you purchase an artificial tree.

Ribbons tied around or dangling from packages can be chewed and swallowed, which can lead to choking or intestinal obstruction. If your cat is attracted to any of the above items or if she attempts to climb your tree, keep the tree and gifts in a separate room that can be closed off when you're not there to supervise. That way, everyone, cats included, can enjoy the holidays safely.

Keep in mind all the extra food during the holidays. Cookies, candies, breads, spicy food, etc. can play havoc with a cat's stomach, so don't leave tempting edibles around. When you place candy and cookies out for company, be sure to put them away when your guests leave. I've witnessed many a sneaky little paw sliding a cookie off the table while the owner was busy playing host.

MICROWAVE OVEN. Keep your cat off the microwave oven while it's operating and have older ovens checked to be sure there are no leaks.

CAT COUNT

Before closing any closet or cabinet door, I make sure no cat has darted in while I wasn't looking. This has become such a habit with me that it takes no effort at all. I also do a "cat count" before leaving my home in case a mistake was made and a cat got shut in a closet. A cat stuck in a closet for a few minutes is one thing, but imagine leaving your home for work and not knowing your cat is locked in a cabinet or closet all day without water or her litter box, not to mention the emotional trauma she'd suffer.

THE OUTDOOR CAT

As you know by now, I don't recommend that you allow your cat outdoors. A small cat is no match for automobiles, large dogs, cruel people, infectious diseases, parasites, pesticides, and other poisons. If you really want your cat to enjoy the outdoors, build a screened enclosure to keep her safe. If you have a screen-in porch, then she can go out there. If you build an enclosure that's connected to your house, you can install a pet door so your cat can go in and out herself. There are many different types of pet doors so you can pick the one that's perfect for you. For instance, the Johnson Pet-Door Panel fits into sliding doors and can be locked. The Pet Screen Door (from Borwick Innovations) fits into a door or window screen. If you're unable to find the right kind of pet door, you can write to Petdoors U.S.A. for a catalog of all of the different models. See Appendix for address.

Cats that are allowed outdoors, even if only in the enclosed cat run, **MUST** have **up-to-date** vaccinations!

If you decide to allow your cat to roam freely outdoors, at least do the following:

■ Make sure she has a collar. It should have an elastic panel in it to prevent strangulation in case she snags it on a branch. An identification tag should also be attached to it in case your cat gets lost. See chapter 10 for I.D. tag information. Also, check the ads in the back of *Cat Fancy* or *Cats* magazine for custom engraved tags.

■ Feed her high quality food so she's less tempted to catch and eat prey, which can be contaminated with pesticides or have parasites. By feeding a high quality diet (see chapter 7), you can at least keep her immune system in fighting shape should she eat contaminated prey or come in contact with toxic substances.

■ Have your cat altered to reduce the chances of roaming, fighting, or unwanted pregnancies.

■ Regularly examine your cat for fleas, ticks, bites, and wounds. Puncture wounds can seal over, causing an abscess (see chapter 13).

■ Make certain your cat has been trained to come when called (see chapter 8).

■ Periodically have your vet do a stool check to make sure your cat doesn't have internal parasites.

■ When the weather is hot, provide your cat with cool water and a shady area while she's outdoors.

■ Never leave your house while your cat is outdoors in case the weather changes, or at the very least, make sure she has adequate shelter.

If you want to allow your cat outdoors only when on a leash, which I feel is the safest way, see chapter 8 under "Leash Training."

THE INDOOR CAT

■ The most important thing is to make sure your cat gets enough exercise so she doesn't get fat or bored. With limited space, you'll have to be creative when it comes to playtime, but make sure your cat gets enough exercise.

■ Indoor cats tend to shed year-round, so be diligent in your grooming.

■ Provide sunshine for your cat, either by an open, screened window, or use a "full spectrum" light. See section on "Sunlight" below.

SUNLIGHT

Natural light from the sun is very important for animals. Sunlight provides vitamin D and many indoor cats lose out on this benefit. Regular fluorescent and incandescent lights don't supply enough, if any, of the essential blue and green rays. Also, the glass in closed windows filters out the beneficial rays.

When the weather is good, keep windows open (screened, of course) so natural light can come in. If you have narrow windowsills, you can buy a carpeted shelf that attaches to the window so your cat can sit and sun herself. Hobar makes one that you can easily attach to the windowsill without using any tools. The shelf is very secure because it has two supports, so it won't tip. The supports don't leave marks on your walls either. It can also be easily removed if your cat likes to follow the sun from room to room. See Appendix for Hobar's address.

You can also look into the idea of buying "full spectrum" lights which will provide the beneficial rays for your cat—these rays are not at all harmful.

IONIZERS

Have you ever noticed how much better you feel when you're outside on a beautiful, sunny day? You feel calm and peaceful when you walk along the beach, near the water, right? One of the reasons for this is that you are surrounded by *negative* ions, which give you these good feelings. When there is an imbalance and the air is filled with more *positive* ions, you may tend to feel more depressed or irritable. When negative ions are in abundance (in sunlight, water sprays, the beach) you feel much better. Pollution, dust, and cigarette smoke can cause an undersupply of these wonderful little negative ions, so I highly recommend you invest in an "ionizer." These machines send out an ongoing supply of negative ions into the air. If you have a cat who is depressed, cranky, or ill, this machine will be a big help. The cat won't be the only one who benefits from this either— you and your family will notice your moods improving also.

Cats who suffer from asthma or other respiratory problems will be helped by the ionizer if you buy one that also *filters* the air. In addition, people who are allergic to cats will breathe easier because there will be less hair floating around. Read labels before you buy an ionizer to be sure it filters the air. The Neo-Life Company makes an excellent ionizer/filter, available through independent distributors (check your phone book).

5

END THE "LITTER BOX BLUES"

When a client calls in a panic, chances are it's because of a litter box problem. Never have I come across a situation that's more stressful than THE LITTER BOX. Oh, those three little words! There's no reason that it should cause such distress and annoyance for both cats and their owners, but unfortunately it does. There are usually very simple reasons for the problems you and your cat may be experiencing and luckily, there are usually very simple solutions.

WHY CATS BURY THEIR WASTE

A cat's urine is very concentrated and has a strong odor. In the wild, this smell can be detected by predators. Wild cats urinate and defecate away from their nest and cover the waste so they don't attract any predators back to their young. For safety, cats don't urinate where they eat, sleep, or hunt. Your cat has those same instincts and that's why you need to supply him with a litter box and litter.

THE BASICS

First you need to buy a litter box—a rectangular pan that's made of plastic, usually measuring 12" x 18". You can buy a standard size or the giant size depending upon what your needs are. Standing in the store, you'll see all kinds, some even have hoods. How do you decide? Well, first of all, if you have a kitten, you don't want to get a box that has high sides because the kitten will have trouble climbing into it to get to the litter. Decide first if you even have enough space for a large covered box before you purchase it. If you have more than one cat, you might be better off with the larger box, unless they don't like to share—in that case you may need two standard boxes. You also have to consider where you're going to put the box.

I use a covered box because my one cat is an enthusiastic digger and kicks half of the litter right out of the box. Another reason I got a covered box was because she likes to squat at the edge of the pan, and all too often would miss the litter completely and leave a deposit on the floor.

If you want a pan with a cover, I strongly advise that you go for excellent quality. You may have to spend more money than you'd planned, but, believe me, I've seen some flimsy covers that lose their shape or are easily knocked over by a cat. I bought the Booda Box brand litter box. It's very sturdy and my cats can jump on it and run into it and still not knock the lid off. The Booda Box has a replaceable charcoal filter in the lid to help eliminate odor. I find the covered boxes do reduce odor quite a bit, but you musn't use the cover to get out of cleaning duty. A covered box can keep the odor trapped inside and the cat may end up rejecting the box because of the odor. If you're interested in the Booda Box, you can probably find it at your local pet supply store. If not, you can order it from the company. See Appendix for address. One word of caution, though, make sure your cat will be able to squat comfortably in a covered box. If your cat is tall, has arthritis, or squats in a very erect manner, a covered box may interfere with his comfort or ability to get in and out of the box.

Litter is next. There are many kinds to choose from so be prepared to be a good shopper. Clay litter is the most absorbent. I know some owners who use cedar chips, sawdust, sand, or even newspaper, but I don't recommend any of those. Sand and sawdust are extremely messy and will stick to your cat's fur and paws. You'll also find it tracked *everywhere* in your house. Newspaper is too smelly and messy. I find clay works the best. There are numerous brands, and many who advertise extra deodorizers.

Being responsible about cleaning will eliminate most odors. Once you buy a brand of litter that your cat likes, don't change brands if you can help it because that can be very unsettling to your cat. Some brands are dustier than others, and I suggest staying away from them because your cat will be breathing that dust as he digs in the litter.

As for price, some litter comes in small and large size bags. Most pet supply stores carry the larger size bags (usually 25 pounds), and if you have the room to store them, buying the larger size can save you money.

A very important part of odor control is how much litter to put in the pan. Many people use either way too much or not nearly enough. If you use too much because you think it will better absorb the urine odor, you're wrong. Using too much will cause the urine to spread out. Not using enough will reduce the absorbency of the litter—also causing potential odor problems. I find that about a 2-inch layer of litter in the pan is generally best.

Plastic liners are sold in pet supply stores and supermarkets and can be a blessing for many cat owners who dread litter box cleaning. You must use them correctly or you'll have more of a problem on your hands. The liners are used to line the pan before the litter goes in. They can prolong the life of the pan and make cleanup easier because you supposedly can just lift the bag out and throw the whole mess away. In theory that's great, but a cat's claws can do dreadful things to plastic—so be advised. When I lift the liner out, I hold the litter pan right up to my outdoor trash can because there are always streams of litter coming through the holes.

When you buy liners, make sure you buy the right size for your litter box. Don't buy the standard size if you have a giant litter box. I also suggest buying "heavy duty" liners. Liners can also add to the odor problem if you don't place them in the box correctly. Make sure there are no folds left where the urine can become trapped, forming little puddles (Yuck! Believe me, this will be a very smelly litter box). Also, be certain the plastic lies flat against all sides of the box so it doesn't interfere with your cat's digging. If every time he tries to cover his waste, he gets his claws stuck in the plastic, he may become miserable enough to find other accommodations. One trick I've learned: After I've put the liner in and filled the box with litter, I tape the edges of the liner that come over the outer sides of the pan. I use masking tape because it holds well. The tape also helps keep the liner flat against the inside walls of the pan.

Among the other tools you'll be needing will be a litter scoop (available at all pet supply stores) for solid wastes. If you scoop up the solid matter a couple of times each day, it will keep things much cleaner. Although the fecal matter isn't what causes the odor (it only smells for a few minutes—whereas urine has a longer lasting odor), scooping it up will keep your cat from stepping on it over and over each time he uses the litter box. It also keeps the litter cleaner, so your cat won't reject it and end up having an accident somewhere else in your home. If you can't find a litter scoop you like, you can use a large slotted spoon. In addition, you should also have an unslotted spoon on hand for picking up very loose bowels or wet clumps.

One handy item I couldn't do without is a little whisk broom to sweep up litter that gets kicked out of the box. I found a little whisk broom and pan that snap together. I keep them right by the litter box for those sudden "litter storms."

LITTER BOX LOCATION

This is extremely important because sometimes "accidents" or random wetting can be attributed to the litter box being in the wrong place. Where's the wrong place? Remember, I told you that wild cats bury their waste *away* from the nest so they don't attract predators. Your indoor cat feels the same way. After all, you may know there are no predators in your home, but he's not so sure. Keeping the litter box near the food and water will probably result in your cat 1) avoiding the litter box and "going" elsewhere, 2) becoming a nervous and picky eater due to the stress of having the box so close, or 3) both.

Another bad location is a noisy, busy area with lots of traffic. Cats like their privacy (just like people), so put the box in a place where your cat won't have to endure kids running all around or hear doors slamming and people passing him. If you don't buy a covered box, you might want to get one of those folding cardboard screens to put in front of the box for your modest feline. Wherever you decide to put the litter box, make sure it's not so secluded that you forget to clean it. Making it convenient to check for solid waste is helpful.

INTRODUCING YOUR CAT TO THE LITTER BOX

Chances are you won't have to do too much work when it comes to this—just supply the box and the litter and your cat should do the rest. Young kittens need extra assistance and supervision, so refer to chapter 12. The main thing is making sure your cat knows where the box is.

When you first bring a cat home, it's a good idea to confine him to a smaller area until you're sure he's gotten the hang of things. If he's slow in catching on or if his mother didn't do such a great teaching job, gently lift him in the box and scratch the litter with your finger—the best time to do this is after he's eaten. You can also gently take his front paw and scratch. Don't push the issue—let him leave if he wants. Chances are his natural instincts will take over and he'll know what to do.

During the orientation I suggest you not use a cover on the box. You want to make the learning process as easy as possible. Also during orientation, if your cat is using the litter successfully, don't change brands because this can be disturbing to him. As for the kind of litter to use during the learning process, choose a neutral clay during orientation so your cat can smell his familiar scent in the box. Sometimes putting a drop or two of ammonia in the litter can help to inspire your cat to use the box, because to a cat, the ammonia smell closely resembles that of cat urine.

Last, but most definitely not least, don't forget the praise and extra petting when the litter is used successfully during training.

THE CLEANUP

If you keep the litter box clean, it won't have that noticeable "There's a cat in this house!" smell. And, despite what you think, keeping the box clean is not such a terrible chore. I keep the slotted litter scoop and the unslotted spoon in a small plastic pail by the toilet. The litter box is near the bathroom and twice a day I check the litter for any solid waste. It takes me only seconds to do. By scooping out the waste, my cats don't accidently step on it, and the litter stays fresher. I pick up the stool, shake off the excess litter, and flush the waste in the toilet. Swishing the litter scoop in the rushing water will help clean it and remove any clinging bits of litter.

I also consider the scooping up of the fecal matter as a chance to monitor my cats' health. Because I check the litter twice a day, I am alerted to potential problems right away. This is the way to easily find out if your cat is suffering from constipation or diarrhea. By discovering something like a loose bowel as soon as it happens, I can more easily recall if any changes occurred in the diet. For instance, if one of my cats had milk that day, it might cause diarrhea. Some cats react to stress with a case of diarrhea or constipation, and being aware of the condition of their stools, I can better determine if a case of loose bowels is maybe the result of a stressful day. I might have had too many noisy guests at once, or perhaps the cat is reacting to a vet visit, etc. Notice the condition of your cat's stools as you pick them up and dispose of them. Do you see any signs of worms? (See chapter 13 for description.) Do you see any blood in the stool? It doesn't take long to do a quick check and it's not as unpleasant as you may think. Knowing it's a job that benefits your cat's health makes it a very acceptable job.

I thoroughly clean the litter box once a week. Some people do it every few days—you'll have to see what works best for you. By having a 2-inch layer of good clay litter and by scooping out all fecal matter, I find the once-a-week scrubbing works fine for me. You can scrub your litter box with a brush or a sponge. Whichever cleanser you decide to use, make sure you rinse and then rinse again to remove every trace of cleanser. Remember how sensitive your cat's nose is. Don't forget to wash the litter scoop, spoon, and pail when you scrub the litter box each week. Make sure the box is completely dry before you fill it with fresh litter.

NOTE: Pregnant women should avoid cleaning the litter box or scooping up feces because of the danger of toxoplasmosis. This is caused by a protozoan parasite, toxoplasma gondii. Cats spread this through egg spores in their feces (more on toxoplasmosis in chapter 13). Have someone else in your house do the litter duties for the pregnant owner. But I must tell you that an excellent reason for having someone scoop up the solids twice a day is that the egg spores of toxoplasma gondii must incubate for several days before they're able to spread this disease. Removing fecal waste right away greatly reduces the chance of getting toxoplasmosis.

DEODORIZERS

Some cats don't like the deodorized litter, so try to be aware of how your cat is reacting to a certain brand. Some litters are very dusty, which is not good because your cat breathes in the dust.

As for special litter deodorizing granules or powders, I've found some to be less than satisfactory. By not neglecting your cleaning duties, you won't have an odor problem. If you want, you can sprinkle some baking soda in with the litter to help absorb odors.

If your cat has a very strong bowel odor and you want to use an aerosol deodorizer, don't spray it while he's near. The sound can frighten him and the scent may be too strong for his sensitive nose. You don't want your cat to associate a negative experience with using his litter box, so if you must use a room deodorizer, wait until he's left the room and don't overspray. Removal of solid waste is the best odor eliminator!

RANDOM WETTING

If your cat has a problem with random wetting, you must first make sure there's no medical problem like cystitis causing it. Frequent trips to the litter box, blood in the urine, or small spots of urine around the house are all signs of cystitis or other urinary problems (for more information see chapter 13). If your cat is not using the litter box, you must have him checked by a vet to determine if there's a medical reason.

If your cat is given a clean bill of health, you have to then play amateur detective and figure out what the problem could be. First, the obvious: Nothing can turn off a cat faster than a dirty litter box. I've seen many cats turn to other areas of the house to relieve themselves because their owners neglected to clean the box. Not only is this situation inconvenient for you, it's very stressful to your cat. Keep the box clean! Second, make sure the box is located in a quiet area, away from people traffic and not near the eating/playing/sleeping places.

Another reason for random wetting can be emotional. If you have more than one cat, notice if one of them is objecting to sharing the box with his roommate. Competition can lead one (or both) of the cats to urinate in specific areas of the house they consider "their's." In that case, you may need two boxes and put them in the cats' own "territories." Other emotional reasons for litter box rejection could be the arrival of a new baby, too many guests at once, a new husband or wife, etc. If there's a new person in your household, don't shortchange your cat. Give him extra love and attention so he doesn't feel forgotten. If your cat is urinating or defecating on your furniture or your personal possessions, there's a good chance he's unhappy with something you've done. When dealing with random wetting, don't overlook emotional causes.

The litter box itself could be the problem. It may be too small, or maybe you bought a covered one and your cat has trouble squatting comfortably. Maybe you didn't rinse all traces of the cleanser away when you scrubbed the box. Remember, a cat's nose is forty times more sensitive than our's. If it's not the box, it could be the litter. Is it too deodorized? Remember that a cat's urine is one way he identifies himself. A litter that smells so strongly of deodorizers or the addition of a powder or granules may interfere with his own scent. When he goes to double-check as he covers his urine, he may get a nose full of chemical deodorizers. This can cause him to seek other places where his nose won't get overwhelmed by the strong and unfamiliar smell. Also, make sure the litter isn't too dusty because this could irritate his eyes and nasal passages. If your cat sneezes several times when he's in the litter box, it's probably the litter that's bothering him. Try switching to a brand that's less dusty.

Elderly cats have less control of their bladders and can't always make it to the box in time. You may want to have more than one box in your house in the locations your cat frequents. Cats who are sick or recovering from surgery or an injury may have trouble getting to their box. Use low boxes for cats unable to climb in. Placing the box a little closer to the cat with limited mobility will help also. If necessary, you may have to assist your cat by carrying him to the litter box several times during the day.

Cats who have been declawed (heaven forbid!) may find it painful to use the litter in the box. It may be easier to use shredded newspaper while your cat heals.

Accidents should be cleaned completely so the cat isn't attracted to the same spot by the familiar smell. I recommend that you buy an odor neutralizer to use on accidents. They're found in pet supply stores. Nature's Miracle is one brand that works very well. Double-faced tape or self-adhesive shelf paper over the spot will also discourage a cat from trying the same place again.

To avoid accidents when your cat is a guest in someone's house, or when you move to a new home, confine him to a small area so he's sure of the litter box location and has become comfortable in his new surroundings.

With a little awareness and responsibility on the part of the owner, there's no reason why the litter box should be a source of problems for anyone involved—cat or cat owner.

THE SCRATCHING POST

Now we come to the most misunderstood aspect of cat training—the scratching post. It saddens me to think of how many frustrated owners have their cats declawed because the sofa or chairs were being used instead of the scratching post. It doesn't have to be that way. Your cat *will* use the scratching post if you get the right kind. I'll explain in detail in a few minutes. Right now I want you to have a better understanding of two very important issues: 1) why cats need to scratch and 2) the consequences of declawing.

UNDERSTANDING THE SCRATCHING INSTINCT

Cats remove the outer sheath of the claws on their forefeet by scratching on objects (hopefully, a scratching post). The removal of the outer sheath makes room for the new growth underneath. This is instinctual in cats and is not, as some may believe, intended as destructive behavior. When a cat stretches up and uses the scratching post, not only are claw sheaths removed, the muscles in the legs, shoulders, and back are kept toned. Being able to stretch up and dig her claws into a scratching post is an important aspect of a cat's physical health.

Emotional well-being is also connected to scratching—it feels good! Using a scratching post also helps unkink muscles after sleeping or helps a cat express her joy at something, like an owner's arrival home. Some cats use scratching as territorial marking. Wild cats sometimes scratch on a tree to announce their arrival. It's nice to provide your indoor cat with a place that's exclusively hers to scratch until her heart's content.

DECLAWING

Many people rush into the decision of having their cat declawed without fully understanding the consequences that may occur. Luckily, many vets are against declawing unless as a last resort. Rather than trying to put this in delicate terms, I'm going to come right out and tell you that the declawing operation is amputation. It's the equivalent of you having the last joint of all of your fingers removed. That's exactly what happens to your cat.

Under anesthesia, the last joint of each of her toes is completely removed. A bandage is put on the legs and remains in place for a couple of days. Most cats continue to experience pain for a few days after the operation. The skin needs about a week to heal, and during that time, the cat needs to be kept in a clean, dry environment. Litter can't be used in the litter box because it's painful to step on and can get stuck in the healing wounds. Torn newspaper or paper towels have to be substituted until the cat has healed.

Once declawed, a cat becomes almost totally defenseless, and some people have the hind claws removed in addition, which leaves the cat *completely* defenseless. Cats defend themselves with their front claws. Swiping at enemies is the natural method of defense. Cats don't defend themselves by biting as often as a dog would. Therefore, a declawed cat *can never be allowed outdoors*. Without her front claws, a cat would be unable to even climb a tree to escape from her attacker. A cat without her claws becomes stressed because she knows she's defenseless. Even though you may keep her safely indoors, you won't be able to convince her that danger won't be lurking around the doorway. Stress can cause a chain reaction, weakening your cat's immune system and inhibiting her ability to fight disease.

Declawed cats are more inclined to become nervous and to bite. I've seen many cats, who had the sweetest dispositions before being declawed, become biters after the operation. This can be dangerous if a cat lives with children, which is ironic because some people have their cats declawed to prevent their children from being scratched.

Declawing can alter a cat's sense of balance and can weaken the muscles of the shoulders and back. Sometimes, if the operation is done improperly, one or more of the claws can grow back in a way that causes the cat extreme difficulty.

One other factor to consider is that by declawing, you deny your cat a natural, enjoyable, and healthy part of her life.

THE SCRATCHING POST IMPOSTER

Clients have called me, saying that they invested money in a scratching post, carried it home, set it up, and the cat used it once and never again. Now I know these well-meaning owners certainly *thought* they were doing their cat a big favor by bringing home this beautifully carpeted little post, and oh, yes, it even had a little toy dangling from it to "entice" the cat. Was I surprised that the cat rejected the post? Nope. You see, most scratching posts are great to look at, but they don't even come close to being what a cat needs for scratching. Let's look at it piece by piece.

First, the carpet on most posts is too soft and dense. Cats don't want nice fluffy soft carpet; they want something rough enough for them to really dig their nails into. This is why your cat may go for your wicker furniture or the tough fabric on your sofa. They need the roughness of the fabric to remove the sheaths on their claws as they pull them through. Next, most scratching posts aren't sturdy enough, so when a cat puts her weight against it to scratch, BAM! Over it goes! Now if I were a cat, that would sure discourage me from using that post again. So back she goes to the sofa to do her scratching because she knows *that* won't topple over.

Moving down the list, my next complaint with most posts is that they're too darn short. A cat needs to be able to stretch out those muscles and how can she do that if you've provided her with this teeny-weeny post? Sometimes I think manufacturers must believe that only small kittens use scratching posts. Finally, my last complaint is with the owners themselves. Many people put the scratching post in such out-of-the-way places that a cat would be a fool to spend her time tracking it down when there's lots of good furniture so conveniently located.

THE SCRATCHING POST OF YOUR CAT'S DREAMS

The best posts I've seen are covered with sisal, which is a hemp product. Just about every cat I know has taken to it right away. Once your cat digs her nails into a sisal-covered post, she won't want to settle for ordinary furniture again. You can usually find sisal-covered posts in a pet supply store. Before you buy it, make sure it's tall enough for your cat to get a good stretch. Ideally the post should be taller than your cat's full-length stretch.

Sturdiness should be a major concern when choosing a scratching post. Make sure it has a large, heavy base and that the post itself is firmly attached. You want a post that can withstand your cat's full weight without toppling over. At home you can increase it's sturdiness by wedging it in a corner or against the wall.

The best scratching posts I've ever come across are available by mail order. They're sisal-covered and come in several sizes. See Appendix for address of The Felix Company. I know that several veterinarians and professional groomers have also recommended the Felix post. I think it will be a very wise investment toward the health of your cat, not to mention your furniture.

You can also make your own scratching post by selecting a strong, heavy base and attaching an upright piece of 4" x 4" wood. Cover the post with the *back side* of a carpet. Don't cover it with the soft front side. Believe me, your cat will prefer the rougher side. Make the post tall enough for your cat to get a full stretch. Rubbing a little catnip on 't will increase its appeal.

Another way to provide a scratching surface for your cat is to cover a large flat board with carpet (back side out, remember) and attach it to the wall. This way you can make it as wide or narrow as needed to accommodate your space limitations, and you won't have to worry about it toppling over. I have both a scratching post and a scratching "wall" in my home and both get used successfully.

If you have the money and want to go all out for your cat, scratching "trees" are also worth considering. If your cat enjoys scratching on bark, she may prefer this. Some companies custom-make the trees to your specifications. They're available through mail order. Some can be found in pet supply stores, but you won't be able to have it customized. Check the advertisements in *Cat Fancy* or *Cats* magazine. Be advised though, your cat may or may not scratch on this tree, she might just use it as a playground. Sisal scratching posts are still your best bet for success.

TRAINING YOUR CAT TO USE THE SCRATCHING POST

There are those cats who don't need any education in what the scratching post is for, but to avoid any confusion I prefer proper training. The first lesson is for the cat owner: Get a scratching post when you first bring your cat home. That's the best way to reduce any chance of behavioral problems. The scratching post should be considered standard equipment, the same way you'd consider the litter box or food bowl. And naturally, training from kittenhood will ensure your cat has the lesson firmly planted in her head.

Now that you've bought (or made) the perfect scratching post, you want to make sure your cat will use it. I've found the best way to introduce the post is to use the post yourself. Yes, you read correctly. I don't know about your cat, but my cats never fail to get into the act whenever they see me doing *anything* new. Just run your fingernails down the post and pretend you're having a grand old time. Usually, the scratching sound alone will bring your cat running over to investigate. In most cases, she'll begin to scratch on it right along with you. Praise and pet her when she uses it successfully.

For cats who need a little extra guidance, turn the post on its side. Stand your cat on it and with a string or other extremely appealing object, create a game by running it all around the post. As your cat digs her claws in to play, she'll realize she just discovered something great. Don't feel bad if your cat then ignores your game and begins to scratch on the post. When she's gotten the idea, you can turn the post right-side up again. Scratch the post with your own fingernails again or use the string to entice your cat to use the post in its upright position. If she stretches up on the post but doesn't scratch, gently stroke her back which will stimulate the scratching reflex. **Never** push her paws on the post because cats hate forceful action and you won't get the results you want. Let her think everything she does is her own idea.

Catnip can be a great aid to entice your cat to use the scratching post. If she's a kitten though, *don't* use catnip because kittens don't react to catnip when they're so young. Rub a little on the post, which should have her ecstatically digging her claws into the sisal- or carpet-backing in no time. By the way, the Felix posts are already treated with catnip (see page 88).

THE PROPER PLACE

Cats generally like to have a good scratch after sleeping or eating. Put the scratching post near your cat's sleeping place so she can stretch and scratch conveniently. If your cat likes to use the post after being hunched over her food dish, then place it nearby. You may even want to buy more than one post. My cats look for something to scratch whenever I come home. That place used to be the leg of my pants until I got smart and put a scratching "wall" just inside the entrance to my apartment.

Make sure the scratching post is convenient for your cat to use. Don't hide it in some corner or in a rarely used room. My cats' post is right in the middle of things and I encourage my cats to use the post whenever we play together right before meals, which helps their appetites. Also, after grooming (when I trim their nails), we all go over to the post to stretch and scratch.

If your cat has been scratching on a piece of furniture, like a sofa or chair, put the post near it. Whenever your cat begins to scratch the sofa, tell her "NO" and bring her to the post. Don't put her paws on it or force her to scratch though—just scratch it with your own nails. When she uses the post successfully, praise and pet her. If you're consistent with this training, she'll get the message that the sofa is a "NO", but the post is a "YES, YES, YES." Chances are that once she's dug her claws into the post, she'll prefer the feeling of it over the sofa, that is if you're using the right post. If you still think she's going to be fooled into using the fluffy-soft post, then you're in for a lot of sofa damage.

If she still scratches on the furniture, put a smooth material over the furniture, such as a sheet or tablecloth. Make sure you tuck it in all around so she can't sneak under and get at the original material. The smooth sheet will be much less appealing and she'll turn to the post. When the training has become cemented into her head, you can remove the sheet.

While you're training your cat to use the post instead of furniture, keeping her nails trimmed will lessen the severity of any damage done to the fabric.

If your cat is one who consistently scratches on your living room carpet and doesn't like the idea of a vertical scratching post, then keep the post permanently on its side and train her to stand on it and scratch.

If you have more than one cat, it might be wise to have more than one post in your home. Cats also use scratching as a way of territorial marking, so this way each cat can have her own post. My two cats love using the one scratching post at the same time. Whenever Albert hears the familiar sound of Ethel's claws on the post, he immediately runs over to join her. He hates to miss out on anything.

Remember, the most effective way to train a cat *not* to scratch where you don't want her to is by providing her with something she'll like better. If your cat isn't using the post you bought, then take another look at it. Is it the wrong post? Is it in the wrong place? Does your cat even know that it's there? Then it's time for you to start from "scratch."

THE ABC'S OF GOOD NUTRITION

When it comes to pet food, many people have two concerns: 1) will their pet like it? and 2) how much will it cost? Walking through the pet food aisle in the supermarket, I find *palatability* and *price* to be the two most common factors which determine what brands most customers choose for their pets. I understand that price is a very legitimate factor when it comes to pet food and that taking advantage of sales and specials is necessary for many pet owners. Unfortunately, these misinformed owners are not always getting the "value" they think. I've also seen well-meaning cat owners pile twelve cans of food (all the same flavor) in their shopping cart because that's the only kind their cat will touch. This can end up being a very costly mistake.

It's important to know when you're actually saving money as opposed to getting an "empty" bargain. For example, you buy a brand of canned food that's always lowest in price. You haven't read the label so you don't know that this particular brand has a very high moisture content (78 percent is considered high). Though you are *paying* less you're also *getting* less in terms of nutrients. Your cat would have to eat more of this food to get the same amount of nutrients as in another brand with a 75 percent moisture content. While this certainly isn't dangerous to your cat's health—the right amount of moisture is actually an important part of your cat's meal— it is something to be aware of before taking advantage of a so-called bargain. I'll give you another example: If you aren't familiar with TVP (textured vegetable protein), or if you don't read ingredient listings, then you might not know that the chunks of "meat" you see in your cat's food are probably not really made of meat at all. TVP is soy flour that is shaped and colored to look like meat. This is a cost-saving measure manufacturers use so they can raise the percentage of protein listed on the label. Unfortunately, cats need protein from animal sources instead of vegetable sources. So if you bought that brand, you really didn't save money because you paid for nutrients your cat can't use.

After reading this chapter, I'm hoping you'll see that the *true* values when purchasing food aren't always the most obvious ones.

When a new client calls and makes an appointment to have their cat bathed, I know there's a good chance a bath is not what's necessary. While there are certainly reasons for bathing cats (see chapter 9), I find some owners think a bath and a brushing are all a dull, dry, or oily coat needs. WRONG!

As I ring the client's doorbell I'm no longer Pam Johnson, mild mannered cat groomer—I have turned into Super Detective (unbeknownst to the unsuspecting client). Upon meeting the cat, I check the coat by sight, touch, and smell. I put my nose right into the fur and take a whiff. I examine the coat for signs of dandruff. The condition of a cat's coat is a pretty good indication of what's going on inside. For instance, a greasy, fishy smelling coat can mean too much fish and too much unsaturated fats in the diet (more on this later).

Continuing the investigation, I check the litter box next to see the cat's stools. Whatever a cat eats will eventually show up here—hopefully as a firm, well-formed stool. A hard, dry stool or a runny, loose one is evidence that something is amiss, either in the diet or medically. Finally, I ask to see what foods are being fed to the cat. By now, the owners usually think I'm a crazy, nosy woman who was just supposed to give their cat a simple bath. This is where a new client gets an unscheduled education in feline nutrition. I know it's more than they bargained for, but they soon learn how the food their cat eats is showing up in a poor coat, besides many other things, like a less than sunny disposition and a lowered immune system.

Being a responsible cat owner means knowing what a cat needs and how to supply it. We're going to do this by first of all clearing up some misinformation.

LEAVING FOOD AVAILABLE

I know this is a subject that's very touchy for some owners. Should you leave food for your cat to nibble at will? Brace yourself, the answer is NO! The quickest way to turn a healthy cat into a finicky eater is by leaving food available. Cats in the wild don't nibble all day—they hunt, eat their prey, and then their digestive system gets to rest. Food isn't lounging around under their noses all day. Your cat's immune system is weakened if food is always available because the blood supply has to work on digestion over and over instead of being able to concentrate on other organs. Even leaving the dirty dish around can be just as harmful. It's the sense of smell that first triggers the digestive system. The smell of food residue in a dish fools the digestive system into thinking more is on the way.

Food left in the dish all day dries out and becomes spoiled, destroying vital nutrients. Would you want to eat meat that was sitting out all day? Many cat owners have called me for advice on their "finicky eater" and when I get to their house, I see food that's been sitting in the dish so long you'd need a hammer and chisel to get it out. My recommendation is two meals a day for adult cats (for kittens, see chapter 12). I'm not in favor of just one meal a day because a cat will have a tendency to gulp. This could cause gastrointestinal problems and might even result in the food coming right back up and making a reappearance on your kitchen floor.

When your cat has finished eating, wash the dish and put it away. I know some cats who recognize their food dishes whenever they pass them (be it on the counter or drying in a dish drainer) and begin the "starving cat" performance, hoping to sucker some unsuspecting human into providing an unscheduled meal.

Another bonus for the two-meal-a-day schedule is it will rid your cat of dandruff. An overworked digestive system causes a backup of waste and it will eventually show up on the skin as dandruff. Two meals a day will help to do away with that.

Now, if you've been leaving food available and are ready to switch over to two meals a day, I warn you, BE TOUGH! Leave food down for a maximum of one half hour, then pick it up. Don't save it for later, prepare a fresh meal. You want to do all you can to make the food appealing. At first your cat is going to be confused and even worried that you've forgotten the routine, but be patient. Eventually he will get the hang of it—trust me—he's not going to starve when food is offered twice a day. If your cat doesn't eat for a day or so, don't panic. He'll start again and on *your* terms. One way to stimulate his appetite is to encourage playtime before meals. Cats in the wild must go through vigorous physical activity during the chase for food. Give your indoor tiger the opportunity to hunt down that ever elusive "mouse," by physical activity for ten minutes before eating.

TYPES OF DISHES

Before getting too involved in the discussion of food, we'd better cover the very important subject of dishes. You don't think that's important? A dish is a dish, you say? Oh, are you in for a surprise! There are several kinds of dishes to choose from and a few things you should watch out for.

SIZE AND SHAPE. It may seem obvious to you, but I've seen some owners use large dishes meant for dogs. Here's this huge dish with this little cat trying to get at the food without falling in. I once spent time painstakingly grooming a beautiful Persian only to watch the owner put her meal in this teeny-weeny bowl that was so narrow and deep the cat had to squish her face right into it to reach the food. Persians and other longhaired cats need to be able to eat without dirtying themselves. Pet shops sell special dishes just for longhairs; it's not as deep and has low sides. Buy the dish that will enable your cat to eat comfortably.

PLASTIC DISHES. They're popular because they're unbreakable. Parents who let their children handle feeding duties usually prefer unbreakable dishes. I don't like plastic for a number of reasons. First, no matter how carefully you wash the dish, plastic holds the smell of food. I don't think it's too appealing for a cat to have to smell a previous (maybe even disliked) dinner from two days ago. A more important reason to avoid plastic dishes is that as they become worn and scratched, the chemicals which make up the plastic can leach through to the food. A scratched dish can also harbor food bacteria. I've even seen some cats who are allergic to the plastic.

CERAMIC DISHES. These are a good choice if you can be certain that the glaze is complete, otherwise there's a chance of lead contamination. I would stay away from ceramic dishes made outside of the United States. I've seen some ads in mail-order catalogs that advertise "lead free" dishes, so if you really want ceramic, I suggest you try one of those. Don't use the dish once it becomes cracked or chipped. A chip could injure your cat's delicate tongue.

STAINLESS STEEL DISHES. An all around good choice, stainless steel dishes are sturdy, unbreakable, and last forever. You can buy them in any pet store. Some dishes come with a band of rubber around the bottom to prevent sliding.

GLASS DISHES. Another good choice, glass is easy to clean and won't hold the odor the way plastic does. Make sure you get a heavy enough dish so your cat doesn't have to follow it all around the kitchen to finish eating. Discontinue use if the glass becomes cracked or chipped to prevent injuring your cat's tongue.

WASHING THE FOOD AND WATER DISHES

Be sure you use a mild dishwashing liquid and *never* a harsh cleanser. Strong cleansers are very dangerous to cats—residue can burn the tongue. Some cleansers leave a strong smell that is very unappealing to a cat's sensitive nose. Thorough rinsing is a must to remove all traces of soap.

PLACEMATS

I know you think I'm getting too fancy here but a washable placemat is helpful in keeping your floor or rug a bit cleaner. You can buy one made especially for pets, or you can use your own. Albert, my cat, is a very enthusiastic eater and much of his food lands outside of his dish. I just have to pick up the placemat, wash it, and my kitchen floor is left clean. After the placemat is dry, I put it back on the floor under the water dish to catch spills. You can also get something called a "pet dinette" placemat which is made of hard plastic and has a raised edge all around. This is good for cats who like to knock their water dishes over.

LOCATION

It might not seem so important, but where you feed your cat is a big factor in how well or how poorly he eats. Cats like to be in a quiet place to eat. Wild cats will drag their prey to a more secluded area to dine. If your cat is a nervous or finicky eater, a noisy or heavy traffic area will only worsen the situation. If you feed him in the kitchen, do it at a time when other family members aren't running in and out.

Cats don't like to eat close to where their litter box is located. So if your cat is being picky about meals, it could be that he doesn't like his food lined up next to the litter. If you absolutely must keep them in the same room, at least put the food as far away from the litter as possible.

Noisy areas can be a big problem. An owner once called me for help with her cat who was a poor eater. After learning that his meals were served in the laundry room, I asked if she ever ran the washer or dryer while the cat was trying to eat. With four kids, the washer was always going she said. All it took was to move the food and water to a quieter room and the problem was solved.

THE MYTHS OF TUNA AND MILK

Yes, we all grew up believing that a saucer of milk and a dish of tuna was all it took for a cat to live happily. Any cat existing on either of those two things is indeed living—living dangerously that is! It's time to learn the truth about tuna and milk.

TUNA. While it's true that fish in moderation is good for cats, tuna is unfortunately a bad choice. The high amount of polyunsaturated fat in tuna may be a blessing for cholesterol conscience humans, but not for cats—they have trouble metabolizing unsaturated fat. A diet too rich in this kind of fat can be harmful to your cat. Tuna robs the cat's body of vitamin E. This can lead to a painful disease called steatitis, where a cat's skin becomes so sensitive it can't be touched. Steatitis is also known as "Yellow Fat" disease because the fat on the animal becomes hard and yellow. Another serious problem with tuna is that a cat can become hooked on the taste and refuse to eat anything else.

Some manufacturers of lower quality food add some tuna into other flavors because the taste is so strong it will entice the cat into eating. You may think you're buying the meat flavor canned food, but if you look closely at the ingredients you may find tuna listed there also. Luckily, good quality pet food companies don't practice this and by learning to read labels, you'll be able to distinguish the good from the bad.

MILK. Kittens, like other babies need the nutrients in milk, but the specific requirements are different. A queen's (mother cat) milk meets a kitten's specific nutritional requirements. It has a higher protein level than cow's milk; queen's milk has approximately 10 percent, while cow's milk has approximately 3 percent.

A diet of whole milk can provide humans with essential amino acids but is low in taurine. For cats this deficiency can be dangerous because they need higher amounts of taurine (more on this amino acid later in this chapter). Another problem with a milk diet for cats is that while whole milk has a high level of fat, and cats do need fat, milk is low in arachidonic acid. Arachidonic acid is an essential fatty acid for cats and *must* be obtained from animal sources, meaning a diet that includes meat. Other animals can meet their fat requirements from dairy fat, but unfortunately cats can't.

The carbohydrate in milk is a sugar known as lactose. In order for lactose to be used by the body, it must be broken down by an enzyme called lactase. Prior to weaning, young kittens have sufficient levels of lactase while they are existing exclusively on mother's milk. After weaning, the amount of lactase in the intestine decreases so a kitten may no longer be able to digest the milk sugar. Diarrhea will be the result if you feed milk to most cats once they are weaned. The inability to digest milk sugar is known as lactose intolerance.

If your cat doesn't develop diarrhea from drinking milk, then it's all right to give him some as a treat. Make sure you give him a small amount because diarrhea can result if fed too much, even if he has the lactase enzyme.

Milk should never be fed as a substitute for water. To do so can cause dangerous dehydration in your cat.

CAT FOOD VERSUS DOG FOOD

Believe it or not, some people feed dog food to their cat and cat food to their dog. If you've been guilty of this, you could be doing serious damage to your pet's health. Cats require about four times as much protein as dogs. By eating dog food, your cat will develop a serious protein deficiency. If your dog eats cat food, he'll be getting too much protein, which could lead to kidney problems.

Taurine, an amino acid which cats *must* get in their diet is missing in dog food because dogs can synthesize taurine in their bodies. So if you've been letting Fluffy share Rover's dinner, it would be better to feed your pets their own particular food.

CAN CATS BE VEGETARIANS?

Cats are natural carnivores. By eliminating meat from your cat's diet it would be very hard to supply enough high quality protein without over-feeding. By "high quality" I mean protein that is actually *usable* by a cat's body.

Vitamin A is a vitamin cats must get from animal tissue—it's called preformed A. Cats can't convert beta-carotene from vegetables to vitamin A the way humans and dogs can. Cats also need arachidonic fatty acid from animal sources. Unlike us, cat's don't have cholesterol problems, and they need to replenish their protein supply daily.

Before we get into the specifics of what nutrients are needed by cats, let me stress that **NO DIETARY CHANGES** should be made unless your cat has been examined by a vet and gets a clean bill of health. You want to be sure that any trouble your cat may be having is not due to a medical problem. It's especially important to check with your vet *before* making any change in diet if your cat is on medication. *Even natural food can alter the effectiveness of a drug!* Also, get your vet's opinion and advice about any of the food and/or food supplements mentioned in this book that you would like to feed your cat.

Pregnant cats, young kittens, and older cats have their own needs when it comes to nutrition. I have included special chapters for each, but I suggest you read through this chapter before skipping ahead to any of the others. A sound background on what good nutrition is in general will benefit your cat at any stage of his life.

KNOWING A NUTRIENT WHEN YOU SEE ONE

Besides protein, cats need other nutrients such as carbohydrates, fat, vitamins, and minerals. The following descriptions will help you to recognize where nutrients can be found and what they do. It may seem confusing at first when you read through each one, but it will give you a sense of how important a complete and well-balanced diet is for your cat.

PROTEIN

Protein is essential for growth, muscle development, repair of tissues, and maintenance of the immune system. It is made up of amino acids. These amino acids combine with nitrogen to form different proteins, each performing different functions. Of the twenty-two known amino acids, eleven can't be manufactured by the body so they must be supplied through diet. These eleven amino acids, known as "essential" are:

arginine	leucine	phenylalanine	tryptophan
histidine	lysine	taurine*	valine
isoleucine	methionine	threonine	

*Taurine has been getting much attention recently due to a study done by Paul Pion, DVM, at The School of Veterinary Medicine, University of California at Davis. The results of the study, published in the August, 1987 issue of *Science Magazine*, reported that taurine deficiency contributes to dilated cardiomyopathy. This is a disease that causes the chambers of the heart to become enlarged, resulting in heart failure because the muscle is unable to contract. Since the announcement of this study's results, pet food companies have responded to the need for higher taurine levels and have fortified their products. Certain cats can still suffer from dilated cardiomyopathy even on high taurine diets, but research continues in to trying to find the solution. Taurine deficiency had previously been known to cause retinal degeneration; taurine levels in cat food are satisfactory for prevention of this. Taurine is found in meat, poultry, fish, and shellfish.

"CRUDE" PROTEIN. On cat food labels you will see protein listed as "crude protein." Not all of this protein can be used by a cat's body. Crude protein indicates all forms of protein included in the particular cat food. You can request statistics on the protein "digestibility" by writing to the pet food company. (See Appendix for addresses.) Digestibility is based on how well protein is absorbed into the intestine. Protein comes in many forms and some are harder for a cat to break down.

CARBOHYDRATES

Carbohydrates are the main suppliers of energy. By supplying adequate carbohydrates, protein can then concentrate on building tissues. Starch, sugar, and cellulose are the primary sources of carbohydrates. Cellulose regulates water distribution in the intestines and provides bulk for intestinal cleansing, preventing constipation and diarrhea. Vegetables and grains are carbohydrate sources.

FATS

Fats serve many functions. They add taste to food and are a concentrated form of energy. Fats transport vitamins A, D, E, and K (the fat soluble vitamins) through the body. Temperature regulation is also aided by fats.

Fats supply essential fatty acids: linoleic, linolenic, and arachidonic.

They promote healthy skin, coat, and also maintain healthy glandular activity. These fatty acids can't be manufactured in the cat's body and so they must come from the diet. Vegetable oils provide linoleic and linolenic fatty acids, but arachidonic fatty acid must be supplied from animal fat.

Buying good quality food and alternating brands will be pretty good insurance that you're providing all the nutrients your cat needs. A good source of fat is "soft" fat, such as butter or chicken fat. Fat that isn't good for your cat is the hard white fat that surrounds beef. This fat, called tallow, is too difficult to digest.

VITAMINS

Vitamins are organic substances necessary for body functioning. They're needed for growth, reproduction, and health. Vitamins are categorized as water soluble (B complex group, C) and fat soluble (A,D,E,K). With a few exceptions, vitamins can't be manufactured by the body and must be supplied through diet. I personally don't believe in achieving this through daily vitamin supplements because they can cause an imbalance. The easiest way to provide vitamins and minerals is through the diet, serving top quality food and varying brands and flavors to ensure sufficient balance of vitamins and minerals. The only time you should give your cat a daily multiple vitamin/mineral supplement is when advised by a vet. My descriptions of the following vitamins and minerals are to familiarize you with a cat's nutrient requirements. The more you know about the food you're serving, the better off your cat will be.

Daily vitamin supplementation is more important for cats who are eating low quality food. Supplements can also be beneficial for cats recovering from illness, injury, or surgery. Your vet will advise you on whether that's needed. Dieting and elderly felines are sometimes put on vitamins also.

More on supplements later. Right now let's learn our nutritional ABC's.

VITAMIN A. Vitamin A is a fat soluble vitamin. To be properly absorbed there must be sufficient fats present. It comes as preformed A (from animal tissue) and provitamin A (beta-carotene, from vegetables). Cats need the *preformed A* from animal sources because they can't convert beta-carotene to vitamin A in the body the way we can. Vitamin A can be stored in the body so it doesn't need to be replenished daily. What this vitamin can do for your cat: It fights infection and bacteria, encourages growth, repairs tissues, promotes healthy skin and coat, aids digestion, and improves sight and hearing. Good sources are kidney, liver, cod liver oil, egg yolks, and butter. A word of caution: Mineral oil robs the body of vitamin A. Never feed your cat mineral oil as a fat source.

VITAMIN B$_1$ (THIAMINE). A water soluble vitamin that must be replenished each day, B$_1$ is needed for normal muscle and heart function and carbohydrate metabolization. Adequate amounts of this vitamin will mean proper growth and muscle tone, stable appetite, and a well-maintained nervous system. Dietary sources include: brewer's yeast, bran, cooked eggs, turkey, beef, and soy flour. Don't feed raw fish to your cat—it will prevent absorption of B$_1$. This vitamin is easily destroyed by heat, food processing, and sulfa drugs.

VITAMIN B$_2$ (RIBOFLAVIN). This water soluble vitamin isn't stored by the body. Riboflavin is used for metabolizing protein, carbohydrates, and fats. It's also needed for cellular respiration and formation of antibodies. What does this mean for your cat? It means healthy skin, less chance of mouth and tongue sores, and prevention of eye problems. Brewer's yeast, cooked fish, kidney, liver, heart, green vegetables, and cheese are good dietary sources. Vitamin B$_2$ can be destroyed by light and sulfa drugs.

VITAMIN B$_3$ (NIACIN, NICOTONIC ACID, NIACINAMIDE). A water soluble vitamin that's needed for protein, carbohydrate, and fat metabolization, B$_3$ helps maintain the health of the digestive system and promotes healthy skin. Good sources are brewer's yeast, white meat chicken, kidney, liver, and egg yolks.

VITAMIN B$_5$ (CALCIUM PANTOTHENATE, PANTOTHENIC ACID, PANTHENOL). Vitamin B$_5$ is a water soluble member of the B complex group. It's needed for the utilization of choline and the production of antibodies. Conversion of fat and sugar to energy is also one of the functions of this vitamin. Vitamin B$_5$ is essential for the maintenance of adrenal glands. In terms of benefits for your cat, B$_5$ promotes healing, fights infection, provides energy, and minimizes the side effects of antibiotics. Good dietary sources include: brewer's yeast, meat, bran, kidney, liver, heart, green vegetables, chicken, and egg yolks. Vitamin B$_5$ can be destroyed by food processing, heat, canning, and sulfa drugs.

VITAMIN B$_6$ (PYRIDOXINE). This is a water soluble vitamin that needs to be replenished. Vitamin B_6 is needed for metabolizing protein, carbohydrates, and fats. It aids in the balance of sodium and phosphorus, and also in the formation of antibodies. What that means for your cat: It helps prevent skin disorders and maintains the immune system. You'll find vitamin B_6 in brewer's yeast, beef, egg yolks, liver, kidney, heart, salmon, brown rice, and cantaloupe (yes, cantaloupe. My cat loves to munch on a little cantaloupe ball.) Food processing and canning can destroy this vitamin.

VITAMIN B_{12} (COBALAMIN). This water soluble member of the B complex is needed for the metabolization of protein, carbohydrates, and fats, and is necessary for the formation of blood cells. This translates into a well-maintained immune system, proper growth, and energy. Your cat will get B_{12} from liver, heart, kidney, cheese, and egg yolks. Enemies of B_{12} are sunlight and water.

VITAMIN B_{15} (PANGAMIC ACID). A water soluble antioxidant that stimulates the glandular system, this vitamin can be found in brewer's yeast, liver, kidney, heart, and cooked eggs.

BIOTIN (VITAMIN H). Water soluble biotin is needed for metabolizing protein, carbohydrates, and fats. It's also important for utilizing other B vitamins and the synthesis of vitamin C. Biotin maintains your cat's nervous system, promotes healthy skin and coat, and aids proper thyroid function. Good sources are brewer's yeast, liver, egg yolks, grains, kidney, and fruit. **NOTE:** Raw egg white contains an enzyme called avidin that combines with biotin in the intestines, preventing absorption of the vitamin. Never feed raw egg white to your cat. Biotin can be destroyed by food processing, water, and sulfa drugs.

CHOLINE. This water soluble B vitamin is an emulsifier and works with inositol to form lecithin. Your cat benefits from choline because it helps rid the body of toxins and promotes a healthy coat. Dietary sources include: brewer's yeast, liver, heart, cantaloupe, and leafy green vegetables. Choline is destroyed by water, food processing, and sulfa drugs.

VITAMIN C (ASCORBIC ACID). Vitamin C is a water soluble vitamin that cats can manufacture in their bodies but only in small amounts. This important vitamin aids iron absorption and helps counteract nitrosamine (cancer-causing substance) formation. What this marvelous vitamin can do for your cat: Vitamin C will help prevent urinary problems and aid in maintaining healthy teeth, gums, bones, and tissues. It also boosts the immune system, guards against the effects of toxins, and accelerates healing from surgery and wounds. Vitamin C is a great stress fighter. Excellent sources include: tomato juice, leafy green vegetables, broccoli, Brussels sprouts, parsley, and turnips. This vitamin is destroyed by heat, cooking, and secondhand smoke. **NOTE:** Add one teaspoon of tomato juice to each meal to keep urine acidic, which will help prevent feline urologic syndrome (see page 175). I know you think I'm nuts, but, believe me, your cat will like the taste. My cat, Albert, would steal tomato juice right out of my glass if I didn't keep watch over it.

I also keep a bottle of vitamin C (100mg) on hand at all times. Since vitamin C is a stress fighter, I crush a pill and put it in my cats' food whenever they're dealing with extra stress. I know that Ethel hates to travel and gets very annoyed when she has to go to the vet, so a little extra vitamin C helps her cope with the situation somewhat better. I find that vitamin C helps my cats when they're under the weather or recovering from any injuries. Be sure you crush the pill and mix it in the food because the acidic vitamin can burn your cat's throat.

If you're a smoker, or if you live where pollution is a concern (as I do, living in New York City), your cat needs more vitamin C. I suggest the daily one teaspoon of tomato juice, and maybe crush a 100mg C tablet into the food three times a week. Be sure, though, to consult your vet first.

Vitamin D (Calciferol, Viosterol, Ergosterol). The "sunshine" vitamin is fat soluble and can be stored in the body. Vitamin D is essential for the absorption and utilization of calcium and phosphorus. This vitamin maintains the nervous system and promotes healthy teeth and gums. Good sources include: sunlight, cod liver oil, egg yolks, and salmon. **NOTE:** Cod liver oil is a good source of vitamin D. Consult your vet first, but I add a ½ teaspoon twice a week to Ethel and Albert's dinners. I **don't** use cod liver oil as a daily supplement because an oversupply can cause hypervitaminosis D (hardening of the lung, kidney, and heart tissue, among other serious dangers). Store your cod liver oil in the refrigerator in a dark glass bottle. The dark glass helps prevent nutrient degradation by light. **Never** feed cod liver oil to your cat if you suspect the oil is going rancid.

Vitamin E (Tocopherol). This marvelous vitamin is fat soluble and can be stored in the body, but not long-term. Vitamin E is made of compounds called "tocopherols." There are eight tocopherols: alpha, beta, gamma, delta, epsilon, zeta, eta, and theta. Alpha is the most effective. Vitamin E is an important element in cellular respiration and in the protection of red blood cells. One of the crucial jobs that this vitamin does is as an antioxidant, fighting the effects of pollution. Statitis ("Yellow Fat Disease") occurs in cats fed large amounts of tuna—vitamin E helps guard against this painful disease. Healing of the skin is accelerated by vitamin E. Two excellent sources are egg yolks and broccoli. Vitamin E is destroyed by heat, food processing, mineral oil, tuna, raw fish, and chlorine. **NOTE:** If you have chlorinated tap water, invest in bottled spring water or buy a water filter. Also, be sure your cat doesn't drink from your backyard pool.

Because vitamin E is destroyed by mineral oil, if you give your cat a hairball remedy, such as Petramalt or Laxitone, be sure to add a little extra vitamin E to the food. These hairball prevention products are mineral oil-based. Check with your vet.

FOLIC ACID (FOLACIN). Water soluble, folic acid is important for the effectiveness of other B vitamins. It helps metabolize protein and is essential for red blood cell formation. Your cat will benefit from a healthier appetite and fewer intestinal problems. You'll find folic acid in brewer's yeast, leafy green vegetables, egg yolks, liver, kidney, heart, and lentils. Enemies include: heat, food processing, sunlight, lengthy storage, and sulfa drugs.

INOSITOL. A B complex vitamin that's water soluble, it works together with choline to metabolize fats. Inositol rids the body of toxins and is also essential for hair growth. Your cat will have a healthy liver and a beautiful coat with the help of this vitamin. Dietary sources include: brewer's yeast, egg yolks, leafy green vegetables, heart, liver, kidney, peas, lima beans, and cantaloupe. Inositol is easily destroyed by water, food processing, and sulfa drugs.

VITAMIN K (MENADIONE). A fat soluble vitamin that cats can manufacture, it's needed for proper blood clotting. Good sources include: leafy green vegetables, yogurt, egg yolks, alfalfa, kelp, and fish liver oil. Vitamin K can be destroyed by mineral oil and air pollution.

NIACIN. A water soluble member of the B complex group that maintains a healthy nervous system and prevents gastrointestinal problems, niacin also increases energy. Good sources of this vitamin are liver, kidney, cooked eggs, and white meat chicken. Niacin can be destroyed by water, sulfa drugs, and food processing.

MINERALS

Minerals work as a group to maintain the body's proper chemical balance and are needed for the cells to move fluids through their walls. Magnesium is the culprit in the formation of gravel that causes urologic blockages. "Ash" is the mineral residue related to feline urologic syndrome. Males tend to suffer from this more often because the urethral passage is narrow and ash builds up (more about this in chapter 13). Many food companies advertise "low ash" and "low magnesium" food, so it's very important to read labels.

Even though minerals, and particularly magnesium, can cause problems, they're still needed by the body in some amounts for proper functioning. Chelated minerals are coated to make them digestible and more easily assimilated. A chelating agent is used to neutralize the positively charged minerals so they can pass through the negatively charged intestinal wall to be absorbed into the bloodstream. A large percentage of nonchelated minerals end up being eliminated.

CALCIUM. Calcium must be in equal proportion with phosphorus. The presence of vitamin D is also needed for absorption. Calcium aids in normal blood clotting and helps maintain the nervous system and heart function. It also promotes the development and maintenance of healthy teeth, gums, and bones. Excellent sources include: dairy products, green vegetables, yogurt, egg yolks, legumes, and salmon. **NOTE:** Calcium absorption is prevented by the presence of oxalic acid (found in chocolate and spinach).

Never feed your cat chocolate candy. It's a good idea to make sure all chocolate is not within reach of your cat. You're not doing him a favor by treating him to a piece of candy—chocolate can be **FATAL** for him.

CHROMIUM. Chromium is a trace mineral used for the stimulation of enzymes in energy metabolization. Good sources of chromium include: brewer's yeast, meat, chicken, and shellfish.

COPPER. Copper is needed for iron absorption and the production of hemoglobin; iron is converted in the body to hemoglobin. Copper also aids in the utilization of vitamin C. Sources are liver, legumes, peas, and shrimp.

COBALT. A mineral essential for the production of red blood cells, cobalt is part of B_{12}. Dietary sources are beef, liver, and kidney.

IODINE. A mineral necessary for proper thyroid function—an important part of the hormone thyroxine—iodine provides energy and promotes proper growth. In the diet, you'll find iodine in seafood, kelp, and seaweed. All cat foods contain sufficient amounts of iodine (iodized salt), so you needn't worry.

IRON. In the body, iron is converted to hemoglobin—a substance in the blood that carries oxygen. Iron maintains the immune system, prevents anemia, aids in protein metabolization, and is important for proper growth. Sources of iron include: red meat, tomatoes, liver, kidney, heart, egg yolks, bran, beets, asparagus, and leafy green vegetables.

MAGNESIUM. Magnesium turns blood sugar to energy and is needed for metabolizing calcium, phosphorus, potassium, vitamins C, B complex, and E. Cardiovascular health is dependent upon magnesium. Sources are shrimp, white meat chicken, soybeans, and corn. **NOTE:** Virtually all cat foods provide an oversupply of magnesium. It's the magnesium in "ash" that is the main cause of urinary tract problems. Buying food with the lowest amount of magnesium will still supply your cat with enough of the mineral he needs.

MANGANESE. This mineral activates enzymes for use of biotin and vitamins B and C. Manganese is also necessary for digestion and the formation of thyroxine (thyroid hormone). Your cat's muscle reflexes are maintained by this mineral. It is found in egg yolks, green vegetables, and whole-grain cereals. Manganese supplied in cat food is more than adequate, so it's another mineral you'll never have to worry about.

PHOSPHORUS. Phosphorus works in conjunction with calcium to build bones and teeth. Phosphorus maintains normal kidney function and provides energy by aiding in protein, carbohydrate, and fat utilization. Too much of this mineral can lead to a deficiency in calcium. Sources are fish, egg yolks, poultry, and whole grains. Your cat will get plenty of phosphorus if you feed him animal protein. **NOTE:** By alternating brands, you ensure proper balance and quantities.

POTASSIUM. Potassium helps normalize heart rhythms and controls kidney activity. Water balance and healthy waste elimination depend on potassium. Diarrhea and diuretics deplete the body of potassium—sugar can, also. Dietary sources include: bananas (yes, bananas), tomato juice, fish, poultry, beef, whole grains, cantaloupe, and leafy green vegetables.

SELENIUM. Selenium is an antioxidant. This mineral helps vitamin E work better. Sources of selenium are brewer's yeast, broccoli, cucumbers, celery, fish, and organ meat.

SODIUM CHLORIDE. SALT! Along with potassium, it's used for maintaining fluid balance. Sodium chloride is an important factor in the health of the muscular and nervous systems. Sources include: seafood (especially shellfish), kidney, and beets. Trust me, your cat is getting plenty of sodium chloride, and I mean *plenty!*

ZINC. Zinc is needed for protein synthesis. It's an antioxidant, promotes growth, and accelerates the healing process for internal and external wounds. It is found in egg yolks, brewer's yeast, beef, wheat bran, and fish.

WATER

Now we come to the nutrient that is all too often overlooked. What does water do? It regulates body temperature, is a solvent in digestion, and is necessary for waste removal. You must always provide fresh water for your cat. I say this because there are a lot of people out there who are under the assumption that cats don't need or like water. CATS NEED WATER EVERY DAY.

I clean the water bowl and change the water every morning for my cats. Anytime you see food particles in the water you should change it to prevent contamination. I also put the water bowl a few inches away from the food bowl because Albert loves to decorate the floor with his dinner.

If you have hard water in your area, your cat is getting extra calcium and magnesium. Buy low magnesium food to compensate for this. You can also buy bottled water, or invest in a good water filter to trap contaminants and metallic impurities from your tap water.

You're now familiar with the basics of good nutrition and the importance of vitamins and minerals. Now let's look at the cat foods available and how to choose what's best.

WHERE DO YOU BUY CAT FOOD?

Supermarket shelves are filled with famous brand-name cat food. These foods are all familiar to you because they're heavily advertised to appeal to *people*. It has been my experience that the quality may be questionable. Most pet food companies use the basic guidelines for nutrient requirements set by the National Research Council. The NRC publishes a document called "Nutrient Requirements of Cats," obtainable for $12.50 from the National Academy Press, 2101 Constitution Avenue, N.W., Washington, D.C. 20418. The document doesn't guarantee the *quality* of the nutrients required, so while a food may meet NRC requirements in quantity, the actual amount that your cat's body is able to use (the "biological value") may be lower.

PROFESSIONAL FOOD

This is food you buy from pet shops, pet supply stores, veterinarians, and breeders. These companies do little advertising, limited mostly to veterinarian and cat magazines. Although you still should read labels carefully, you stand a better chance of getting higher quality here.

TYPES OF CAT FOOD

CANNED FOOD

■ *WHAT'S GOOD ABOUT IT?* Well, it can be all natural, is higher in fat, and the high moisture level (approximately 75 percent) is beneficial for cats with FUS problems (see page 175). Canned food has a longer shelf life.

■ *WHAT'S BAD ABOUT IT?* Some vets believe a diet of canned food exclusively does not promote good dental health. Heat and processing can destroy vitamins. Canned food must be refrigerated after opening.

"GOURMET" CANNED FOOD

■ *WHAT'S GOOD ABOUT IT?* Convenience is number one with this food because it comes in single serving cans. You don't have to deal with leftovers and neither does your cat. These foods are also very palatable to cats.

■ *WHAT'S BAD ABOUT IT?* It's expensive! "Tasty" flavors, like tuna, are added for palatability. They usually contain TVP (textured vegetable protein) which is shaped and colored to look like meat. In some cases, these foods may not be complete and balanced.

DRY FOOD

■ *WHAT'S GOOD ABOUT IT?* It's cheaper than canned, easy to serve, and can be left in the bowl longer. Some vets believe that dry food promotes healthy teeth by preventing the build-up of tartar. Most cats love dry food.

■ *WHAT'S BAD ABOUT IT?* Dry food has a higher ash content and causes urine to be more alkaline. It's *acidic* urine that prevents cystitis and dissolves stones. Also, the nutrient content of certain ingredients may be reduced by drying. Dry food is more susceptible to insect infestation.

SEMIMOIST

■ *WHAT'S GOOD ABOUT IT?* Not much! If I have to say something good, then I'll tell you it's very palatable and convenient—just tear open the pouch in most cases.

■ *WHAT'S BAD ABOUT IT?* It has a high level of sugar for taste and to prevent bacterial growth. Excess sugar increases your cat's chance of becoming hooked on sugar and increases the risk of diabetes. Semimoist has lots of artificial colorings and some are carcinogenic. Why they add these colorings is beyond me because I have yet to meet a cat who would refuse food based on "color." Lots of salt is added to semimoist and you won't find "low magnesium" advertised on the labels. Oh yes, one more thing—what do you think keeps semimoist food able to sit in a dish all day and stay "moist?"—CHEMICALS!

HOMEMADE

■ *WHAT'S GOOD ABOUT IT?* You can control the quality of ingredients.

■ *WHAT'S BAD ABOUT IT?* Homemade meals sometimes are imbalanced and lacking the vital vitamins and minerals cats need. I would recommend that you consult your vet about homemade food. Table scraps, though, are a real no-no because they are usually too spicy and throw off the balance of vitamins and minerals.

CHOOSING THE RIGHT FOOD

Reading the labels on cat food will be the most important step in choosing the right food for your cat. I'm going to show you how to compare products and to recognize vitamins, minerals, colorings, and preservatives on labels. When you're not familiar with the names, they can be very misleading.

READING LABELS

Any cat food you buy should state on the label that it's "complete" and/or "balanced" and that it *meets* or *exceeds* all NRC requirements. The label should give the manufacturer's name and address. Some labels will say the product was tested in accordance with standards set by the Association of American Feed Control Officials (AAFCO). This is a national organization that provides the pet food requirements that serve as the standard for state regulations and laws. The AAFCO provides testing regulations so manufacturers can prove that the nutrition and safety of their food meets state requirements. A pet food company using the AAFCO testing standard must sign a sworn affadavit that the procedure was followed and the nutritional claims on the label can be supported by the test results. It is required that animals involved in the tests be given a thorough physical examination after each test. All tests and physical examinations must be done under a veterinarian's direction.

So if you see that the label states AAFCO testing standards were followed, then that's more of plus for that brand. If you have any questions about the testing procedure, and especially if the label doesn't state, write and ask how and where the product was tested. (See Appendix for manufacturers' addresses.)

Protein and fat will be listed in minimum amounts on labels. "Protein" doesn't necessarily mean animal protein. Remember, cats need protein from animal sources so check the list of ingredients and make sure that at the *top* of the list is more than one source of protein of animal origin. Be aware that ingredients are listed in the order of the quantity in the food. If the only source of animal protein is low on the ingredient list, often you can pretty much assume that this is a poor quality brand and will not provide your cat with adequate amounts of the protein needed. You also don't want to see something like soybean meal as the very first ingredient—you want to see animal protein at the top of the list.

Preservatives are used to prevent fat from turning rancid. Some companies use more preservatives than others. Some use highly suspicious ones. Check to make sure only *one* preservative is used. I have included a list of common preservatives in this chapter. You also should try to eliminate foods that list artificial coloring. And, because some vitamins and minerals can be destroyed during processing, you need to see added vitamins and minerals listed on the label.

Protein is listed as "crude protein" which unfortunately means not all of it can be used by your cat. I suggest you write to the manufacturer and request the "total protein digestibility" of their product. Comparing the statistics of different brands will help you in determining which products are best for your cat.

Labels should state total number of calories. If not, write and request the information. I wouldn't hesitate to write a manufacturer with questions, comments, praise, or complaints. (See Appendix for addresses.)

Make sure you see "low ash" and hopefully "low magnesium" on the label. As a guideline, the maximum ash should be 3 percent for canned and 8 percent for dry.

FOOD ADDITIVES

Why are they used?
1. To improve quality
by preventing rancidity of fats
by retarding growth of bacteria
by replacing nutrients damaged during processing

2. For appeal
by enhancing flavor
by enhancing color
by enhancing or masking aroma

3. For processing
to emulsify ingredients and keep liquids evenly mixed
by using stabilizers to create desired consistency
to control acidity/alkalinity

Not all additives are bad—you have to become familiar with what they're used for.

LIST OF COMMON INGREDIENTS

ANIMAL FAT/CHICKEN FAT	Source of fat
ASCORBIC ACID	Vitamin C used as an antioxidant
BEET PULP	Carbohydrate used for fiber
BHA (Butylated Hydroxyanisole)	Controversial preservative that retards rancidity. Supposedly safer than BHT — try to avoid
BHT (Butylated Hydroxytoluene)	Preservative that retards rancidity, can cause allergic reaction among other unpleasant effects — try to avoid

BLUE NO. 2	Artificial color that's been inadequately tested — try to avoid
CARMEL COLORING	"Natural" coloring made from burnt sugar — usually manufactured with sulfiting agents
CELLULOSE	Carbohydrate used for fiber and thickening
CORN GLUTEN MEAL	Digestible carbohydrate
CORN MEAL	Digestible carbohydrate
DIGEST	Also known as predigest — it's meat that's been liquified and sprayed on food to add flavor
EDTA (Ethylenediaminetetraacetic)	Antioxidant that traps metallic impurities and prevents rancidity and discoloration — considered safe
ETHOXYQUIN	Preservative — considered safe by the FDA
FISH OIL/COD LIVER OIL	Source of fat
GROUND CORN	Digestible carbohydrate
GUAR GUM	Natural binder, carbohydrate, and thickener — considered safe
LECITHIN	Nutrient that acts as an emulsifier and antioxidant, keeping oil and water from separating
MEAT/BEEF/ POULTRY BY-PRODUCTS	Good source of protein if from a quality manufacturer

A note about meat by-products — the AAFCO defines them as the nonrendered, clean parts, other than meat, from mammals. This includes, but is not limited to: lungs, kidneys, spleen, liver, brain, blood, bones, stomach, and intestines (empty of contents). Hair, horns, teeth, or hoofs are *NOT* included.

MEAT MEAL	Good source of protein
MSG (MONOSODIUM GLUTAMATE)	Flavor enhancer — can cause allergic reactions
PROPYLENE GLYCOL ALGINATE	Thickener derived from seaweed — considered safe

PROPYL GALLATE	Preservative used to retard spoilage of oil and fats — often used in conjunction with BHA and BHT. The word on this preservative is "caution"
RED NO. 40	Widely used artificial color that has caused cancer in mice — try to avoid
SODIUM BISULFITE	Preservative that prevents bacterial growth — can destroy B_1 in food and can cause allergic reaction
SODIUM NITRATE	Preservative used to prevent botulism growth — also used for coloring and flavoring, may be connected to production of cancer-causing nitrosamines — try to avoid because it also depletes the body of vitamin A
SODIUM NITRITE	Same as sodium nitrate
SOYBEAN FLOUR	Used to raise protein level on label, but it's not the protein needed by cats
SOYBEAN MEAL	Protein used to raise level on label
SOYBEAN OIL	Source of fat
SULPHUR DIOXIDE	Preservative that prevents bacterial growth
TITANIUM DIOXIDE	Coloring
TVP (TEXTURED VEGETABLE PROTEIN)	Soy flour that is shaped and colored to look like meat, used to raise the protein level on label
WHEAT FLOUR	Digestible carbohydrate
WHEAT GERM OIL	Source of fat
WHEY	Derived from milk, used to raise label's protein level
YELLOW NO. 5	Poorly tested artificial color that can cause allergic reaction — try to avoid

VITAMINS MAY BE LISTED AS:

Alpha Tocopheryl Acetate (E)
Alpha Tocopheryl Acid
   Succinate (E)
Alpha Tocopheryl
   Concentrate (E)

Inositol (part of B complex)
Lecithin (Choline and Inositol)
Menadione (K)
Niacin (B_3)
Niacinomide (B_3)

Ascorbic Acid (C)

Biotin (part of B complex)

Calciferol (D)

Calcium Pantothenate (B$_5$)

Choline Chloride
 (part of B complex)

Cobalmin Concentrate (B$_{12}$)

D-Activated Animal Sterol
 (source of D)

D-Alpha Tocopheryl (E)

D-Calcium Pantothenate (B$_5$)

D-Pantothenate Acid (B5)

Ergocalciferol (D)

Phytonadione (K)

Pyridoxine (B$_6$)

Pyridoxine Hydrochloride (B$_6$)

Riboflavin (B$_2$)

Sodium Ascorbate (C)

Thiamine Hydrochloride (B$_1$)

Thiamine Monoitrate (B$_1$)

Vitamin A Acetate (A)

Vitamin A Palmitrate (A)

MINERALS MAY BE LISTED AS:

Bone Meal (Calcium and Phosphorus)

Calcium Carbonate (Calcium)

Calcium Gluconate (Calcium)

Calcium Iodate (Calcium)

Copper Gluconate (Copper)

Copper Oxide (Copper)

Copper Sulfate (Copper)

Ethylene Diamide Dihydriodide (Iodine)

Ferrous Fumarate (Iron)

Ferrous Gluconate (Iron)

Ferrous Sulfate (Iron)

Iodized Salt (Iodine)

Iron Carbonate (Iron)

Iron Sulfate (Iron)

Magnesium Phosphate (Magnesium)

Magnesium Sulfate (Magnesium)

Manganese Sulfate (Manganese)

Phosphoric Acid (Phosphorus)

Potassium Chloride (Potassium)

Potassium Glycerophosphate
 (Potassium)

Potassium Iodine (Potassium)

Sodium Selenite (Selenium)

Tricalcium Phosphate (Calcium)

Zinc Acetate (Zinc)

Zinc Sulfate (Zinc)

For the most part, all of the popular brands of cat food that you're familiar with meet NRC requirements, but as I said, it's the *quality and digestibility* of ingredients that may be questionable. By just taking the time to read labels you can also be aware of what brands use artificial preservatives and colorings or unusable proteins.

Science Diet canned and dry food from Hill's Pet Products is an excellent quality food and is always my first recommendation to clients. The canned food comes in three varieties, Feline Maintenance (for adult cats), Feline Maintenance Light (for overweight adult cats), and Feline Growth (for kittens, pregnant, and lactating cats). The Growth formula has a higher amount of protein and fat plus the special balance of vitamins and minerals needed during growth, pregnancy, and lactation. Science Diet is low in magnesium and the protein is of excellent quality with high digestibility. This brand has added taurine, vitamins, and minerals. The dry food from Science Diet comes in the same varieties as the canned and is also top-of-the-line when it comes to nutrition.

Another dry food I've had wonderful results with is Iams. They make an adult cat formula and a kitten formula which is low in magnesium and has added vitamins and minerals. If you're unfamiliar with these companies I suggest you write to them and request literature on their products. One "hard to find but worth the effort" brand is Natural Life. My clients give this one glowing reports. Write to them for information (addresses are listed in the Appendix).

Whatever brands you decide on, make sure they pass your checklist of quality. Don't stick to one brand *exclusively* no matter how great it is. Alternating a few top quality brands is a better guarantee of providing the right balance of nutrients and the best way to prevent a cat with a fixed food preference.

In the Appendix is a list of some companies who manufacture several of the popular cat foods on the market today. Write to them with any questions or comments. Some have toll-free numbers so you can call to request literature.

BUYING AND STORING CANNED FOODS

Before buying a can of food, check for any signs of swelling—this could mean the vacuum seal has been broken. Dented cans are basically safe as long as you give them a thorough once-over, but my personal advice is not to buy them.

Once an unfamiliar canned food has passed my label inspection in the store, it has to pass my inspection at home. I open both ends of the can and push the contents onto a plate and spread the contents with a fork. I look carefully at the contents, checking the consistency. I shouldn't see any large globs of fat separated from the rest of the ingredients. There should be no hair, feathers, hulls, or other suspicious parts in the food. Any large blood vessels, tendons, or other connective tissues in the food is an indication of inferior quality.

One very important thing I do is *smell* the food. Now I know you're already wrinkling up your nose at the thought, but despite what you've been led to believe, good quality canned cat food shouldn't smell bad. I admit the smell doesn't make me want to run for a fork and dig in for myself, but it shouldn't smell rancid or offensive. The brands that smell horrible might be using a lot of poor quality ingredients, questionable protein sources, or fat that's turning rancid.

After opening canned food, refrigerate unused portions. Don't store leftovers in the can, because once opened the can reacts to oxygen, causing changes in the food. Glass jars that seal tightly are the best choice. Don't store leftovers for more than two days.

Always allow refrigerated food to come to room temperature before serving.

BUYING AND STORING DRY FOOD

Before buying dry food, make sure the bag has no holes or slits. You should reject any bag that shows signs of oil coming through—the bag will look or feel greasy. I'm very fussy and never take a bag that looks like it's been sitting on the shelf a little too long.

At home, when you open the bag it shouldn't smell rancid. Be aware of any signs indicating that insects have been in the food. Check for mold (green, blue, or white-colored food). Spread some pieces of food on a sheet of paper and check for any signs of hair or insects.

As for storage, keep dry food in a sealable container (preferably glass) once the bag has been opened. This prevents insects from getting at the food and will keep it fresh longer. Don't buy more dry food than you'll use in a month.

FOUR WEEKS TO FELINE FITNESS

At this point you should have a pretty good idea of how to purchase quality cat food, and, hopefully, I've convinced you not to leave food available all day. Now, there are just a few other suggestions I have.

Even though you're buying good quality food, there's always the chance that some of those delicate nutrients may have been destroyed during processing. As I said before, I don't recommend daily vitamin supplements for your pet, unless advised to do so by your vet, *but* there are some things you can do to improve your cat's chances of getting everything he needs.

THE "VITALITY" MIX

Years ago, my husband and I started adding bran, lecithin, and brewer's yeast to our diet. We had heard such wonderful things about how they improve health. It didn't take long to see and feel the results. We noticed that the daily stress of city living was no longer taking such a toll on us physically. We had more energy and seemed to have better resistence to illness. I knew of some vets who were recommending that pet owners add these same things to their pets' food, so we started the routine. Within weeks our cats' coats got fluffier and silkier.

I started recommending this dry mix to my friends and clients. Marvelous things started happening. Clients whose cats had dandruff noticed it was disappearing (due to the lecithin) and coats were getting gorgeous. Dry, dull fur was becoming glossy and healthy; greasy coats were becoming cleaner; thin coats were getting thicker. Cats who had repeated bouts of diarrhea or constipation began leaving normal, regular stools in their litter boxes (due to the bran fiber). Perhaps the most amazing change was that cats who had been bothered by fleas were no longer playing hosts to the little pests (due to the brewer's yeast). Another unexpected surprise was that the owners who had previously been allergic to their cats' shedding hair were discovering that they weren't sneezing as much. Lecithin, brewer's yeast, and other goodies in the Vitality Mix made the coat so healthy that the amount of dander was reduced. This mix is only for adult cats. Do not feed to newly weaned kittens. Also, consult your vet before adding this mix to your cat's diet.

Here is the official recipe for the Vitality Mix.
1 cup brewer's yeast
1 cup bran
1 cup lecithin
½ cup bone meal

I've given you the ingredients in these measurements so you can mix up a large amount and store it in one container, since you don't want to be opening four containers each time you feed your cat. I store my mix in a large glass jar. Be sure to keep it refrigerated, and each time you feed your cat mix in a ½ teaspoon into his meal. Don't take a shortcut and mix a whole bunch into a can of food. You want to add it FRESH to the food each time.

The Vitality Mix will provide your cat with extra B vitamins, which are not stored in the body, so you don't have to worry about oversupplementing. Brewer's yeast is a great source of B complex vitamins, which can be so easily destroyed by the heat used in food processing. The bran in the mix is for fiber—it absorbs water and creates bulk, which cleanses the intestines and stimulates movement of food through the intestines to prevent constipation. The lecithin is a fat emulsifier, breaking up fat globules and ridding the body of wastes and toxins. Lecithin will create a stunning coat on your cat and end any dandruff problems. Bone meal supplies the calcium and phosphorous needed for healthy bones and teeth. *Make sure you use bone meal and not dolomite.* Dolomite doesn't supply enough phosphorous.

All of the ingredients for the Vitality Mix can be bought at a health food store. If any of the ingredients you buy come packaged in bags, make sure you check them over for any holes. Most importantly, don't buy any product that looks like it's been sitting on the shelf too long. I also stay away from packages that have been sitting in a sunny location.

HOW MUCH FOOD SHOULD MY CAT EAT?

Clients ask me that all the time. My advice is that you should feed enough food to maintain your cat's healthy weight. Only you and your vet can make that decision. Requirements vary due to a number of factors. Specific breeds may naturally eat less food. Knowing the physical characteristics of a breed is extremely important. Siamese, for instance, are long and slender, whereas other breeds may have cobby bodies. Requirements will also change as cats age. Active cats will probably eat more than sedentary ones.

I think, too, many people overfeed their cats. With the help of your vet, you can determine approximately what your cat's ideal weight should be and how much food is needed to maintain that weight. Another factor to be considered when feeding a cat: Just as your appetite increases or decreases depending on time of year, mood, weather, etc., so will your cat's. Don't get upset if your cat turns his nose up at food when the thermometer hits 90°F. Remember, a cat's stomach is not that big. If you feed good quality food, providing your cat with nutrient-rich calories, then he won't have to eat such a large portion to meet his nutritional needs. This is where a good quality food and the Vitality Mix are important to ensure every calorie your cat eats is a healthy, usable one. If you are in doubt about how much to feed, ask your vet for help.

MAKING THE CHANGE

When I help a client to introduce the new food to their cat, I know it's going to be emotional for everyone concerned. After all, your cat's been used to his old favorites for a long time. The changeover should be done gradually to reduce the amount of complaining your cat will probably do and also to reduce the chance of stomach upset, due to increased fiber and nutrients. Basically though, because cats are creatures of habit, it will go much smoother if you introduce the new food gradually. The changeover period should take about ten days. Start by using 3 parts old food to 1 part new food for the first few days. After that, *gradually* decrease the amount of old food and increase the amount of new food so that by the tenth day your cat is eating all new food. If your cat has a fixed food preference or is a complete tuna junkie, it may take a few extra days. Remember, no abrupt changes.

Now we come to the hard part. What if your cat totally and completely refuses to eat the new food no matter what? Then after a half-hour if your cat hasn't touched the food, then pick it up and throw it away. I know you hate to waste it, but don't save the food. Prepare a fresh meal for the next time. *Appeal* is crucial at this point. The odds are, if your cat refuses a couple of meals, he eventually will get hungry enough to try this new food. I warn you, BE STRONG and don't fall prey to his pitiful looks, mournful cries, and dramatic attempts to win your sympathy. Your cat won't starve himself, believe me, he's too intelligent for that. When he sees he's not going to get his way, he'll eventually walk over to the food and eat. Even if he refuses to eat for a couple of days, you needn't worry. Cats in the wild fast when there's no prey to be found. It may even do some good for your cat if he's a bit on the pudgy side. Just make sure you have fresh water available and under no circumstances are you to sneak treats to your little darling!

FATTY ACID SUPPLEMENTS

Remember I told you about the essential fatty acids? To be sure your cat is getting enough of them, I recommend that you start providing him with a well-balanced fatty acid supplement. They're usually wheat germ, safflower, and sunflower oil-based. Depending on the size of your cat, add either a ½ or whole teaspoon into one meal each day. Dosage instructions are on the label. Be sure to consult your vet.

There are several brands available. Linatone and Mirracoat both use

BHA as a preservative so I try to stay away from them. If you can find an all natural brand, that's the best one to use. I recommend a supplement called Super Felerol (Nutra Vet Research) and also Kingdom Coat (Noah's Kingdom). Both are good quality fatty acid supplements that come in dark glass bottles.

Cod liver oil is a good addition. Put a ¼ teaspoon into one meal twice a week. Don't give cod liver oil more than twice a week because you will be oversupplementing vitamins A and D and causing a deficiency of others. Store the cod liver oil and the fatty acid supplement in the refrigerator. Both of these products should be kept in dark glass bottles to prevent nutrient degradation by light.

Butter is a good source of fat for cats, so I add a little (and I do mean a *little*) dab of it once or twice a week to my cats' meals. Remember, cats don't have cholesterol problems.

If you would like to try all of these supplements, alternate them. Do not use all of them everyday.

By the end of the changeover period you should be feeding a high quality professional food, alternating a few brands and several flavors to ensure proper nutrient balance. A ½ teaspoon of the Vitality Mix should be added to each meal and fatty acids should be supplied daily. This is how we turn a finicky eater into a cat with a healthy stable appetite. The only one who should be "finicky" about what a cat eats is the cat's owner. Yes, *you* can never be too finicky about the kind of nutrition your cat is getting. That's why I know by now you're asking yourself if there is anything else you can do to be sure your cat gets what he needs. YES! YES! YES! Read on.

VITAMIN/MINERAL SUPPLEMENTS

If you're feeding your cat good quality professional food with the Vitality Mix and the fatty acid supplement, you shouldn't need to give a daily multiple supplement. Certain factors such as age, illness, surgery, or diet can require the addition of a multiple supplement though. **NEVER GIVE A VITAMIN/MINERAL SUPPLEMENT WITHOUT A VET'S**

ADVICE. Remember, certain vitamins and minerals can alter a drug's effectiveness and can upset nutritional balance.

If you are advised to give a vitamin/mineral supplement and your vet doesn't specify a particular brand, be sure to buy one made especially for cats. Beecham Laboratories makes Pet Tabs-Feline. For more information on this product you can ask your vet or write to them (see Appendix for address). Felobits by Norden Laboratories is another good choice. Bene-Pet Pet Care Products makes a supplement called Felo-Pet (see Appendix for address). There are many good brands available.

I have never seen a cat reject the taste of a supplement, but if your cat does, you can crumble it in his food.

OTHER GOOD ADDITIONS

Providing some fresh additions to food can be very beneficial and tasty for your cat. I don't suggest adding meat or anything that might upset the protein balance of the food. Though occasionally, when Ethel is feeling a little under the weather, I might treat her to a bit of cooked egg in her food or a few pieces of chicken, but it's considered a real treat and I do it sparingly. The additions I usually put in are extra means of fiber, extra boosts of the easily destroyed vitamins, or extra surprises to provide a little fun "crunch" to a meal.

CUCUMBERS. You're laughing, right? I've seen more cats go crazy for a slice of cucumber. Ethel will just about do a nose dive into a bowl of salad to steal a few cucumber slices. Cucumbers provide a little "crunch" to a meal and contain lots of water so they're good for cats with urinary problems. I chop up a couple slices into small pieces and mix them into the meal.

In most areas, the cucumbers you buy will have been waxed. If that's the case, peel the skin before slicing. Don't buy a cucumber that feels mushy—it will have a bitter taste and the seeds will be tough.

GARLIC. "Garlic?" I can just hear you now. You're sure I've lost whatever remaining marbles I had. Garlic is very good for your cat. Yes, unfortunately you may have to endure his garlic breath. Garlic contains vitamins B and C. It can purify the blood and rid the body of excess glucose. Garlic makes the blood undesirable to parasites so if you put some in your cat's meal a couple of times a week, then those little fleas won't bother him.

Another garlic bonus is that it helps cats who suffer from arthritis. If your cat's garlic breath really bothers you, chop up a little parsley in the meal when you add garlic.

When buying garlic, look for compact heads with plump, firm cloves. Avoid garlic with shriveled cloves or soft brown spots.

ALFALFA SPROUTS. Live, organic vegetables, yum! Alfalfa sprouts provide vitamins A, B, C, D, E, and K. My cats love them chopped up in the meal. You can use other kinds of sprouts, but I've had the most success with alfalfa. Buy a sprouter from your local health food store along with a package of tiny seeds. Growing your own sprouts is fun and the best way to guarantee the freshest sprouts possible.

If you don't want to grow your own, you can buy a package of sprouts from a health food store or supermarket. When buying packaged sprouts, the ones to choose are bright in color and have a "lively" look, you'll know it when you see it. Check the bottom of the package to be sure the sprouts aren't too wet or packed too tightly. Sprouts need some circulation of air so they don't become moldy.

CARROTS. Even though cats can't turn the beta-carotene in carrots into vitamin A, a little grated carrot mixed in the meal adds fiber to help with intestinal cleansing. Tip: Before storing in the refrigerator, cut the tops off because they drain moisture from the carrot. Don't bother peeling the carrot before grating. A healthy scrub is all you need to remove dirt. The outer skin of the carrot is rich in nutrients.

VITAMIN C. After consulting with your vet, keep a bottle of 100mg vitamin C handy at all times. Although I don't put it in the meal everyday, I do crush one pill and mix it in two or three times a week. When my cats will be encountering a stressful situation, such as travel, vet visits, etc., a little boost of vitamin C is a help.

TOMATO JUICE. We talked about the wonders of tomato juice earlier. I couldn't get along without this marvelous juice. I mix one teaspoon into each meal to help keep the urine acidic and prevent cystitis. I've been recommending this to cat owners for years with much success. Cats love the taste and it provides vitamin C.

If you buy tomato juice in a can, make sure to transfer it to a glass jar once it's opened. I've already mentioned that storing foods in cans is not advisable and this especially applies to anything acidic like tomato juice. Storing the juice in an opened can increases the amount of iron it accumulates and it will develop a metallic taste.

COD LIVER OIL. (See page 72.)

VITAMIN E. After consulting with your vet, keep a bottle of vitamin E capsules in the refrigerator. Whenever I feel my cats need a little extra boost, I prick the contents of the capsule and empty some into the meal. If you give your cat a hairball medication, which is mineral oil-based, on those days give him extra vitamin E (15 IU). You can also buy vitamin E bottled as a liquid with a dropper. I feel the capsules preserve the contents better, but use whatever is best for you.

I also keep the vitamin E for use in ear cleaning instead of using baby oil, which is just mineral oil. I find it keeps the delicate skin of the ear in better condition. So you see, one way or another vitamin E will come in handy for you.

BROCCOLI. Steam a little broccoli for your cat sometime when you're preparing the vegetable for yourself. Broccoli is such a wonderful source of vitamins C and E, plus calcium, potassium, and iron. I know many cats who love the taste of a little chopped broccoli in their dinner.

If you buy fresh broccoli, look for stalks that are firm but not thick or tough. The tops shouldn't be yellowish or wilted. Your cat won't enjoy the vegetable if it's tough or stringy.

GREEN BEANS. Try a couple of chopped green beans in a meal. Whenever I'm steaming some for myself, I never forget to share a couple with my cats. To be most appealing to your cat (and you), stay away from beans that look like the seeds are bulging out—they'll be too tough.

By the way, a green bean makes a great toy for your cat.

LIMA BEANS. I hated lima beans when I was a kid. I still need to summon up courage to eat them, but I've seen cats go crazy for the taste. Sneak a few into your cat's dinner and see what happens. **ALWAYS COOK** lima beans before serving because heat is needed to destroy an antinutrition agent that's present in them.

PEAS. Several of my clients' cats love a few peas in their meal. One cat I know is particular and only eats mashed peas. My cat, Ethel, likes to roll a pea around the floor before deciding to eat it. Of course she never neglects to lose a couple for me to find squished under my foot as I walk into the kitchen.

CELERY. Albert hates it, but Ethel's a celery enthusiast. Chop up celery into very small pieces because it has those long fiber strands that can get caught in a cat's throat.

TREATS AND OTHER GOODIES

BREWER'S YEAST TABLETS. You want to give your cat the greatest treat? Go to the health food store and buy a bottle of brewer's yeast tablets. Give one of these tablets to him instead of commercial treats that may be full of chemicals. Cats love brewer's yeast tablets. Give them only as treats though—meaning **one** tablet not a whole handful.

I personally think they smell awful and taste even worse, but my cats come running from the farthest corner of the house if I so much as touch the bottle. I always bring brewer's yeast tablets as a peace offering when I go to a new client's home. I make instant friends with the cat by giving out one of these. I also use one as a reward after each grooming session.

ASPARAGUS. A cooked asparagus spear can be a fun treat for your cat, especially if he's on the "ample" side. You don't want to feed your cat a spear that's stringy or tough, so don't buy asparagus that's limp. Look for firm spears with tips that are compact.

WHEAT GRASS. If your cat is nibbling on your houseplants, which is extremely dangerous, then I've got the solution for you. Cats seem to have this natural instinct for internal cleansing and so they eat grass if they're outdoors or your houseplants when they're indoors. You can provide your cat with what he needs by growing a little wheat grass in your home. You can buy commercial wheat grass kits made especially for cats at most pet stores. Just follow the easy directions and in a few days you'll have grass for your cat to nibble. By placing the grass in front of a plant that your cat normally chews, you'll encourage him to go for the good stuff and not the bad. If he doesn't know what to do with the grass, pluck a blade and play with him, eventually he'll bite it, like it, and want more.

If you can't find a wheat grass kit, you can make your own. Buy wheat berries and soak them overnight in water. The next day, sprinkle them on top of a pot or tray filled with potting soil. Try to evenly space the berries. Cover lightly with ¼ inch of soil. Keep the soil moist by watering daily and pretty soon you'll see grass poking up.

Don't let your cat eat outdoor grass because of fertilizers, pesticides, weed killers, and other dangerous chemicals. Keep an ongoing supply of wheat grass indoors and hopefully your cat will prefer that to the outdoor grass.

CANTALOUPE. I can think of a dozen cats I know who love cantaloupe. Try giving your cat a little cantaloupe ball—it's full of vitamins. Albert usually licks it, plays with it, and ends up losing it under the refrigerator, but I still think it's worth the trouble.

CUCUMBERS. I mention these again (see page 73) because a cucumber slice is a great treat to offer your cat. Cucumbers are low in calories which is great for your fat cat, high in water which is great for cystitis-prone cats, and just plain delicious. Unfortunately, once your cat gets the taste of it, your salads will never be safe again!

YOGURT. A tablespoon of yogurt is a wonderful and healthy snack. Buy plain, unflavored yogurt—your cat won't miss the fruit flavors.

THE BAD GUYS

There are some foods that are not good for your cat and in most cases can cause serious problems.

TABLE SCRAPS. I don't recommend feeding table scraps because most are too spicy and rich for a cat. By adding table scraps to a cat's food, you run the risk of upsetting the nutrient balance. By sneaking a table scrap to your cat while you're eating, you are doing two very destructive things: 1) encouraging the habit of "begging", and 2) ruining your cat's appetite for his own dinner, thus, creating a finicky eater.

RAW MEAT. Never feed your cat raw meat, raw poultry, or raw fish. Salmonella bacteria forms on raw meat and raw poultry, and if eaten, causes an acute intestinal disorder. Salmonella can also be on cooking surfaces and utensils, so after preparing raw meat or poultry for cooking, always thoroughly wash all utensils and surfaces. Don't forget to wash your hands immediately after handling raw meat or poultry. Salmonella is destroyed by the cooking process so you needn't worry about meat once it's cooked.

Raw meat can also harbor toxoplasma gondii, and the parasites can infect your cat causing toxoplasmosis.

BONES. Don't give your cat bones of any kind! Small bones, like chicken bones, can splinter and get stuck in the throat or pierce the narrow intestinal wall. You may think large bones are safe, but you're wrong. Chewing on large bones can break teeth. If you were hoping to use bones as a way of keeping your cat's teeth clean, feed a good quality dry food a few times a week instead. A balanced diet, regular examinations by the vet, and at-home maintenance done by you are also ways to achieve good dental health.

MILK. As you read before, most cats lack the enzyme needed to digest the lactose in milk and this may result in diarrhea. Kittens, pregnant, or lactating cats need more milk, but the adult cat doesn't need it because he'll be getting all his nutrients from a well-balanced diet. Yogurt is a good substitute for milk if you want to give your cat a treat. You can also give milk as an occasional treat if diarrhea isn't a problem.

CHOCOLATE. The oxalic acid in chocolate prevents calcium absorption. Also, chocolate contains theobromine which is toxic to both cats and dogs—it can cause seizures and death. Remember, what seems like a small piece to you can be **FATAL** to your cat.

ALCOHOL. It's not cute or funny to let your cat take a taste of your drink—it's dangerous. Alcohol depletes the cat's body of extremely important vitamins and minerals and can cause liver damage.

MICE AND OTHER RODENTS. The reason I mention rodents in this chapter is because many people allow their outdoor cats to catch and eat them. The pesticides and poisons swallowed by mice and rats will be swallowed by your cat if he catches and eats one. The poisons build up in the cat's system. Hopefully, by feeding your cat a well-balanced diet, you can discourage his desire to eat any prey he may catch.

TUNA. Mentioned in the beginning of this chapter, it deserves repeating because of the severity of complications it causes. Tuna is high in unsaturated fats—the kind cats have trouble metabolizing. Tuna robs the body of vitamin E. Absence of vitamin E leads to steatitis (see page 178). Cats become addicted to tuna and turn into the worst finicky eaters you've ever seen. Pure canned tuna (the kind humans eat) **CAN BE FATAL FOR A CAT!**

RAW EGG WHITE. If you want to put a little egg in your cat's food as a treat, always cook it first. Raw egg white contains an enzyme called avidin that prevents the absorption of biotin in the intestine.

MEALTIME TIPS

■ Don't serve cold food. Always let it come to room temperature first. Cold food is less appealing and can cause stomach upset.

■ Alternate brands and flavors of cat food to ensure a balanced diet. This way, if one brand is lower in a certain nutrient, you have a better chance of covering it with another brand. Alternating brands also helps avoid the finicky eater syndrome.

■ Feeding at the same time each day helps maintain a healthy, stable appetite and promotes regular bowel movements.

■ If you have more than one cat, make sure each has his own dish. This prevents a dominant cat from nosing out a less aggressive partner. If your cats get used to their own dishes in the *same* place every time, you can better monitor appetites and add individual supplements if needed. For example, I wouldn't dream of putting celery into Albert's food when I add it to Ethel's.

■ Organ meat shouldn't comprise more than three or four meals within one week. Too much organ meat leads to oversupplementation of vitamins A and D, which can be as dangerous as a deficiency. Remember, when an animal devours his prey, organs constitute a small portion of the meal.

■ Don't leave dirty dishes down after meals. Clean with a mild dish detergent—strong cleansers are toxic to cats. A cleanser that is too harsh can leave a residue that can burn the cat's tongue. A strong cleanser will also leave a smell that may be offensive to your cat's sensitive nose, causing him to reject even his favorite meal.

THE WEIGHTY PROBLEM OF FAT CATS

Have you stopped referring to your cat as "Little Kitty" and found yourself calling him names like "Blubber Belly" or "Porky Puss?" Has it become a major effort for your cat to even raise up his body after a nap? Do the dishes in the cabinet rattle when he walks into the kitchen? Well, your cat isn't the one to blame for the excess baggage. YOU have allowed your cat to become a fur-covered mountain.

It's difficult to give a definite amount that your cat should weigh because you have to take into consideration such things as the particular breed (some are naturally large), age, and health. Through my experience, I've found the *average* cat to weigh about seven to eleven pounds. The best thing to do though is to be familiar with the breed, and along with your vet, determine the correct weight for your particular cat.

Obesity is dangerous. It can shorten a cat's life by creating serious health risks, such as diabetes and heart disease to name just two.

If your cat is a bit overweight and you're just beginning the change-over to the high quality food, that may be all the "dieting" your cat may need. Hopefully, if you've started your cat on the good food, adding the Vitality Mix and vegetables, you've already noticed a change in him. Many clients who had been feeding lower quality food and leaving food available all day, especially mounds of dry food, were surprised when I told them that their cats were overweight. Some people actually thought the fat was just an extra thick winter coat. When I had the owners put their cats on the better foods and the Vitality Mix, their cats lost those extra pounds.

First of all, with high quality food, the cats didn't have to eat as much to get the nutrients they needed. Also, the lecithin in the Vitality Mix helped emulsify the fats and rid the body of toxins. The bran cleansed the intestines and aided in regular bowel movements. And, not leaving food available all day allowed the blood supply to concentrate on other organs and created a stable, healthy appetite.

EXAMINE YOUR FULL-FIGURED FELINE

How do you know if your cat is overweight? Take a good look at him. Does his face look puffed out? Has he developed noticeable jowls? Has your cat's neck gotten thicker? Does his underside hang low to the ground? If you answered "yes" to any of these questions then I think your cat could stand to lose a little weight. Now, take your fingers and try to feel your cat's rib cage without pressing. If you can't, then you have a fat cat.

Once you've realized that you've allowed your cat to become too heavy, I'd advise you to take him to the vet. It's best to have the vet determine the cause of the weight gain. Certain endocrine disorders could cause a cat to become overweight and it's best to have that diagnosed and treated immediately. If the vet concludes that the obesity is due to just plain old "pigging out," then you have to start making some serious changes.

Depending upon how overweight your cat is, your vet may establish a diet for him using prescription food. He or she may also prescribe a multivitamin/mineral supplement at this time. Find out from your vet what he or she feels your cat's optimum weight should be. With that information, you can weigh your cat regularly to maintain the proper amount. Be patient though, the diet will progress gradually since we wouldn't want to put our pets through the awful crash diets we torture ourselves with. Realize, too, that a pound is a relatively large amount of weight for a small cat to lose. Remember, too, that it took time to become overweight, so it has to take time to lose the extra pounds. Never sacrifice nutrition for the sake of losing weight.

One way to prevent obesity is to feed two high quality, well-balanced meals per day, limiting snacks to special occasions, and choosing low calorie, healthy treats like a cantaloupe ball or a cucumber slice instead of fattening treats. Also, try giving extra love and attention instead of food treats. The bran in the Vitality Mix helps satisfy your cat by creating a feeling of fullness because of the water-absorbing fiber. And, as you are already aware, vegetables are a great low-calorie addition to a meal.

Diet is not the only factor in obesity. EXERCISE, or should I say, the LACK of it is one very important reason cats get fat and flabby. Playtime is really exercise in disguise. You should make sure to set aside time for play each day for your cat. Your participation is essential when it comes to exercise to guarantee a good workout. Use the Kitty Tease, the Cat Dancer (see page 86), a Ping-Pong ball, or anything else that will get your cat burning those calories. If your cat is already overweight, then playtime is absolutely a must!

PUTTING YOUR CAT ON A DIET

Keeping tabs on your cat's weight is the way to avoid the shock of trying to lose several pounds. If you weigh your cat on a regular basis you can catch an extra pound and nip it in the flabby bud without too much trauma. It's easy to weigh your cat. First stand on the scale by yourself to get your own weight. Next, hold your cat, stand on the scale, and read the weight. The difference between the first and second weight is the weight of your cat. I weigh my cats once a month, but twice a month during the holidays when guests may sneak food to them. What you should do is have an idea of what your cat's ideal weight should be. Your vet can help you there. Losing weight will have to be gradual, but a pound will disappear more easily if combined with exercise. In fact, in some cases an increase in exercise may be all that's needed to trim a flabby feline. Sedentary cats need your encouragement and participation when it comes to exercise.

If your cat has a couple of pounds to lose and your vet doesn't prescribe a professional reduced-calorie food, then all that's involved will be a few simple changes on your part. First, examine whether 1) you've just been feeding too much food, 2) you've been feeding low quality food, or 3) your cat is too inactive. The first thing to do is make the change to the good quality food, serving a specific amount twice a day. Your vet can advise how much you should be feeding. Usually, the safest dieting recommendation is to reduce the caloric intake by approximately 15 percent. You can also use reduced-calorie food, such as Science Diet Feline Light Formula. By serving top quality food, you won't have to feed as much for your cat to satisfy his nutritional requirements. And, of course, by now you know how detrimental it is to leave food available all day.

Also good during dieting is the water content of the vegetable addition in the meals, so don't forget to chop some cucumber, grate some carrot, or dice some celery. Combine this new way of eating with the much overlooked regular playtime/exercise schedule and your cat is on his way to a sleeker figure and feline fitness.

Your vet may also recommend a vitamin supplement during this time, but don't take it upon yourself to give one unless advised to do so.

HELP YOUR CAT WITH GROOMING

It's very upsetting when I see a cat that is so overweight he can no longer groom himself. Cats are such fastidious creatures and grooming serves many tension-smoothing functions. The decline in hygiene because a cat is so obese he can't do his regular grooming will cause him stress and frustration. As you know, stress takes its toll on internal and external health. Before you know it, you're dealing with a chain reaction of problems caused by obesity. An outward sign may be a dull or matted coat, even sparse in places. Another thing you'll notice is that your cat will no longer have that nice clean scent. These outer signs mean something is happening inside. Regular grooming will keep him looking good and feeling less stressful.

Finally, don't forget to give lots of love, affection, and encouragement to help your beloved companion through this sensitive time.

AIN'T MISBEHAVIN'

GETTING TO KNOW YOUR CAT

Introduce yourself to your cat by giving up your giant stance and go down on her level. Get on all fours and go nose-to-nose with her. This shows trust on your part and thus begins the bonding process. Let your new kitten sniff your face and conduct her own investigation. Start petting gently and before you know it, you'll be hearing that little engine purr.

THE PROPER WAY TO PICK UP A CAT

Never just walk up behind a cat and scoop her into your arms because you could easily startle her. Think about how you'd feel if someone (a very large someone, I might add) suddenly came up from behind and lifted you in the air without any warning. Your cat deserves the same consideration that you'd expect.

To get your cat accustomed to being held, practice the following procedure a few times a day. First, approach your cat so she can see you. Never pick up a cat with one hand—no matter how tiny she is. You must support her body. Put one hand under the chest, just behind the forelegs. Put the other hand under the stomach, in front of the hind legs. Gently lift the cat up and transfer her into a comfortable position with your hand supporting her hindquarters—this is very important. Hold the cat securely, but never squeeze her—make it comfortable for her to sit there. When you're teaching your cat to accept being held, you'll have more success and will build trust if you only hold her for a very short time. Let her down BEFORE she starts to squirm to get out of your arms. When you place your cat back down, do it gently. NEVER just let your cat jump from your arms because she could easily get injured. In addition, you don't want to teach your cat that it's acceptable to leap from your arms when she's being held. When you place her back on the floor, praise her for her patience.

When your cat is sitting in your lap, never stand up suddenly when you want her to leave. This can cause injury to your cat and is especially dangerous for a kitten. The safe way to do it is to use your hands to place her back on the floor.

CALLING YOUR CAT BY NAME

As much as you may want to give your cat the importance she deserves by bestowing her with a grand and lengthy name, a shorter one will be easier for her to recognize. Start teaching your cat her name every time you play with or stroke her. Repeat the name softly so she'll begin to associate nice feelings with the name. After doing this awhile, call your cat from another room and when she comes, reward her with a healthy treat, stroking, and much praise. When she's learned to respond to her name, you no longer have to supply a treat, but keep up the praise and the petting.

GOOD TOYS, BAD TOYS

Every pet store has a vast array of toys. Unfortunately, many of them are unsafe. Any toy with glued-on pieces, such as plastic eyes, is hazardous. These pieces come off very easily and can be swallowed. If you have any of these toys at home, pull off the glued-on pieces before your cat gets to them. Other dangerous parts on toys are the strings and yarn attached to the toys as tails. These can be pulled off and swallowed. The image of a little kitten playing with a ball of yarn is classic, but, unfortunately, is also very dangerous. You should only allow your cat to play with yarn, string, or ribbon when you're supervising and put it away when playtime is over.

Packages advertising "catnip scented" toys are the ones I stay away from. I've found the quality of the catnip to be less than ideal. I grow my own catnip from seeds, but I also will buy a bag of it if it looks fresh. I rub catnip over a toy to create my own "catnip scented" mouse or whatever. Be careful that you don't overdo the catnip scenting because cats become immune to its effects if left around under their noses too much. Also, do **not** use catnip with kittens.

Having been the purchaser of many cat toys in my life, here are my favorites.

The **Kitty Tease** (my #1 favorite) is a marvelous and irresistible toy for your cat. The idea is basically that of the old "string on the end of a stick" fishing method. A piece of denim dangles from a heavy gauge line which is attached to a fiberglass pole. It sounds ridiculously simple, but the inventor did some homework and came up with a well made, durable, and fun toy. If you dangle this piece of denim in front of your cat, she'll soon be leaping, doing somersaults, and having a heck of a good time. You can also make the piece of cloth move across the rug like a cricket or little mouse, which will drive your cat wild.

The pole on the Kitty Tease is so light you can make the little dangling cloth come alive with just the slightest movement. Replacement line is available should your cat get through it, but it's really very strong. My only note of caution with the Kitty Tease is that you MUST put it away when playtime is over or your cat will demolish it. My Kitty Tease serves double duty because in addition to my cats, my little dog always gets into the act. Kitty Tease is available by mail order. Write or call the Galkie Company for information (see Appendix for address). By the way, this is a fun way to help your flabby tabby trim down!

The **Cat Dancer** is another surefire way to exercise your cat. The Cat Dancer is a wire with tight rolls of paper at the end. You can make the toy move like a bug in the grass, hopping unpredictably, or like a fly, buzzing in the air. The Cat Dancer is another toy you must put away when playtime is over or it, too, will be demolished. This toy is available in just about all pet stores. If you can't find the Cat Dancer in your area, check the ads in the back of *Cat Fancy* or *Cats* magazine because it's almost always available by mail order.

Buy a box of **Ping-Pong balls** and roll one lazily along the floor where your cat can see it. A Ping-Pong ball is great because it's so light that it just takes one tiny tap with a paw to send it into motion. My cats play hockey with one in the kitchen, usually at about 2:00 A.M. The Ping-Pong ball is best on floors, but it will also work well on carpet. If your cat bites and punctures Ping-Pong balls, then only allow supervised play.

I advise you to periodically check under sofas and behind furniture to retrieve lost balls. When I walk into the living room and see my cats' hindquarters up in the air and their heads under the sofa, I know there's a family of Ping-Pong balls hiding there. You can provide your cat with entertainment that will keep her busy for quite awhile if you drop a Ping-Pong ball into an empty tissue box. When she sticks her paw in there and plays with the ball, make sure you have your camera ready!

A **peacock feather** can be a wonderful way to play with your cat because it's so light and enticing. Put the feather away when playtime is over because a cat can pull out the feathers and swallow them.

The **cardboard roll** from toilet paper is light and lots of fun to bat around. Next time, don't throw it away—toss it on the floor for your cat.

A **plastic drinking straw** gets raves from my cats whenever I drop one or two on the kitchen floor. Supervise your cat though.

Cats are attracted to **aluminum foil balls** because they're shiny and make an interesting sound as they skitter across the floor. You can let your cat play with one as long as you carefully supervise.

A **crumpled-up piece of paper**, innocently tossed on the floor, has sent my cats into many hockey matches.

Open a **paper bag** and place it on its side. This is a *classic* for cats!

PLAYTIME

THE PREDATOR. Kittens begin practicing their skills by stalking each other and pouncing. The way cats play is actually training them to become efficient hunters. Your outdoor cat will use her hunting skills on mice, butterflies, birds, or insects. She slinks along the ground, going from cover to cover, until she gets close enough for an ambush. Her pupils become dilated as she watches her prey, and other than a twitching at the end of her tail, she's perfectly still. When she senses it's the right moment, her hindquarters raise up, she starts treading with her hind feet, and then she's off.

Watch your indoor cat as she plays with a toy, or if she spots a bug, you'll see the fascinating predator in her.

PLAYING WITH YOUR CAT. Playtime is a wonderful way to get close to your cat. Remember, when you come home from work, your cat, who has been alone all day, really looks forward to this time together. Playtime is also exercise in disguise, and after sleeping most of the day, your little kitten could use a run around the house. Exercise is important to maintain a healthy appetite, increase circulation, tone the body, and send oxygen to the tissues. With playtime/exercise, your cat's digestive system will function better and she'll have a sunny disposition.

The trouble with many of those great toys you so generously bought for your cat is that they don't do anything. They just lay on the floor day after day. That's why your cat needs YOU to play with her. Your cat is attracted to sudden movement, which is why the Kitty Tease or the Cat Dancer are tops on my list. It's your job to make the toy come to life and act like proper prey should. If a little mouse got loose in the room, what would he do? He might scurry to a hiding place (under the couch, maybe?), then perhaps poke his head out now and then to see if the coast was clear. Maybe he'd creep along the floor, trying not to attract attention, stopping to hide behind a paper bag, and then making a mad dash. The key is to move the toy like prey. Rolling a ball at your cat will do nothing—she's not going to play like a dog. Remember, think PREY.

Don't forget to let your cat "capture" her prey so she doesn't become frustrated and give up. Otherwise you're just teasing your cat. I find that by allowing Ethel and Albert to successfully catch their "mouse," they really look forward to playtime and they're both in wonderful moods when the game is over.

CATNIP. Cats love catnip and when exposed to it, they become harmlessly intoxicated by the aroma. Catnip will bring out the "kitten" in your sluggish feline and is a wonderful treat for her. She'll sniff it, eat it, rub her head all over it, and entertain you with her antics. You can buy dried catnip in any pet supply store or you can grow your own from seeds. I grow mine and when the plants reach the right height (instructions will be on the packet), I harvest the leaves and dry them. To dry: Spread the leaves on a flat baking sheet and put it in a dry place for 3-5 days—far away from your cat. When the leaves are dry, separate them from the stems (discard the stems), crumble, and put them in a sealed container. Don't crumble them too much because you want to save enough aroma to release when you use the catnip.

I also save one or two catnip plants to keep by the window for my cats to nibble on. This keeps them happy and away from my houseplants. I grow so much catnip in fact, that I always bring a plant or a container of dried catnip as a gift when visiting cat-owning friends. A nice gift idea is to package some homegrown dried catnip in an attractive container and put your own "label" on it.

A note of warning: Keep catnip locked up tightly in a sealed container to prevent your cat from getting to it. Don't think a little plastic bag will deter your cat. Don't leave catnip around because your cat can then become immune to the effects. Provide your cat with it as a scheduled playtime treat, and when she's exhausted herself, take it away until next time.

You can use catnip in several different ways. Sometimes I put some in an old cotton sock, knot the top, and dangle it a few inches away from my cats. There are the times when I just sprinkle some on a paper plate and watch my cats sniff, snort, lick, roll, and in general, act like nuts! I also rub some on the scratching post occasionally if I feel they've been neglecting the post. Hint: To release the aroma in catnip, rub it between your fingers.

The reaction to catnip will vary from mild enjoyment to total ecstasy, depending on the individual cat. The effects, which usually last about 10-15 minutes, are totally safe and not habit-forming. Kittens don't like catnip, so **don't** attempt to entice them until they're older. And, for some reason, Siamese cats, in general, aren't susceptible to catnip either. I guess a Siamese thinks she's perfect just the way she is. I have also come across the occasional cat who just doesn't care for catnip, so if your cat doesn't respond, don't think there's something wrong with her.

MISBEHAVING

You must teach your cat what is acceptable behavior in your home. It will be easier to do this with a kitten, but if you're consistent in your training, you'll be just as successful with an adult cat—it may just take more patience. A strong "NO!" is the best way to deal with a misbehaving cat. She'll learn to interpret your harsh tone of voice and that one word with disapproval. You can also keep a spray bottle filled with plain water and give your cat a quick spritz if she does something wrong, like chewing houseplants. Never hit a cat because she'll soon associate your hands with punishment. This can even create a fear of you. The message you want to send to her is that you disapprove of her *actions*, not *her*. If your cat runs away after being scolded, let her—she got your message and is going off to avoid further embarrassment. Don't chase after her because you'll make her afraid of you.

When you discover something after the fact, don't punish your cat because she won't know why you're angry. For instance, if you come home and find the chair has been scratched, instead of punishing the cat, which won't work anyway, make the chair unappealing so she won't be tempted to scratch there again. Put a sheet over it, tucking all corners in so she can't get under it, or you can even temporarily cover the chair with some self-adhesive shelf paper. Then put a scratching post nearby so she'll go for that instead of the chair.

Since scratching is a vital part of a cat's health and well-being, you'll have a more peaceful household if you deal in rewarding rather than punishing when it comes to scratching. Stay calm and plan your strategy. Determine the correct place for your cat to scratch (i.e. the scratching post) and praise her whenever she uses it. For more specific information on scratching behavior and scratching posts, refer to chapter 6.

As discussed in chapter 4, electrical cords pose a very serious threat to cats. If your cat continues to chew on the cords, use the very firm "NO!" and clap your hands loudly. You can also put bitter apple on the cords (sold in pet supply stores). The unpleasant taste of the bitter apple, in most cases, will keep your cat away.

Consistency is the most important factor in successful training. For example, if you don't want your cat to walk on the counter, then take her off with a firm "NO!" every single time she's up there. You'll just confuse your cat if you sometimes weaken and let her go up on the counter. Make sure all family members understand what's acceptable behavior and what isn't, so they can contribute to consistent training. It's best to sit down with your family right away before your cat has a chance to develop bad habits and establish the rules. This is important, especially if you have children because they are notorious pushovers. If you don't want your cat begging at the dinner table, then instruct your children that they must not feed table scraps to her. As a child, I was a sucker for my dog's big sad eyes and couldn't put another bite of food in my mouth until I shared some. My mother didn't like that the dog begged at the table and knew my sister and I were responsible. My mother was such a softie that she didn't have the heart to get mad at us. She should have set down definite "house rules" regarding our dog's behavior.

In dealing with something like begging, I suggest you explain to your children and other family members that you feed your cat the food that's specifically made to keep her healthy and that table scraps can cause stomachache, diarrhea, and obesity. Whenever I have company over and they start sneaking treats to my cats, I very tactfully tell them how I provide a specific diet of high quality cat food and how table scraps upset that balance. Many times people become very interested in the fact that I've researched cat food. I've sent many guests home with samples of cat food, Vitality Mix, and fatty acid supplements (see chapter 7), along with feeding instructions. I always seem to get a phone call about a month later, telling me how much better their cats' coats look, how all dandruff has disappeared, and there's no more constipation.

FORGETTING LITTER BOX TRAINING. A behavioral problem that several new clients call me about concerns litter box training. If your cat seems to be forgetting her training, make sure her litter box is not too dirty. I find this to be the most common reason why a cat will seek other accommodations rather than use a dirty, smelly box with soggy litter and mounds of solid waste.

Another reason why your cat may not be using the litter box might be due to a change in litter. Any changes you make should be done gradually by mixing the old brand with the new. Litter box location is also very important to a cat. If the box is too close to where she eats or sleeps, she may refuse to use it. Refusing to use the litter box can also be due to emotional upset or stress. Litter box training, including how to deal with problems is covered in chapter 5.

Do not rule out a medical problem when it comes to your cat soiling the rug or furniture. Infections such as cystitis can be the cause of random wetting because a cat finds urinating painful and only tiny drops come out. This is serious and can be fatal if not treated. For more on urinary disorders, see chapter 13.

BITING AND SCRATCHING. A finger makes a very convenient toy when you're playing with your tiny kitten, but what you'll be doing is training her to think that it's okay to bite and scratch people. A little kitten's tiny teeth may not do damage, but your little kitten isn't going to stay little forever. Biting people (even in play) should not be allowed. Don't ever use your fingers as toys. When your cat bites or scratches your hand, you need to say a firm "NO!" and then provide her with an acceptable object to bite, specifically a toy.   To avoid scratches, never try to hold a cat who is struggling. Teach children the proper way to handle a cat and make sure they don't provoke her or use fingers in play. Keep your cat's nails trimmed to lessen any damage done by a scratch. It's the tip of the nail that punctures the skin so easily.

CAT SCRATCH FEVER. This affects people, not cats. In most cases when you are scratched by a cat, you can just disinfect it and in no time, it heals. If you are scratched and bacteria gets under the skin, you may experience swollen lymph nodes nearest the scratch, pain, and fever. These symptoms show up somewhere between one to three weeks after being scratched. The chances of getting this infection are low, and if you keep your cat indoors, it's even less likely to occur. You can also get the infection directly from soil, if you prick or scratch your finger while gardening.

Clean any cat scratches (no matter how small) with soap and water, followed by hydrogen peroxide. For serious scratches, or if you notice swollen lymph nodes, see your doctor.

PICA. Pica, or eating nonfood material can be caused by nutritional deficiencies, so make sure you're feeding excellent quality food. See chapter 7 "The ABC's of Good Nutrition."

At about four months old, a kitten may chew to relieve teething pain. The permanent teeth start pushing out the temporary ones at this time. You may notice your kitten chewing on clothing, so to save your favorite sweater you might want to give her an old woolen sock. DON'T GIVE YOUR KITTEN ASPIRIN FOR THE PAIN!

Other reasons for chewing can be boredom, so be sure you provide your cat with daily playtime and give her interesting things to do when you're not around. Keep curtains open so she can look out the windows, rotate toys, and consider getting another cat so she'll have a playmate.

DRINKING FROM THE TOILET. The first rule is to always keep the lid down. Although a cat probably wouldn't drown, she may panic and then drowning could occur. Keeping the lid down also eliminates the chance of something being knocked into the toilet. I know a cat who dropped his toys in the toilet. Always provide fresh water for your cat so she won't need to resort to drinking the toilet bowl water. If you suspect your cat may like taking an occasional drink from the toilet, be sure you never use bowl disinfectant and remind all family members to close the lid.

THE TOILET PAPER DEMON. Some kittens love to play with the toilet paper hanging from the roll. It might seem adorable to watch your kitten batting and unrolling the paper, but it may lead to a very undesirable habit later on when you walk in and discover most of the paper unrolled on the floor. Discourage this behavior with a firm "NO!" and be consistent—don't weaken and let her play with it "just this once." If you're unable to break your full grown cat of this habit, you can buy a special holder that prevents pets from unrolling the paper. These holders are usually advertised in the back of *Cat Fancy* or *Cats* magazine.

SPRAYING. A cat sprays to mark territory. This is mostly done by unneutered males. In most cases, having your cat neutered before this habit begins will prevent the undesirable behavior. Sometimes females and neutered males will spray when there are competitive cats living in the same household. It's usually an aggressive reaction to a territorial threat. Your indoor male might be looking out the window and see a strange cat in the backyard. Spraying is different from usual urination. The cat's posture is different for spraying—he doesn't squat. He stands with his tail straight up in the air, wiggling or twitching it, and the urine gets sprayed out on the targeted area.

If your male cat sprays in the same place each time, try putting an unappealing material (wax paper or self-adhesive shelf paper) over the area. The trick is to make the spot undesirable as a spray target. You can also try putting his food and water bowls there because cats don't like to eliminate where they eat. I know some owners who have had success by hanging orange rinds over the area, so if all else fails you could try that. If the spray target is a small piece of furniture, you can try removing it from the room and placing it in an area that's off-limits to your cat.

Don't hit or punish the cat who sprays because he may just resort to doing it when you're not around—this is very often the case. Some vets prescribe progestin (a female hormone) for males who spray, but this can only be given short-term. The only practical solutions are neutering and behavior modification. As for commercial repellents, many people I know have not had much success with them, myself included.

THE SOCIAL CAT

Cats and babies. Cats DO NOT, I repeat, DO NOT steal the breath from sleeping babies. This, and any other old wives' tales you have heard are so ridiculous that I don't even want to dignify such slanderous statements by trying to disprove them. I've been around cats and babies enough to see what a wonderful relationship they can have. Cats are so gentle and careful when they approach a baby. Can you say that about your big dog, who in his enthusiasm, dashes up to the baby to plant a big kiss?

Include your cat in your activities with your baby and you'll never have a jealousy problem. Talk to your cat and tell her what you're doing with the baby—mention your cat's name often so she feels a part of the action. Spending time grooming your cat will also prevent her from feeling ignored. And, no matter how tired you may be after doing all that's needed for your new baby, try to set aside time for playing with your cat and showing her her usual amount of attention.

CHILDREN. You need to make your children understand that a kitten or cat needs tender and gentle handling. Help your children learn how lightly to pet—no squeezing, no teasing, no fast moves, and no pulling on the tail.

Demonstrate how to pet gently with an open hand and explain that a pet is not a toy. Children should learn that when the cat is sleeping, eating, or using her litter box, she is off-limits. A cat loves her private, cozy bed and she needs to have a place to go to get away from children or other activity. Make sure your cat's favorite places are not disturbed.

Playtime between cats and kids can be fun, but a cat must never be FORCED to play and children must not "roughhouse" with her. Squealing, shouting, or other loud noises that children tend to make while playing will easily frighten your cat. Don't allow a child to go running up to the cat and grab her. A cat will only scratch if she's frightened and feels threatened.

It's fine to assign cat-care duties to children provided they're old enough to understand the importance of this responsibility. Never let an animal suffer because of the child's neglect in filling the water bowl, cleaning the litter box, or serving dinner. Monitor a child's duties toward all pets. It's also important that you do regular health checks and make sure your cat remains healthy. A child may not notice if a cat is straining to urinate (signs of feline urologic syndrome) or is constipated.

VISITORS. When you have visitors staying over, make sure they understand about checking before closing doors and cabinets, being careful about windows, and leaving things around. Don't be embarrassed about the "rules of the house." It would be very tragic if your cat ingests something that was left out or gets locked in a closet, especially where there are mothballs, because you were embarrassed to tell your company a few guidelines.

People who come to my apartment and tell me they are allergic to cats are shocked that they have no symptoms while visiting. There have even been times when my "allergic" guests have been in my apartment all evening and didn't even realize I owned cats! I truly believe the high quality diet I feed them, plus the Vitality Mix and fatty acid supplement (see chapter 7) reduce the dander, which is what aggravates allergies. The fact that I groom my cats regularly also controls the amount of hairs left on the sofa and chairs.

INTRODUCING ANOTHER CAT. You have to plan this out in advance if you want to avoid as many disruptions as possible. The first thing is to make sure your resident cat is up-to-date on all her vaccinations and is in good health. Your soon-to-be newcomer should also be in good health and free of parasites. Have the newcomer tested for feline leukemia and make sure she's been vaccinated before bringing her home (for more on infectious diseases, see chapter 13).

Because you don't want to threaten your cat's "territory" any more than you have to, you should buy your newcomer her own food and water bowls, litter box, a bed (can be a cardboard box lined with a towel), and a few toys. Nothing extravagant for toys—maybe just a Ping-Pong ball and a little mouse.

Because cats are territorial, brace yourself for a rather inhospitable greeting from your current cat. I'm going to tell you how to do it as painlessly as possible, but be prepared for some hissing, muttering, and general crankiness from your cat. There are always those occasions when a resident cat welcomes a new arrival with open paws, but most often a cat views the intruder with extreme caution and suspicion until she's sure this stranger poses no threat to her established territory.

There are many ways to bring in a new cat, but I've found this method to work the best: Have someone else carry the new cat into the house in a carrying case. This way your cat won't hold *you* directly responsible for this outrage. The carrier should be brought into a room you have designated as the "nursery," equipped with the new cat's litter box, bowls, bed, and toys. Leave the new cat in the carrier and let your current cat sniff around. Probably, she'll be grumbling the whole time. Then take your current cat out of the room, close the door, and try to distract her with play, affection, or dinner. Don't be insulted if she ignores you. The person who brought the new cat in for you should let the new cat out of the carrier and make sure she's comfortable. Leave the new cat in that closed room so 1) she can get accustomed to her new surroundings and 2) your current cat feels that only a part of her territory has been threatened.

After a few days, let them introduce themselves. Open the door and let them check each other out. Don't hover over them, but make sure you supervise the goings-on. Don't reprimand or hit your cat for hissing. On the very rare chance that a major fight breaks out, you can stop it by squirting water at them from a spray bottle. Usually though the only physical contact will be an occasional warning swipe with a paw. Now, this is the hard part: DON'T PET THE NEW CAT! I know it's very hard to resist, but you mustn't show the newcomer any attention or there will be hell to pay later from your resident cat. You don't want to give her any more reason to resent this intrusion, so don't make her feel like she's being replaced. Don't worry about the newcomer feeling hurt because you're not playing with her. She's got enough on her mind with the strange new surroundings and your hostile cat to deal with.

When you go to sleep at night or leave the house, close the newcomer in her room until you're sure there won't be any major skirmishes. Once the situation is under control, you can allow her the run of the house, showing her where the official litter box is located. The length of time it takes for your cat to accept the new cat will vary, depending upon individual personalities. I've seen cats hit if off instantly, and I've also known cases where it took a year for the two cats to become friends. Then, of course, there are those cats who really do prefer being the only pet in the house. You'll have to be patient and allow your cat time to adjust to the change in her lifestyle. You may have to feed the cats in separate places for awhile, or you may have to keep two litter boxes until the cats become friends. Each case is individual.

When I first brought Albert home as a playmate for Ethel, she wouldn't allow him to eat in the kitchen with her. He had been eating in his "nursery" room, but after a while I decided it was time to start letting him eat with the "adults." At first, the closest Ethel would let him get was the hallway outside of the kitchen. Each day, I gradually moved his dish closer, an inch at a time, until one day he was eating right by her side and she accepted it without a fuss. She even helped groom him after dinner. I also used bribery as a way of bringing them together. I discovered that both cats went absolutely wild over yogurt. They'd practically run me down if they saw me eating a container of it. They'd be totally oblivious to anything around them. I took advantage of that and spooned a little yogurt into a saucer. They both gobbled it up immediately, and in the process ended up with yogurt all over their faces. And, being the greedy little devils that they are, they started licking each other's faces to get every last drop of yogurt. By the time they realized what they were doing, they discovered it wasn't so bad to be friends. Ever since, Ethel has carried on the tradition of licking Albert's face after meals. I know it's probably on the chance that she'll discover an extra morsel of food on his chin, but it makes him feel wanted and he purrs like crazy.

LIVING IN HARMONY WITH DOGS. If you are under the assumption that cats and dogs can't live happily together, you are very wrong. All it takes for animals to live peacefully in the same household is a little organization and sensitivity on your part. Introduce the pets gradually and always supervise them until you're sure they've become friends. For the first couple of weeks, don't leave them alone when you're not in the house. Keep your cat's nails trimmed to prevent serious injury should the dog catch a swipe across the nose for getting too close.

Since dogs go outdoors, they can bring fleas and ticks into the house which can infest your indoor cat, so keep on top of the situation by checking your dog regularly. Use a flea preparation on him if needed (ask vet for proper one) and groom him. Don't forget to examine your cat if you see any flea "dirt" (excrement from the flea) on her, then do a thorough once-over because your cat probably has fleas, too. For more on fleas and ticks, see chapter 13.

Cats and dogs have different nutritional requirements. Cats need more protein, fat, and taurine (an amino acid) than dogs. Make sure each animal eats only her own food and don't allow one to finish the other's leftovers. One of my clients has a dog who gobbles his own food very fast, then sits and waits for the cat to finish so he can clean up what's left. Sometimes he doesn't even wait for the cat to finish, he just sticks his nose right in and pushes poor Mikki out of the way. Mealtime must be supervised to be sure all goes smoothly.

LEASH TRAINING. What? Leash training for a cat? Yes! Your dog isn't the only one who can be trained to walk by your side on a leash. If you want to take your indoor cat outside for walks on a leash, I recommend that you use a harness instead of a collar. A harness usually feels less threatening because you tug at the cat's shoulders instead of her throat. There are special harnesses made just for cats, known as "figure eight." Don't use a dog harness because it won't fit properly. Take your cat's girth measurement to be sure of getting the correct size harness.

The key to successful leash training is to keep it a positive experience. Before you attempt to put the harness on your cat, lay the harness on the floor and let her investigate it. She'll sniff it, paw at it, and maybe even play with it—that's okay. Let her do what she wants. Leave it on the floor for a few days so that your cat becomes used to it. The next step is to loosely slip it on her. Play with your cat while you're doing this and talk reassuringly to take her mind off the fact that she's now wearing what she thought was one of her toys. Put the harness on your cat everyday for short periods, gradually increasing the length of time she wears it. Stay close by, in case she panics, and remove the harness before she gets annoyed by it. Don't even try to use the leash until she's totally accepted the harness.

All leash training must be done indoors where it's safe and where you will have your cat's attention. Buy a leash (either nylon or soft leather) that has a bolt on the end that attaches to the harness. When you first put the leash on, let your cat walk where she wants. When she's comfortable with the fact that she's connected to you by this strange object, you can begin leash training. Have some treats in your pocket, preferably healthy ones like brewer's yeast tablets. Walk a few feet in front of your cat, hold a treat at her eye level so she can see it, and *gently* tug on the leash. Do this several times. As you can probably guess, a cat's normal reaction to being pulled will be to put on the brakes and resist. Of course leash training is a breeze when you're in agreement on which direction to walk—the hard part comes when you want to go one way and your cat wants to go another.

When you tug on the leash, your cat may react wildly, rolling over and maybe even biting the leash. By offering the treat, you will be teaching her to walk in the direction you want. Don't pull or drag her and definitely don't baby your cat by picking her up. Release the tension on the leash until the rebellious little cat calms down. Then walk a few feet in front her, hold the treat at her eye level, and eventually she'll get the message that it pays to be cooperative. When your cat is walking with you and responding to your tugs, you can stop using treats and replace them with much praise and stroking. Give your cat at least three weeks of indoor leash training before taking her outdoors.

When you take your cat outside, make sure you have her I.D. tag attached to her harness just in case something were to happen. Walk your cat in a fenced-in yard or a secluded area so she doesn't become frightened by cars whizzing by, dogs barking, or worse, a dog running up to her, children playing, or some other scary distraction. Remember: While you're walking your cat outdoors, she could possibly get fleas or ticks, so during warm months be sure to check your cat after her walk.

As for tethering a cat outdoors, I'm really against it unless:

1. your cat has absolutely learned what the "tug" response means. Otherwise, when she reaches the end of the tether she may thrash and struggle.

2. you are there to supervise. A tethered cat is at a *very* severe disadvantage should an attacker get into the yard. Your yard should be fenced-in, so no dogs can run up to your cat. Even being bothered by a bee could cause your cat to struggle against the end of the tether.

3. your cat is tethered in a safe area. If she's tethered near a tree or fence she could climb up and accidently hang herself. In warm weather, you must provide adequate shade and fresh water for her.

A FEW TRICKS. Dogs aren't the only ones who can do tricks—you can also teach your cat. It's not difficult, provided you remember that PATIENCE is extremely important. Don't attempt to work on tricks until your cat is about four months old because you'll want to be sure she's mentally alert enough. It's best to start with simple tricks and only work on one at a time or you'll just frustrate your cat.

The two most important things to teach your cat are 1) her name and 2) to come when called. If you do nothing else, at least teach those two commands which were discussed earlier in this chapter.

"Sit" can be taught after your cat has learned to come when called. Kneel on the floor with the cat facing you, say "sit," and gently push her hindquarters down. Give her a reward and much praise. Repeat this about five or six times and then stop. Do it again later in the day or the following day. Eventually your cat will sit on command without you having to assist her. When she does it successfully without your help, make a big fuss, reward her, bestow lavish praise on your brilliant student, and end the session on that positive note.

"Roll Over" is an easy trick because cats do it themselves anyway. Usually when you're stroking your cat on the floor, she'll roll over so you already know she can do it! Start the training by stroking her. Say "(*cat's name*), roll over." Give the cat a very gentle push to assist her rolling over, then when she's done it, reward her with a brewer's yeast tablet. Stop when she's successfully performed the trick for you. Lavish her with praise and leave her with this positive experience.

TIPS FOR TEACHING TRICKS

■ Make sure your cat is in the right mood for lessons. Don't do it when she's tired, cranky, or distracted.

■ Find a quiet spot to conduct training sessions, away from distractions and other pets.

■ Teach only one trick at a time, and make sure it's successfully learned before moving onto the next.

■ When your cat has successfully done the trick for the first time without your assistance, use praise and a reward, then *end the training session on this positive note.* Once she's done it right, don't make her do it again.

■ Don't attempt to show the trick to family until you're sure your cat has successfully learned it. The distraction of other people around could frustrate her.

■ When the cat has perfected the trick, substitute affection and praise for the food reward.

STRESS

We all know how owning a pet reduces the effects of stress in our lives, and studies indicate that pet owners live longer. What about the stress our pets go through? Pets do suffer from this, too, in case you didn't know.

Stress alerts the body to be on guard. This means the heart pumps more blood, extra hormones get secreted, muscles tense up and, in general, internal mechanisms must work harder. Unrelieved stress can leave the internal balance in a cat's body out of sync. Continued stress also lowers the body's resistance to illness, causes personality changes, and depletes energy, among other pitfalls.

You may not have associated stress with pets, but take a look at an animal's life through her eyes and you'll discover such stressful situations as: being left alone too long, being left at a kennel, not knowing when or if your owner is coming back, sitting in a vet's waiting room with lots of unfamiliar and BIG animals, cat shows, a new house, a new baby, lots of strangers in the house, injury, illness, death of a household member (person or pet), a noisy household, or even an unclean litter box. The list could go on and on, but what's important to remember is that the things that stress us, also stress our pets; your four-footed companion feels those same things. For animals, even minor changes can result in stress, such as a sudden change in diet or a different brand of litter.

How stress affects each cat varies, depending on the individual. Age, general health, and personality are all factors that come into play when dealing with the impact that on-going, unrelieved stress will have on a cat. I don't want to scare you because a certain amount of stress is unavoidable and you'll never be able to create a totally stress-free life for your cat, but what you need to do is eliminate or minimize the situations within your control.

SYMPTOMS OF STRESS. The first thing you may notice is a change in your cat's behavior. For example, a usually playful cat may no longer be eager to play, or she may start hiding. Another symptom of stress can be a decrease in appetite. You may also notice a change in the condition of your cat's coat. Stress very often is behind a dull coat or excessive shedding; it can also be a poor diet, so you have to be a good detective. Cats under stress may groom themselves to such an extent that they create bald spots.

HELPING YOUR CAT COPE WITH STRESS. First of all, whenever you suspect stress, you should have your cat examined by the vet to rule out any physical problem. After that's done, you need to find the cause or causes of the stress—don't overlook anything. For instance:

■ *Has there been an addition to the family?* This includes a new pet, spouse, or baby. If so, make sure your cat's personal space is not violated. Give her extra love and affection to reassure her that no one could take her place in your heart. If you've recently gotten married, you can also help your cat to accept this stranger in your house by letting your spouse share in the handling of feeding duties. If the new addition is a baby, then make sure your cat gets extra attention and don't shut her out—let her investigate this strange-looking, tiny person. I've seen cats and babies develop such bonds. Since you'll be holding your baby so often, to avoid feelings of rejection on your cat's part, include her in activities, talking to her as you take care of your child.

■ *Have you moved to a new house or apartment?* Setting a cat loose in a new home can be overwhelming for an animal who values her own territory. In addition to it being unfamiliar, there could be smells left over from previous animal residents. Allow your cat time to adjust to the change by confining her in one room with her food, water, litter box, scratching post, bed, and toys. Gradually introduce her to the rest of the house. For more, see section on "Moving" in chapter 10.

■ *Have you changed jobs recently which causes you to come home at a different time?* If so, make sure you make a big fuss over your cat when you arrive home. I would also recommend that you consider a playmate for your cat to keep her company during those long hours while you're at work.

■ *Have you changed your cat's diet?* An abrupt change can be very disturbing, so make adjustments gradually by mixing the old food with the new food. See chapter 7 to learn how to provide your cat with stress-fighting nutrition. If you have more than one cat, there could be some display of dominance going on during meals which could cause stress. If you suspect that this is the case, feed your cats farther apart—maybe even in separate rooms, so the less dominant of the cats no longer feels threatened.

■ *Could the litter box be the problem?* Have you changed brands of litter? This can be very disturbing to a cat. If you must switch litter, do it gradually by mixing the old litter with the new litter each time. If it isn't the litter that's causing the problem, it could be that the box is too dirty. Be responsible about your cleaning duties by removing solid waste daily and scrub the box regularly. See chapter 5 for more on litter boxes.

■ *Do you have toys for your cat or is she left alone all day with nothing to play with?* Provide her with toys, rotate them to prevent boredom, and PLAY with your cat everyday to make her time without you more tolerable. Also, open your curtains, shades, or blinds so your cat can look out the window.

■ *Have you neutered or spayed your cat?* If not, your male or female is going through LOTS OF STRESS! See chapter 11 for more on this very important subject.

■ *Do you travel often and have someone come in and feed your cat?* If so, consider getting another cat so your cat won't be lonely. Also, ask your sitter to spend time with your cat, playing with her and providing affection. For more on cat sitters, see chapter 10. When you travel, I urge you to find someone who will come to your home rather than putting your cat in a kennel—you'll cut out a lot of stress that way.

To find the cause of your cat's stress you really have to exhaust your brain to think of any little thing that could be bothering her. Don't overlook anything, no matter how minor. It could be that you moved her bed from one corner to another; it could be the sound of the vacuum cleaner; it could be the dog next door who keeps coming into your backyard; or it could be that you don't feed your cat at the same times each day.

LOOKING GOOD

As you already know, cats spend a great deal of time grooming them-selves. What you may *not* know is that they aren't always doing it for cleansing purposes. There are also psychological reasons behind grooming activity. If you scold your cat for doing something forbidden, such as scratching on the furniture, he will probably start grooming himself to displace the energy he would rather spend scratching your sofa. If a cat would like to do something, but wouldn't dare because he knows it's not allowed, he will groom himself to suppress the forbidden desire. Cats also groom to help heal or cleanse a wound. Roommate cats may groom each other as a show of affection. A bored cat or one under stress may groom himself excessively, even pulling out his hair. A situation like this requires more playtime or the addition of another pet to help ease boredom. So you see, hygiene is just one part of a cat's grooming behavior.

HAIRBALLS

I mention hairballs up front in this chapter because I believe it's such an overlooked and ignored problem. I've met cat owners who have accepted their self-grooming cat coughing up hairballs as a normal part of feline behavior. They never put it together that a little brushing on their part would reduce, and in most cases, eliminate hairballs.

The bad part about self-grooming is that the cat swallows lots of hair. This hair can accumulate in the stomach or intestines, developing into a hairball. Cats can't spit out the hair they've licked because of tiny backward-facing barbs on their tongues. Because of the direction the barbs face, the hair that's licked only has one way to go—down! Some small hairballs can pass out of the body and some are regurgitated, as the cat will have trouble keeping food down until the hairball is vomited up. If a hairball passes out of the stomach and can't get through the intestines, a blockage results. This is serious business because if the hairball can't get through, then neither can the stool. The result will be constipation. Your vet may give your cat a laxative or try removing the hairball through an enema. If the hairball is still unable to pass, it will have to be removed surgically.

Even with daily grooming, some longhaired cats may still require a hairball remedy. If your cat is an excessive self-groomer, it might be a good idea to give a hairball remedy like Petramalt, twice a week. Just be sure you add a little vitamin E into the food on those days because the mineral oil-based product robs the body of vitamin E. If your cat gets a hairball, even though you've been grooming him faithfully, don't be discouraged—just think of how many hairballs you've prevented.

OTHER REASONS TO GROOM YOUR CAT

Brushing distributes the natural oils and removes dead hairs and loose dander. Brushing will bring out the shine in a cat's coat. You'd be surprised at how the dead hair left on the body can make a coat look dull and drab.

Cats shed. People sneeze. You can reduce the amount of both of these things by regularly brushing your cat. It will also cut down on the amount of loose hairs you find on your furniture. A note of caution concerning radiators: Cats love to sleep on them, but it's something you shouldn't allow. Sleeping on a radiator can increase shedding and will dry out the hair, causing it to break.

Cats shed the most in the fall (preparing their winter coat) and spring (preparing their summer coat). Cats also shed when they're under stress. This could be due to illness, emotional upset, strangers in the house, the arrival of a new pet, vet visit, or being left alone too long.

Grooming time is also "health check" time. This is the perfect opportunity to give your cat the once-over. Check for scrapes, wounds, and parasites. Check the ears for signs of infection, redness, or ear mites (for treatment see chapter 13). As you look over your cat's coat, separate the hairs so you can examine the skin for fleas or ticks. You may not see the fleas themselves but you might notice the flea "dirt" (excrement). Check the rectal area for signs of irritation or redness. If you see what appear to be pieces of rice around the rectum, that means your cat has tapeworms (see chapter 13).

Continuing your examination, look in the eyes to make sure they're bright and clear with no sign of discharge. Check the nose for any scrapes or discharge. Examine the pads of the paws for any signs of injury or swelling. Don't forget to also check *between* the toes because that's where the sneaky tick can hide. Go over every inch of your cat's body.

My favorite reason for grooming a cat is to use it as a time for closeness and affection. When I groom my cats, it's an expression of my love for them. I rub them in their favorite places, check them over to be sure they don't have any problems that need attention, and in general, do my part to make sure they stay healthy and looking their best. Some cats look forward to grooming sessions because they know they're going to get lots of attention. I try to teach my clients to view grooming time as a positive and loving experience so that the feeling is transferred to their cat. If you dread grooming, believe me, your cat will pick up on that and dread it also.

GROOMING

GETTING STARTED

First of all, if you've been following my recommendations on nutrition and feeding, your cat's coat should be in good condition to begin with. The coat should be neither dry nor oily, with no signs of dandruff. By feeding good quality food twice a day and not leaving food available, you encourage a healthy, glossy coat with a clean scent. If you've been neglecting your ownership responsibilities, your cat probably has a less then desirable appearance with either a dry, lifeless coat or a very oily one. Let me tell you, a cat with an oily coat will attract every piece of dust and dirt in his path like a four-footed dust mop!

The easiest way to ensure stress-free grooming is to begin the procedure while your cat is still a kitten. If you do this, you will find that by the time your cat is an adult, he will be so used to being handled that you'll both breeze through the process. If your cat is already full-grown, then you have to be very sensitive to his suspicions about this new adventure. For the first few sessions, don't do anything but get the cat used to being handled. Run your fingers all over his body, petting him in all of his favorite places. To get him used to having his paws touched, so you'll be able to clip his nails later, just gently stroke them, then work up to the point where he'll let you hold them (gently) for several seconds.

PROFESSIONAL GROOMERS

If you've never groomed a longhaired cat before, it's a good idea to have a professional groomer come to your house and do the first grooming session. The best and quickest way to learn is to watch a professional. Groomers are very willing to explain each step as they go through it because you'll have to do the daily maintenance. If your cat's coat is in poor condition, or if it's matted, I strongly advise that you have a professional handle the job. Detangling and cutting mats is tricky business and a groomer can do it more efficiently and with less stress to your cat. Once the groomer has gotten the coat in good shape, then you must do daily grooming (a few minutes a day is all it takes) to keep mats from reforming.

The best way to find a professional groomer is through personal recommendation. If you don't know any owners who use groomers, then ask your vet. Once you find a groomer, make sure you're present during the first grooming session. In addition to watching his or her technique so you can learn the procedure, you also want to watch *how* your cat is being handled. The cat shouldn't be given any tranquilizers or be held with any restraints. Gentleness and patience are two essential qualities that any groomer should have. I also encourage owners to be close by to offer their cat reassuring words and petting during sessions.

THE RIGHT PLACE TO GROOM

The best place to groom is one that's quiet and away from distracting activity. You'll have a greater chance at successful grooming if you choose a time and place where no other pets or family members will make your cat feel that he's missing out on anything. Don't turn on the TV during grooming—try to keep the place quiet. If you work better with music, turn the radio on low to a classical or soft-music station. The important thing is for you to be relaxed which will in turn relax your cat.

You can groom your cat just about anywhere. You can put him on a table or a counter. If you choose a table for grooming, make sure it's sturdy. Don't use a TV snack table or a wobbly card table. Hobar Manufacturing Inc. makes a sturdy folding table for grooming (see Appendix for address). If you decide to groom your cat on the kitchen counter, make sure it's clean and dry. I don't recommend putting a towel down because two seconds after you place your cat on it, the towel will end up a jumbled mess. If your cat feels more secure with a sure grip, then place a rubber bath mat on the grooming surface.

Keep grooming sessions short so you don't test the limits of your cat's patience each time. By completing the grooming *before* your cat gets fidgety, you stand a much better chance of him becoming more and more cooperative with each session.

In the beginning, just get your cat comfortable with being placed on the counter or table. Use your hands to stroke him and a soft soothing voice to reassure him. Keep these sessions short, and don't let him jump off the table when you're through. It's important that *you* establish when grooming time is completed—not your cat, so lift him off the surface and place him on the floor. Always end every session with lots of praise and a treat.

GROOMING A LONGHAIRED CAT

TOOLS

cotton swabs or cotton balls (for ear cleaning)
vitamin E oil or baby oil (for ear cleaning)
fine-tooth comb
medium-tooth comb
wide-tooth comb
nail trimmers
blunt-nosed scissors
soft bristle toothbrush (for facial area)
baby toothbrush or gauze (for teeth cleaning)
baking soda (for teeth)
natural bristle brush
detangling spray or liquid

Before you get all nervous at the thought of so many tools, just realize that you won't have to use everything each day. For example, schedule it so you don't do ear cleaning on the same day you clip the nails. This will make it easier on both you and your cat.

Store all your tools in a plastic caddy (available in any hardware store), which will keep everything conveniently organized. The vitamin E capsules are what I use for ear cleaning because I feel the oil helps keep the skin on the inside of the ear in good condition, but you can use baby oil if you prefer. Keep the caddy well-stocked. When you're running low on something, replace it. Once I put the cat on the counter and begin grooming, it would be very inconvenient to interrupt the session to go looking for a piece of gauze or a cotton ball.

Before you even begin to use a single tool, first use your fingers by gently running them up and down your cat. This is done for good reasons: It will relax your cat while giving you the opportunity to do your "health check," and lets you feel for anything you need to be aware of before grooming, such as mats. If you're new at grooming, use this finger massage as an opportunity to become familiar with your cat's body—all the bumpy bones, crevices, possible wounds, sensitive areas, etc., which could cause your cat pain if you just rake a comb across these spots. If you do encounter a mat upon your finger inspection, then you must take care of it before going any further. Turn to the section on "Mats" to learn how to remove them.

Once you're sure the coat is free of any mats you can begin grooming. First use the wide-tooth comb with a light touch. This way you can double-check in case you come across any tangles. When the wide-tooth comb goes through the coat freely, you can then switch to the medium-tooth comb. When that goes through the coat smoothly, then move on to the fine one. Be careful that you don't start the comb right down at the skin until the outer layers can be combed freely. Work your way toward the skin, section by section.

The best way to make sure your cat cooperates is to start by grooming the back of his neck or under his chin. These are usually a cat's favorite spots and by doing one of these areas first, I can pretty much guarantee you'll hear some purring. Then move on to the throat and chest area. Lift one of the forelegs to reach the upper stomach. Use a soft toothbrush for the facial area. When combing the back, be aware of the way the spinal bones stick out. Don't run over them with the comb. Comb on either side of the spine, using short strokes. Your free hand should be used to hold the skin while you comb. Move skin away from any protruding bones so you can comb that part of the coat. Pay particular attention to potentially troublesome areas like the abdomen, under the arms, and the hindquarters. To comb the inside of the leg and abdomen, brace the cat against your chest, lift the outside leg, and reach over him. Most cats are sensitive about having their stomachs groomed, but don't neglect those areas. Be very gentle and watch out for the nipples. If your cat cries out, stop immediately because chances are you hurt him. Start again *very* gently. Do the tail last, going section by section—be very careful. Comb in the direction the hair grows. Finally, you can use the soft natural bristle brush, fluffing out as you brush to lift the hairs. Never use a synthetic brush because it could damage the hairs.

I don't believe in using any coat conditioners. A good quality diet, exercise, and regular grooming will be the best "conditioner" your cat's coat will ever get. If your cat's coat isn't in top condition, you need to work on the *inside* first.

MATS

Mats that remain in the coat will cause your cat much pain. If the cat scratches himself, he can get his nails caught in the mat. To disengage them, he may end up pulling out clumps of hair and even tearing the skin. Mats can be very painful because they pull the cat's sensitive skin. As I mentioned before, if your cat's coat is very matted or if you're a novice at grooming, it's best to enlist the help of a professional groomer.

If the mat is not so bad, you can first try detangling it with your fingers. Saturate it with a detangling liquid or spray safe for cats, then, using your fingers, try separating the hairs. The most important thing to do first is to provide relief for your cat. Try to separate the mat into sections so it isn't pulling on the skin. If you can, gently start to comb through quarter-inch areas. If possible, pinch the hairs close to the skin so your cat doesn't feel the pull of the comb.

If you can't detangle the mat, you'll have to cut it. Use your blunt-nosed scissors for this. I recommend you have an assistant on hand, if possible, so you'll have both hands free to work. To protect your cat's skin, place a fine-tooth comb against it, behind the mat. Do this very carefully. Always cut close to the edge of the mat, as far away from the comb as possible. If the mat is in a place where you can't slip the comb in, then *always* make sure you can see the skin before you cut. Snip a few hairs at a time. Remember, a cat's skin is very loose and can easily be mistaken for the mat when cutting. Having an assistant hold the cat can be very helpful because you need to be able to concentrate on what you're doing. If the mat is on the underside of the cat, place your fingers over any nipples to prevent cutting them. If the cat moves around too much, don't attempt to cut the mat. Try another time when you cat is more calm.

NAIL CARE

By keeping your cat's nails trimmed, you lessen the severity of any damage he may do should he scratch the furniture or more importantly, a human or another pet. If you're thinking the easiest solution would be declawing your cat, you're very mistaken. Declawing can cause many other problems, both physical and emotional. I urge you to read the section of this book on declawing (chapter 6) before you take any action.

As you remember from chapter 6, a scratching post plays an important role in maintaining the health of your cat's nails. If you haven't provided your cat with a sturdy scratching post, you'd better pay a visit to the local pet supply store immediately. When a cat uses a correct scratching post, the outer sheath of the nail is shed, making room for the new growth beneath.

Start the routine of nail trimming at an early age so your cat becomes used to the procedure. Five to six weeks old is a good age to start.

To begin, just pet the paws and learn how the nails extend and retract. This will build trust and your cat will become comfortable when you're holding his paw. Do this little exercise each day. Become familiar with the look and shape of the nails themselves before you ever attempt to trim them.

To extend the nail, put your finger on the paw pad and thumb on top of the paw. By gently pressing, the nail will automatically extend. Keeping gentle pressure will prevent the nail from retracting again. Now look at the nail. The pink area is the "quick," which is where the blood supply is. If you trim to the quick, you will cause pain and some bleeding, even possible infection. Trimming to the quick and hurting your cat will also undo all the trust and relaxation you have worked so hard to instill in him. Some of the nails on dark-haired cats may be too dark to see the quick, so be very careful. When in doubt, trim only the very tip, don't go beyond the curve.

Get the nail extended by pressing on the paw as described above and put the trimmer in position. Before squeezing, double check that you aren't near the quick or that you haven't caught any part of the paw pad. If you should accidently clip the quick, apply pressure to the bleeding nail with a piece of sterile gauze for a few minutes. After you're done, don't feel insulted if your cat runs to his scratching post—he just wants to try out his new manicure.

Some cats have extra toes. Most cats have five on the forefeet and four on the hind feet. Make sure you don't neglect trimming the extra nails because they don't get worn down like the others. The extra nails can curve inward, which can cause pain and possibly an infection.

Your cat's nails won't need trimming every time you groom. Most cats usually need it about every two weeks. If you are absolutely unable to trim the nails, have your vet or a professional groomer do it because it should be done.

DENTAL CARE

Cats suffer from the same dental problems as humans. Tartar can build up on teeth which can lead to problems such as gingivitis. A balanced diet and serving good quality canned and dry food will help keep teeth and gums in good shape. Make sure your vet checks your cat's teeth and gums during each visit.

It's important that *you* regularly check your cat's mouth. Teeth should be white, gums should be pink. Your cat's breath should not smell like the inside of a garbage can. If his breath is foul, have him checked by a vet. Lift the upper lip and check the teeth and gums. Pull the jaws apart (gently, please) to check the back molars.

To clean your cat's teeth, put a little baking soda on a dampened gauze pad or a baby toothbrush and wipe over the teeth. If your cat can't tolerate the brush or the gauze in his mouth, use your finger until he gets used to the procedure. **NEVER** use toothpaste meant for humans to clean a cat's teeth because it's too harsh and can burn the throat and stomach. If your cat absolutely can't tolerate the baking soda, you can buy Petrodex brand toothpaste which is made especially for cats. This toothpaste is malt-flavored for appeal. If you see a little tartar build-up on the teeth, you can scrape it off with your fingernail. The regular cleaning that you do should in no way replace veterinary checkups.

If your cat requires a professional teeth cleaning, it's done with ultrasonic cleaning equipment and the cat is given an anesthetic.

EYE CARE

The cat's eyelid has glands in it which secrete a fluid for lubrication, providing easy movement over the eyeball. You may not even realize your cat has an eyelid because of the covering of hair—but it's there. The cat's eyeball also gets protection from his "third" eyelid, known as the nictitating membrane or haw. This thin eyelid slides upward from the inner corner of the eye. You may occasionally catch a glimpse of it. Seeing an exposed portion of it is normal, but if it stays in the unfolded position without returning to the corner of the eye, your cat needs to have his eyes checked. He may have an injury.

For peke-faced cats, such as Persians and Himalayans, whose eyes may tend to tear, you have to prevent the discharge from accumulating. Do this by cleaning the area with a cotton ball, gauze, or cotton swab moistened with water. You can also use sterile boric acid; this helps prevent the discharge from causing stains on the fur and will also help prevent infection.

EAR CARE

For the ears, use a cotton ball moistened with pure vitamin E oil—you also can use baby oil. Never use alcohol. When cleaning the ear, be careful that you don't go *into* it, which is why you should use a cotton ball instead of a swab until you're used to the procedure. If your cat makes a sudden move or shakes his head, as many cats do during ear cleaning, by using a cotton ball you won't have to worry about causing injury to the ear. Only clean the section of the ear you can see.

While you are cleaning the ears, check for ear mites. Signs of ear mites will be a crusty black material or redness in the ear. Your cat may also shake his head and scratch his ears a lot. For more on ear mites, see chapter 13. Be careful when checking and cleaning the ear that you don't pull on the ear flap because you risk injuring the inner ear.

If your cat is uncontrollable during ear cleaning, enlist the help of an assistant. Wrap the cat in a towel, extending his legs straight downward, leaving his head exposed. Have your assistant hold the cat while you clean the ears.

GROOMING A SHORTHAIRED CAT

TOOLS

slicker wire brush (or a rubber brush)
soft bristle brush (for underside)
fine-tooth comb (to check for fleas)
chamois or velvet cloth (optional)
nail trimmers
vitamin E oil or baby oil (for ear cleaning)
cotton balls or swabs (for ear cleaning)
baby toothbrush or gauze (for teeth cleaning)
baking soda (for teeth)

The basic difference between grooming longhaired and shorthaired cats will be the tools you need. The beginning section on grooming longhaired cats applies here also, so use that as a guideline to familiarize yourself with your cat's body and how to organize your grooming tools.

Shorthaired cats are a breeze to groom because their coats don't mat or tangle. You'll want to groom your shorthaired cat about two to three times a week to remove dead hair and keep the coat glossy and healthy. Something to keep in mind if you have both a long- and shorthaired cat: If they groom each other, then the shorthaired one is ingesting long hairs and can develop the same hairball problem that longhaired cats suffer from.

First dampen your fingers with warm water and work them through the coat to loosen dead hairs. Then use what is called the "slicker" wire brush (the *gentle* one—it's found in just about every pet store) on the coat. Use light strokes and never flick the brush up at the end of a stroke—that will hurt the cat because the wire bristles dig in. For cats with very short coats, you can use a rubber brush. Always brush lighter than you think you should and go in the direction that the hair grows. As the brush fills with hair, take the time to clean it. Never use the slicker brush on sensitive areas like the cat's underside. Use the soft bristle brush for that and be gentle— most cats aren't too crazy about having their stomachs brushed. Don't use the slicker brush on the tail or legs because it will hurt. Use a fine-tooth comb or the soft bristle brush.

After brushing, use the fine-tooth comb, which will also remove dead hair. If you suspect your cat may have fleas, use the fine-tooth comb *first*, before brushing. The closely spaced teeth on this comb will trap fleas. For more on flea control, see chapter 13.

For shorthaired cats, nothing brings out the gloss on a coat like a soft chamois or even a piece of velvet. After brushing and combing, rub the cloth over the coat. This is great for cats with very short, tight coats, like the Siamese.

Nail trimming, ear cleaning, and dental care are the same for both short- and longhaired cats, so use the information on the preceding pages. Eye cleaning is not the same because shorthaired cats rarely suffer from runny eyes the way peke-faced longhaired cats do. For your shorthaired cat, just check the eyes and clean away any dirt that should accumulate. If the eyes have any discharge, you should contact your vet.

BATHING YOUR CAT

If you faithfully groom your cat and provide high quality food, you probably won't ever need to bathe him. Some longhaired cats do need occasional bathing, though. If your cat gets into a greasy, oily mess, he'll need a bath. There are also medical reasons for bathing a cat, for instance, when there's flea infestation. If your cat needs a bath for medical reasons, your vet will provide specific instructions as to what products are needed and how to use them.

Before bathing your cat, you must first groom him to be sure there isn't so much as one little tangle left in his coat. *ALL MATS MUST BE REMOVED* before bathing. I can't stress that strongly enough. You cannot get rid of mats by bathing instead of brushing.

You can use the kitchen sink for bathing, or you can place a plastic pan in the bathtub or put it in the sink, whichever method will make it easier on both you and your cat. Wherever you choose for bathing, make sure the room is warm and draft-free. If possible, close the door to keep the warmth in the room, and in cool weather, turn up the heat.

The shampoo you'll use will depend on the reason for the bath. If your cat has a flea problem, refer to chapter 13 for shampoos to use and the proper bathing procedure. If your cat is just plain dirty, use a pure castile shampoo. You can usually find one in the pet supply store, but if not, you can use one intended for people. Don't use a shampoo with chemicals or built-in conditioners.

Your cat will probably feel more comfortable during the bath if he can get a steady grip by digging his nails into something. Put a small rubber bath mat in the bottom of the sink or pan. This will also help him to keep his balance. As you do with grooming, it's best to have all of your supplies handy so you won't have to leave your cat for any reason. Have three or four absorbent towels ready. For rinsing, you can use a plastic cup or bottle (no glass, please) or a hose attached to the faucet. If you use a spray attachment, keep it close to the coat because many cats are frightened by the sound. Keep your cat's comb and brush handy because you'll need them after the bath. You'll also need a portable hair dryer. My advice is to invest in a very quiet one with multiple settings. Have it set up and ready in the place you'll be drying your cat.

Before putting your cat in the bath, test the water as you would for a baby's bath by running it over your forearm. It should be "baby bath" warm. You'll also want to make sure the shampoo is room temperature. Put a piece of a cotton ball in each ear to prevent water from getting inside the ear canal. A drop of mineral oil or plain eye salve goes into each eye to protect them should any water or shampoo accidently get in. You should be *extra* careful to avoid getting water or shampoo into the ears, eyes, nose, and mouth.

Talking in soothing tones, put your cat in the sink, hind legs first. If he starts to panic, stay close and keep reassuring him with your voice. Start by wetting his back, hind legs, and sides, working your way up. Keep a good grip on your cat—an assistant would be a great help here. Use the hose, plastic cup, or plastic bottle for wetting the coat. Keep the water running all during the bath so you don't have to fidget with the faucets and readjust the temperature. Running the water throughout the bath will also help your cat get used to the sound. Make sure you saturate the coat before applying shampoo. Some cats' coats are resistant to water, so be sure it's wet enough. If the cat doesn't have fleas, don't wet the head until the body has been shampooed. If your cat *has* fleas, you have to wet the head *first* to prevent the fleas from running into the ears and mouth.

When the coat is wet, apply the shampoo. Use a massaging action to be sure you're getting down to the skin. Some cats enjoy this massage. Every now and then pour a bit of warm water over the body so the cat doesn't get chilled. When the body, tail, and legs have been shampooed, you can wet the head. When washing the head, be extra careful to avoid getting shampoo or water in the ears, eyes, nose, and mouth. For extra protection, place your hand over the cat's ears when rinsing the head. If your cat's coat is very greasy, you'll have to do a second lathering.

When it's time to rinse, remove *all* traces of shampoo. If you fail to do this, it will result in a dull coat. Start rinsing at the back of the head and work your way down the body. Rinse and rinse and rinse, until the water that runs off the body is crystal clear. When the coat is totally free of shampoo, press the wet hair against the skin to get out the excess water. Gently squeezing the legs and tail will remove the excess water from them. Use the first towel to blot more of the water. Change towels as they get wet (about two or three times). Towel dry carefully so you don't create tangles. Make sure the cat doesn't get chilled. Use as many towels as needed to get him as dry as possible. Then, with your cat wrapped in a towel, carry him to where you have the hair dryer set up.

The hair dryer should be used on the low setting, but make sure it's not just cold air. Never use the high setting because it will burn your cat. Always keep the dryer far enough away from the body because the heat can easily burn the skin, even on the low setting. Keep the dryer moving over the body, never hold it in one place. When drying the head, shield the eyes, nose, and ears with your hand, and never blow the air into the cat's face. For longhaired cats, gently comb as you finish drying, using a wide-tooth comb or a natural bristle brush. Lift the hair to be sure the undercoat gets dry. For shorthaired cats, use either a rubber or natural bristle brush as you dry, brushing in short strokes. Make sure the cat is completely dry before allowing him to walk around the house again, or he'll just end up attracting dirt.

When you're finished, go all out with praise! Make the biggest fuss over your cat, telling him how beautiful he looks. This is also the time for you to reward your wonderfully patient feline with a treat.

ALTERNATIVES TO BATHING

If your cat is too difficult to handle and you're unable to bathe him yourself, seek out a professional groomer or ask your vet. Don't rely totally on dry shampoos to take the place of a bath. If your cat can't be bathed because of age, illness, or some other reason, you can try one of the dry or no-rinse shampoos made especially for cats. These products are nontoxic to cats so don't use anything else, except cornstarch.

To use the dry shampoo, first stand your cat on a towel. Apply the powder and leave it on for a few minutes to absorb the oil or dirt, then brush it out. The label will have specific instructions. There are also shampoos that you don't have to rinse out. After lathering, you towel dry following label instructions. I personally find that the dry and no-rinse shampoos are poor substitutes for a bath, but in a pinch they're better than nothing.

If your cat gets tar, gum, or another sticky substance on his coat, you can remove it with mineral oil. Rub the oil in the area and let it soak into the substance. Don't allow the cat to lick the oil because mineral oil robs the body of vitamin E and is a laxative. After you remove the tar or gum, you can wash the area with a castile shampoo. Make sure you rinse thoroughly. If the tar or gum was covering most of the coat, then after removing it with the oil, your cat will need a bath.

Greasy coats can be helped by sprinkling a little cornstarch into the hair. Let it sit for a couple of minutes before brushing it out. Make sure that you are *also* addressing a greasy coat by changing the diet so that it doesn't become a recurring problem.

HAVE PAWS, WILL TRAVEL

THE CARRYING CASE

There are many types of carrying cases to choose from. The ones I like best are the Kennel Cab and the Vari-Kennel. These carriers are made of high impact plastic with a grill ventilated front door. The sturdy latch is spring-loaded. They're easy to clean and can be taken apart for storage—the top and bottom unscrew by hand. I think this type of carrier provides more security for a cat. She can see out, but still feel hidden from view. The carrier is leakproof, and if you put a towel in the bottom, it will absorb any wetness, making for a more comfortable ride.

This carrier can also serve double duty at home if you want to use it as a bed or cozy hideaway. Unscrew the top to remove the door if you prefer, and then set the carrier in a corner. My two cats often use their carriers for daytime napping.

Another type of hard carrying case is the one with a clear plastic dome lid. The top opens for loading and the ventilation holes are located on the side. If your cat loves to see everything that's going on, then this is the case for her. I don't recommend it for timid cats.

Another popular carrier is the soft-sided nylon kind with mesh ventilation. The side opens by way of a double zipper. The double zipper lets you open it a little on top to reach in to pet your cat or to give her a treat. This carrier is very light to handle and is washable.

For on-board airline travel you need a case that fits specific require-ments. This is covered under the section "Traveling By Air."

When buying a carrying case, don't select one that's too large or your cat will just end up getting bounced around while inside. She should be able to stand up and turn around inside the case. When you bring the case home, leave it out so your cat can get used to it. She will most likely find it a cozy place to nap.

PUTTING YOUR CAT IN THE CARRYING CASE. First, line the bottom of the carrier with an old towel to absorb accidents. You can also use a disposable diaper, which is good for long trips because you can throw the soiled one away and reline with a fresh one.

The first rule when putting your cat in her carrier is to BE CALM! If you're nervous, your cat will be nervous also. Put your cat in front feet first. Gently, but quickly, push her hindquarters in and make sure all body parts are inside—don't forget the tail. Don't slam the door or shut the lid until you're absolutely positive that no part of the tail, whiskers, paws, or ears are sticking out.

Let your cat get used to being carried around. Start by walking around the house and yard. Then take your cat on short car trips. It's very important that she be used to travel before you take her on a long journey.

IDENTIFICATION

The most common means of identification is the I.D. tag. It can be made of metal, ranging from stainless steel to sterling silver to brass, or reflective plastic. The tag should have your cat's name and your name and phone number. You may wish to include your address, too.

The only problem with I.D. tags for an outdoor cat is that if you use the breakaway collar, which is safest to prevent a cat from hanging herself should she snag a branch, then the tag will stay with the collar when the cat gets loose. But if you do allow her out, by all means make sure she has an I.D. tag. In the Appendix is a list of mail-order companies that make and engrave many types of I.D. tags. Write to them for information.

Another good precaution is to keep all of your cat's papers together with several clear pictures of her. Also, take the time to write a brief description of her. This will be essential should your cat get lost or stolen. Tattooing inside the ear can also be done for identification. (See page 127 and page 128.)

TRAVELING WITH YOUR CAT

First, make sure your cat is healthy before attempting to travel with her. Don't travel with a sick, weak, pregnant, or very nervous cat. Don't travel with a cat who is in heat, either.

Make sure you have the right size carrying case with the proper I.D. on the top. Cats travel better inside a carrying case—they feel more secure. You should also have your leash and harness (with I.D.) with you in case you take your cat out of the carrier at any time. Bring your cat's medical history booklet with you (see chapter 2) in case she needs medical attention on your trip. You may even want to take along your first-aid kit.

While you're away from home, you should also bring your own supply of food and water. Changes in water can upset a cat just as it can a human. And, don't rely on being able to buy your usual brands of cat food while traveling. You may not find them, and now isn't the time to introduce a new food to your cat—so bring a good supply. Don't forget the Vitality Mix and the fatty acid supplement, and the tomato juice, if you can. Don't let good nutrition slide just because you're on vacation. You may even want to bring extra vitamin C (100 mgs) to add to the food each day to help your cat cope with the stress of travel.

As for tranquilizers, try traveling without them. Most cats travel well without needing to be tranquilized. If through experience you know your cat will be unable to tolerate the trip, then speak to your vet about medication. Don't take it upon yourself to administer *any* kind of tranquilizers not prescribed by your vet. Follow his or her dosage instructions carefully. The medication will have to be given an hour before leaving home to give it time to work, so be sure to plan ahead for this. Realize that the first few times your cat travels will be the roughest.

If you're traveling by public transportation, always inquire beforehand if pets are allowed. Many trains and almost all buses don't permit animals on-board. Also, if traveling to another state, ask your vet about getting a written health certificate. Certain states require it, plus some require proof of rabies vaccination.

In very hot weather, you can buy one of those small plastic ice packs, wrap it in a towel, and put it in the corner of the carrying case. Be sure to wrap it in a towel because it must not come in contact with your cat. In cold weather, put a soft towel in the carrier so she can snuggle. You can also tape a thin towel over the ventilation holes to cut down on drafts. If you use the carrier with the grill door, tape a small towel over the front in cold weather.

Don't forget grooming duties when you're traveling with your cat. For longhaired cats, this is a must. Your cat will be under enough stress without having to deal with mats, too.

TRAVELING BY CAR. Feed your cat at least six hours before travel time to avoid any stomach upset. Cats, in general, don't get carsick, but they can become extremely anxious. If your cat becomes too excited or gets motion sickness, speak to your vet. Don't take it upon yourself to administer any kind of tranquilizer. In most cases, if you allow your cat time to get adjusted to car travel by taking her on short trips (10-15 minutes and then gradually increasing the length of time), she'll probably be just fine without medication when it's time for the longer journey.

The safest way for your cat to travel by car is in her carrying case (see section on "The Carrying Case"). If you allow your cat to run loose inside the car, she could interfere with the driver and cause an accident, or jump out of an open window. She will stay calmer in the car while inside her case. Being loose and looking out the window at everything whizzing by might make her very anxious. If your cat is calm in the car and you want to hold her in your lap, keep her leash on for control, in case she starts to bother the driver.

Unless you walk her on a leash, carry your cat to and from the car in her carrier. The cat who is so docile in your home may just surprise you by bolting when she gets outside if you have her in your arms.

For long trips, bring the leash and harness (I.D. tag attached) in case you want to take your cat for a walk. Walk your cat only in safe, secluded areas. Also bring a small litter box along in the car. You can buy a "cage size" litter box at most pet supply stores. Make regular stops to allow your cat to use the box.

In addition, for long trips you should bring dry food because you don't want to be dealing with opening cans and trying to store leftovers when you're riding in a car. Keep a thermos of cool water for your cat and offer her sips regularly from a small container. This is especially important in hot weather.

If you want, you can also use a cage for car travel. There are large cages available that can accomodate a small litter box and a bed. These are great for traveling in station wagons.

WARNING: Never leave an animal in a parked car in warm weather. Even in the shade, the temperature inside can soar, turning into an oven in minutes. MANY PETS DIE THIS WAY! For more on heatstroke, refer to chapter 13. I personally don't recommend leaving an animal unattended in a car even when there's no danger of heatstroke. There are too many thieves out there who will steal ANYTHING left in a car and pets are often stolen to be sold to research laboratories. Please don't leave your cat in the car ever!

TRAVELING BY AIR. About putting your cat in the cargo area, I've heard many horror stories about pets arriving dead or in very bad shape, and then again I've known people who've shipped their pets this way with no problems. Just the thought of my cats being locked in the cargo area, which is often very cold, with the possibility of something falling on them, surrounded by strange animals, is enough for me to say "NO WAY!" Luckily, there is an alternative for owners of small pets, which I'll explain later. But if for some reason you must put your pet in the cargo area, make sure you have a VERY sturdy, well-ventilated case that is labeled "LIVE ANIMALS" and that proper identification is affixed to it. Book a direct flight, if possible, to reduce your cat's anxiety as much as possible. Line the carrier with newspapers or a towel. Feed the cat a light meal six hours before the flight and don't give any water within two hours of boarding time, except on a very hot day. If possible, avoid traveling on very hot or cold days. Exercise your cat before the flight.

Here's the best way to fly: You can get permission to bring your cat on-board with you if you reserve this option in advance—sometimes there's a charge. Find out from the airline what's required, such as a written health certificate and vaccinations. The cat must be in a case that can fit under the seat. Many companies sell carriers for this specific purpose. You can also buy one from the airline, but if you do, purchase it in advance so your cat can first get used to it at home. For the carrier to fit under the seat it must measure 17" x 12" x 8". Many of these carriers have a ventilation grill on top with a 4" x 4" opening to let a tiny head poke up, or for you to pet your cat. Put some newspapers, a towel, or a diaper in the bottom of the case to absorb any wetness.

Feeding instructions on-board are the same for traveling in the cargo area: Feed a light meal six hours before the flight and withhold water within two hours of boarding, unless it's a very hot day.

FOREIGN TRAVEL. Foreign travel is especially tricky. Many countries require lengthy quarantines. Consult the embassy for your destination country. Speak to your vet about specific vaccinations and a written health certificate.

The ASPCA publishes a booklet called *Traveling With Your Pet*. It provides tips, plus includes regulations for foreign travel. To order the 36-page booklet, send your request, along with $5.00 to: The ASPCA, Education Dept., 441 E. 92 Street, New York, NY 10128.

ARRIVING AT YOUR DESTINATION. When you reach your destination, confine your cat to a small area with her litter box, food, and water. Let your cat spend the night there before you allow her to go exploring. Don't just drop your cat in this room and go off. Spend a good amount of time comforting and playing with her. Let your cat know that you're with her every step of the way on this journey.

Before you allow your cat out of the room, do a check to make sure she won't get into any danger, such as windows without screens, etc. Stress to everyone the importance of being careful about closing doors and closets. This is important if you're visiting friends or family who have never owned cats.

If you're in a hotel or motel, make sure the maid is aware that a cat is in the room so your cat doesn't get out by mistake. A reminder on the door may be helpful, but make sure you speak to the maid in person, too. If possible, arrange to pick up your towels and bed linens yourself or to be in the room when the maid comes in to clean. When staying in a hotel or motel, make sure you don't open any windows without screens.

To be more considerate during your hotel stay, bring a few plastic bags for disposal of used cat litter or food cans. Be certain to bring your litter scoop, too. Sweeping up scattered litter with a little whisk broom and dust pan (the small kind that snaps together) will help keep the bathroom cleaner.

SHIPPING YOUR CAT ALONE BY AIR

If a situation comes up where you must ship your cat by herself by air, there are pet shipping companies who can help you with the arrangements, domestic and foreign regulations, and vaccination requirements. They can make the flight arrangements, pick up your cat, and provide board before or after the flight if needed. Many are members of the Independent Pet and Animal Transportation Association, which is a network of companies that work together on both ends of the flight to pick up and deliver your pet.
In the Appendix are names of some pet shipping companies around the country. Write to them for information.

WHEN YOU MUST LEAVE YOUR CAT

PET SITTERS. You can board your cat in a kennel or sometimes with the vet, but being left in a cage for a week could be very traumatic, especially surrounded by unfamiliar animals and people. With the vet, if your cat is boarded near sick animals, it could be dangerous. Your cat needs her familiar routine to comfort her in your absence. Having a friend stay with your cat or hiring a pet sitter is the easiest and least stressful way to leave her. If a friend is unavailable, you can, in most cases, find a sitter through your vet. If you use a professional groomer, ask him or her for a recommendation because they usually know several reliable sitters. In a pinch, you can check the yellow pages. In that instance, though, check references.

Have the sitter come over before your trip so you can explain the routine and introduce your cat. Go over the feeding instructions and leave written instructions as well. Don't be afraid to ask that the sitter do all the "special" things you do. Your cat needs her good nutrition especially while you're gone.

Show the sitter how to scoop out the solid waste in the litter box and how to clean the box and change the litter if needed.

Instruct the sitter to rotate toys to ease boredom. Show him or her how to use those special toys like the Kitty Tease or the Cat Dancer to give your cat her daily exercise. Be sure you stress that these toys MUST be put away after playtime. You can also show the sitter how to throw a catnip party for your cat as a midweek surprise. As an extra treat, buy a few new toys for your sitter to introduce. Each day should involve a game for your cat so she'll look forward to each visit by the sitter.

Have your cat's carrying case in a convenient location and show the sitter how to put her inside. Have your veterinarian's name, address, and phone number by the phone, along with the name, address, and phone number of an emergency hospital, if different from your vet. Also provide the phone number where you can be reached.

If you feel your cat will be very lonely in your absence, ask the sitter to leave a radio or TV on for a couple of hours during the day. If you have a timer on your radio or TV, the sitter can set it to stay on for a specific amount of time. Have him or her leave a light on at night, too, or buy a timer so it can be set to go on and off at the right times.

With a longhaired cat, light grooming must be done everyday to prevent mats. In this case, you may be more comfortable with a professional sitter than a friend because a sitter may be more knowledgeable in grooming. You can also arrange to have your professional groomer come in to do a thorough job.

LEAVING YOUR CAT FOR ONE NIGHT. In a pinch, if no one is available to take care of your cat, or if you're called away suddenly, you can leave your cat for one night. To do this you must be prepared in advance. Buy a water dispenser to make sure your cat doesn't run out of water. They're sold in every pet supply store. These dispensers always keep the dish filled. As for food, you can set a bowl of dry food down to cover the meals you'll be absent for, but make sure it's low magnesium, high quality food. Try not to make a habit of this because it can lead to overweight and finicky eater syndrome. If you're worried that your cat will eat all the food the second you put it down, you can try using one of those covered bowls with a timer on it. At a specified time, the lid comes up and your cat can eat. Some models can keep food cool, so you can fill them with canned food if you prefer.

Only leave your cat this way if you have no other option and are unable to find someone on such short notice. And, never do it for more than one night because it's a risk when you leave an animal unattended for such a long time.

Leave a light on a timer and maybe even the radio for your cat if she's going to be staying home alone. Put some new toys out and make sure the litter box is clean before you leave. Keep the curtains open so your cat can pass the time by looking out the window, preferably an upstairs window, so no one can look in at night and see that the house is empty.

BOARDING YOUR CAT. If you're unable to find a friend or a pet sitter to stay with your cat, then sometimes the only option is to board your cat at a kennel. I urge you to *first* search high and low for someone trustworthy to stay with your cat, or even someone who would let you bring your cat to their house. It would be less lonely for your cat and less stressful.

If you must board your cat, go personally and check out a number of kennels before deciding on one. Sometimes vets will board animals—if you choose this, make sure your cat is kept separate from sick animals. Find the kennel that looks the cleanest. What kind of care do the animals receive? Does the kennel require proof of vaccinations? If your cat is on medication, will it be administered as directed? Are the cages roomy enough for a cat to move around freely? Is there a place for exercise and will the cat be taken out for play each day? Notice the attitude of the staff. Do they seem to like animals? How do the animals look? How's the room temperature? Do you see any insects around?

Make reservations for boarding well in advance. The best kennels are heavily booked. Before boarding your cat, have her examined and vaccinated if needed. Get a written health certificate from your vet. Some kennels require this (a good practice), but it's also good protection for you. Provide the kennel with a copy of your cat's medical history record, the phone number of your veterinarian, and the phone number where you'll be. Only board a healthy, well-adjusted cat. A sick, old, weak, or nervous cat should be kept at home. You should also bring along your cat's own food, familiar food bowl, feeding instructions, her bed, and your brand of litter. Don't forget a few of her favorite toys!

When it's time to say goodbye, be calm. If you get too emotional, your cat will sense something's up and that maybe this is a final parting. Keep the farewell light and reassure her that this is just a brief separation.

MOVING

During all the hustle and bustle that goes along with preparing for a move, your cat is likely to encounter some stress. Do all you can to maintain her normal schedule at this time. Plus, with the activity, a cat could easily climb into a box and get caught, locked in a closet, injured by furniture being moved, or accidently let out of the house. Confine your cat to one room where there are no boxes or moving activity. Put her food, water, bed, litter box, and scratching post there. Visit her regularly.

If you allow your cat outdoors, keep her inside during those last few days before the move. Animals can sense the upheaval and your cat may run away. You don't want to be searching for your cat on the day you're scheduled to move. It's also a good idea to have a new I.D. tag made with your new phone number on it.

On moving day, confine your cat again to a room where the movers won't be, such as a bathroom or an already empty room. This will prevent the tragedy of a mover accidently letting your cat out or injuring her. Put a note on the door of the room instructing people to stay out.

In your new house, set up a room to confine your cat until things get settled down. This way you'll give her time to adjust to the new surroundings. If you set up a room with a few pieces of familiar furniture from the previous home, it will be a comfort for your cat. Introduce more of the unfamiliar territory gradually. Make sure you "cat proof" your new home as well as you did your previous one.

For an outdoor cat, only allow her outside on a leash, until you're sure she's acquainted with the area and you're certain there are no dangers. If you've moved to a busy street, I advise you to reconsider letting your cat out. The safest place for a cat is indoors and with patience on your part, you can retrain her to accept that way of life.

By the way, before, during, and after the move, supplement your cat's diet with vitamin C (100mgs) to help her body deal with the stress.

FINDING A NEW HOME FOR YOUR CAT

Placing a pet up for adoption is a very difficult and painful decision to make. It could come about because of a move to an apartment where pets aren't allowed, or it may just be that cat and owner are unable to come to terms with each other. These things happen. I only ask that you try not to rely on your local humane society to find a home for your cat. These shelters are already filled with animals in desperate need of homes. In the best interest of your cat, *you* should try to find a home for her.

For whatever reason, if you must give up your cat or kitten, you want to be absolutely sure that she will be adopted into a caring, loving, and responsible home. Realize that a good home will probably not be found overnight. It will be even more difficult to place an adult cat, so don't get impatient. If you can't place your cat with someone you know and trust already (the best choice), you can put advertisements in vets' offices, churches, and pet supply stores.

If you put an ad in the paper, make sure you don't offer the cat for "free." Put a price on your cat to discourage people who answer ads to get pets to sell to laboratories. This happens more than you would believe and these people are very convincing. Kittens and cats have even been used to train dogs to fight, such as the unfortunate case of the Pit Bull Terrier. So put a price on the cat, $25 or $30 will be sufficient. Believe me, it's in your cat's best interest.

When someone calls on the phone, ask lots of questions. For instance: Do they already own a cat? Have they ever had a cat before? If so, what happened to her? Are there children in the house? If so, are they gentle with animals? Are there any other pets in the house? If so, how will they take to a new addition? A person who truly wants to love and care for a pet won't resent such questions, so don't be afraid to ask anything you feel is important. It's also better to get a lot of this initial screening done over the phone because it's easier to turn someone down that way rather than in person. You should also tell the person about your cat's personality. If your cat demands affection, say so. If she's always been allowed on the furniture, you'd better find out how the prospective owner would feel about that. In the case of an older pet, be sure the person would be willing to follow the feeding schedule your cat is used to so her routine doesn't get upset too much.

When the person comes to see your cat, observe carefully what their reactions to the cat are. Do you sense a chemistry? Let them know how much your cat means to you. Inform them of any conditions that must be followed, such as no declawing, not allowing cat outdoors, etc., and make sure you're satisfied with the reaction.

One very important thing to find out about, if the prospective owner has had pets before, is what happened to them. If you find out that previous pets were hit by cars or ran away, I don't think you'd want to leave your cat there.

When you think you've found the right person, *you* should bring the cat to their home. Check out the environment for yourself. Does everyone in that family seem to want this cat? Does the house look safe? Will they have time for the cat?

If the prospective owner has never had a cat before, but you trust them and believe this would be a good home for your cat, then help them learn about food, the litter box, scratching post, safety, etc. If done tactfully, it will be very welcome information.

Finally, make an agreement with the new owner that if things don't work out, they will return the cat to you. I'm sure you don't want them finding out in two or three weeks that they don't want the cat and taking her to a shelter or giving her to a stranger, or worse, letting her loose.

FINDING YOUR LOST CAT

Before a tragedy happens, make sure you have followed the suggestions in the "Identification" section on page 118. You don't want to be trying to remember details after the cat is lost and you're emotionally upset.

If you allow your cat outdoors, a collar and I.D. tag are a must. You can also have your cat tattooed (done inside the ear) and registered with a registry organization. Sometimes, stating on the I.D. tag that the cat has been tattooed will discourage thieves because you'll be able to prove ownership.

Here are some steps to take when trying to locate a lost cat.

■ Ask everyone—neighbors, children, mail carriers, EVERYONE! Even if they haven't seen your cat, they can help keep an eye out. Offer a reward.

■ Post notices everywhere in your neighborhood. Also post them in vets' offices, stores, and on community bulletin boards. The notice should say "LOST CAT" at the top in large letters. Below that should be a clear picture of your cat. Put the date, where the cat was last seen, and give a clear, brief description of her (sex, age, breed, colors, and whether she was wearing a collar). Give the name your cat answers to and then your name and phone number. I suggest you also offer a reward.

■ Go to all the shelters in your area. Leave a copy of your cat's picture with your name and phone number or a copy of the notice. Ask to see all the cats in the shelter personally—visit every cage, if possible. Don't depend on someone to remember if a cat fitting that description was brought in. Go back and check all the shelters everyday.

■ Report the loss to your police, especially if you suspect that your cat was stolen.

■ Put ads in the local newspapers.

■ If your cat has been registered with an organization, call them right away. These organizations act as networks to identify your cat and assist in recovery.

Here are the phone numbers of organizations that help recover pets.

Pet Find Inc. (800-AID-A-PET). You must register your cat in advance.

Tattoo-A-Pet (800-TATTOOS)

Petfinders (800-666-LOST). Call Monday-Friday between 9:00 A.M.-2:00 P.M. and between 4:00 P.M.-5:00 P.M. You should register your cat in advance, but they'll help you find her even if she isn't registered.

ACTION-81 (703-955-1278). This nonprofit organization can provide you with names of laboratories in case you fear your cat was stolen to be sold for research.

THE INTIMATE DETAILS

❦

If you're undecided about whether to neuter or spay your cat, consider this: The overpopulated cat world results in too many unwanted cats roaming the streets leading short and violent lives, and many unwanted cats also end up being destroyed. Unless breeding is going to be done, unaltered cats suffer great stress and *cause* stress to their owners. Unless you're planning to breed a purebred for a specific purpose, it's best to leave the job to the professionals who have the knowledge and ability to provide the cats with the needed surroundings. You may have been mistakenly informed that having a litter of kittens is healthier for a female, or that altered cats become fat—this is inaccurate information.

First, not only is having a litter of kittens adding to overpopulation, you could be risking the life of your cat. Weak or small mothers may not survive the birth process. Plus, the mating ritual itself can be violent and a female can be hurt if the male is too aggressive.

Some people want their children to witness the miracle of birth and feel it will help teach responsibility. Unfortunately, it's always more difficult than they thought to find homes for the kittens, once they're old enough to be adopted. I've seen many people promise they'll take a kitten only to change their minds. Plus, some people who think a kitten is "so cute" no longer want him once he becomes grown and has lost his "cuteness."

The next myth is that cats will become fat after altering. Neutered cats require less food, so to prevent obesity all you have to do is feed good quality food twice a day and encourage playtime. It's as simple as that!

THE FACTS

❦

MALES

Unaltered cats become so preoccupied with their sexual urges that they will not be good pets. First of all, you'll have to deal with the fact that males will spray when they reach sexual maturity. Males mark their territory by spraying a stream of very strong smelling urine on vertical objects. Once you smell the urine of an unaltered male, you will never forget it! Don't think you can easily train him not to spray because you can't—spraying is natural to unaltered males and you'll have a very hard time trying to break him of that need.

Unaltered males who are allowed outside go in search of a female in heat. This can involve infringing upon the territories of other males. The result? Territorial fights. Once a male has picked up the scent of a female in heat, he'll probably have to fight the other males for the right to mate with her. These fights are violent, causing injury, such as torn ears, slashed eyes, and even death! Males who are deprived of females become noisy and take out their frustration at home by turning aggressive in play.

Neutering your male cat will increase his resistance to illness and reduce his chance of developing prostrate cancer. It will bring out the affectionate side of him and usually eliminate his habit of spraying. Your outdoor male will be less likely to roam after neutering.

Neutering is done when the male is about six to nine months old, after he's become sexually mature (smell of urine will change), but before he starts to spray. The sooner neutering is done after he reaches sexual maturity, the less chance of him developing bad habits. The operation, called an orchiectomy, is done under general anesthesia. It involves removal of the testicles (scrotum remains) and tying the spermatic cords. Some cats require an overnight stay, but many cats go home that same night. The vet will probably tell you to keep him quiet for a day. In Albert's case, he didn't seem to realize that he'd even had an operation and lost no time in resuming his routine leaps from chairs to tables to windowsills.

FEMALES

A female in heat becomes very vocal, issuing throaty sounds. She rubs up against everyone and everything, rolling on the floor and then crouching with her rear end in the air. An unspayed female is very nervous, and, at times, might become so concerned with her sexual frustration that she may even forget her litter training. Females who go through repeated heat periods, without their eggs being fertilized, can develop cystic ovaries. Spaying will make her a better, more affectionate pet who is no longer plagued by repeated frustration. Spaying also eliminates the chance of uterine diseases such as pyometra, and the chance of developing breast tumors is reduced. Having your female cat spayed will also eliminate the gathering of male suitors who camp outside, fighting for her attention.

The time to spay your cat is usually between six to seven months of age, after her first heat period. The spaying operation, called an ovariohysterectomy, is done under general anaesthesia. It involves the removal of the ovaries, uterus, and fallopian tubes. One overnight stay is required with a follow-up visit to remove the sutures. You have to watch that your cat doesn't pull at her stitches; the vet will advise you to keep her relatively quiet until the stitches are removed. When you bring her home after the operation, make sure she's warm enough and let her get comfortable in her favorite sleeping place.

THE MATING PROCESS

Even though I *strongly* advise that you alter your cat, I'd like to explain the mating and birth process because it may give you a little better insight into cat behavior.

The female comes into heat a few days before she's ready to mate. Males pick up on her scent and gather outside fighting for the right to mate with her. The female's hormonal changes gradually build during each phase of the heat period and she starts to spend a lot of time rolling on the floor and rubbing up against people. Eventually she'll get into a crouched position, treading her hind legs and issuing her "call" for a mate. Her behavior will reach such a peak that certain owners can no longer stand it and will open the door and let her outside.

Once outside, the female ignores the advances of the males until she's ready. Meanwhile, the males fight for the honor of being the chosen one. When she's made her selection, the ritual begins. She entices the male, he approaches, and she runs away. If he doesn't follow, she may roll over in front of him and start purring. If the male is too quick in his approach, she will hiss or swipe at him with her paw. When she's finally ready, she crouches, raising her hindquarters and shifting her tail to one side to provide access to her vulva. The male pounces on her and grips her with his teeth by the loose skin on the nape of her neck. Putting his forelegs around her at shoulder level and his hindquarters around her flanks, they both begin to tread. He will thrust with his penis and when a successful entry is made, ejaculation *and ovulation* take place within seconds. As he withdraws his penis, the tiny backward-facing barbs on it tear at the female's delicate tissue. This causes her to emit a scream, free herself from his grip, and attempt to strike him with her paw. The reason for the tiny barbs is to induce ovulation, stimulating the ovaries to release egg cells. Because ovulation in cats occurs *during* the actual mating, a female who mates with more than one male can have a litter of kittens with different fathers.

After mating, the female rolls on the ground, rubs her head on nearby objects, and licks her genitals. The male also licks himself and waits for her to be ready for another mating. After a brief rest, the process will begin again. They may mate five to ten times within a half hour. As time goes on, he may tire of her and move on in search of another female. At that time, other waiting males may try to mate with her.

PRIOR TO PREGNANCY

Before your cat gets pregnant, it's important to have her examined by the vet to be sure she's free of any internal and external parasites; bring a stool sample with you. Your cat will also be given booster vaccinations to increase her immunity and to prevent infectious diseases in her kittens. Before breeding, make certain your cat is in good shape and at her optimal body weight. Don't allow her to breed before she's fully mature because it can affect her growth. Most cats reach maturity around twelve months.

FEEDING THE PREGNANT CAT

After mating, the female returns home and seems to be her old self again. After a few weeks, you may notice her licking her abdominal and genital area more than usual. Also around the third week, the nipples start to enlarge and turn pink.

If your cat has been eating good quality food with highly digestible protein, then you really won't have to change too much of her diet. If you haven't been feeding good quality food, then you'd better start now. The amount of food your pregnant cat needs gradually increases. Protein needs increase so that the fetuses are supplied with adequate nutrients without depleting the mother's body. You can feed your mother-to-be two or three meals a day. Three is preferable (dividing her regular daily amount into three meals), making digestion easier for her during pregnancy. In the second month, gradually increase her food by approximately 25 percent. The exact amount will depend on her size. With the increased food, three meals a day is a better schedule to avoid overloading her abdomen. Your veterinarian can specifically advise you on how much to feed your cat.

There are commercial foods available for pregnant and lactating cats. You can get them at pet supply stores or from your vet. I strongly recommend that you do this because it's the best way to ensure your cat is getting enough protein for herself and her fetuses. Mothers also need to continue getting good quality food during lactation to be sure milk production will be sufficient.

Spicy, greasy foods are a no-no for any cat, but they are an extra big no-no during pregnancy because they upset the digestive system—foods such as salami, bacon, pepperoni, luncheon meats, etc. One vegetable that's also on the taboo list is spinach because the oxalic acid it contains inhibits calcium absorption. If you want to give your pregnant cat a treat, stick to healthy ones:

- a tablespoon of yogurt (good source of calcium)

- a small piece of mild cheese (good source of calcium and protein)

- a cantaloupe ball (vitamins B and C)

Your vet may recommend a vitamin/mineral supplement for your cat during pregnancy. Don't take it upon yourself to give *any* supplements unless advised to do so by your vet.

CARING FOR THE MOTHER-TO-BE

Your cat shouldn't get any medications or vaccinations during her pregnancy unless advised by the vet. If she should become infested with fleas, don't use anything on her because it could be ingested when she licks herself. Ask your vet for specific advice for flea control when your cat is expecting.

A pregnant cat needs exercise, but don't allow her to jump from high places during the last few weeks. If you allow your cat outside, keep her in during her pregnancy. Sometime around the end of the sixth week you'll notice her swollen abdomen. You can continue to encourage moderate exercise, but make sure it doesn't involve jumping. Advise children not to lift the cat because a fall could cause a miscarriage.

Because of her size, the mother-to-be may not be able to groom herself. Keep her coat in good condition by brushing and combing it a little each day.

The gestation period is usually 63-65 days and as the time gets close, the cat will begin her search for a suitable spot for delivery. About one or two weeks before the due date you can prepare a box for her. Find a clean cardboard box that's big enough for her to stretch out and stand up, and will accommodate her litter. Cut an entrance three to five inches from the bottom so she can get in and out, but will keep her kittens in. Don't make the entrance so high that the mother might have trouble jumping through it to get in and out. Leave the top on the box attached on one end so you'll be able to open it to monitor the activity inside. Line the box first with newspapers and then absorbent towels on top of that. You'll have to change the paper and towels after delivery because of discharges. Place the box in a warm, dimly lit spot away from noise, drafts, pets, and people, like a closet that you could keep open for her.

Hopefully, your cat will approve of this box and choose it instead of your laundry basket. If she does decide to give birth in a place other than the box you've selected, don't disturb her! Let her give birth where she wants. Bring the box over to her after the kittens are born and gently put the kittens inside. Carefully move the mother into the box and leave it in the spot where she gave birth.

THE DELIVERY

It's a good idea to make sure your veterinarian knows when your cat is due just in case some help is needed.

One helpful thing you can do for a longhaired cat is to trim the hair around the vulva and anus. This will make delivery a little more sanitary. While you're at it, carefully trim the hair around the nipples also.

Restlessness is usually an indication that labor is close at hand. Your cat won't eat and will go in and out of her box, rearranging the bedding. She'll lick herself quite a bit and make frequent trips to the litter box to urinate. There will also be a slight discharge—first it's colorless and then slightly bloody. If the discharge is very bloody, smells foul, or is greenish in color, you need to call the vet right away!

During the contraction stage, the cat will probably change her position often. She'll settle into a squatting position with her rear end turned slightly so she can see the birth of her kittens. The time for each kitten's birth can vary. It can take as little as a minute or as long as forty-five minutes. You'll see her abdominal muscles contract and she'll start to push out the kitten, which is surrounded by an amniotic sac. Some mothers cry during delivery and some are very quiet. If your cat screams in agony during delivery, you should contact your vet.

Each kitten is born surrounded by a thin transparent sac. The fetus develops inside this sac. It also allows for an easier passage through the birth canal because of its natural lubrication. Even with this lubricated sac, there are those few times when a kitten can get stuck halfway out during delivery. If after fifteen minutes the kitten is still stuck, take a little K-Y jelly and lubricate the mother's vaginal opening. Hold the part of the kitten that's exposed with the tips of your fingers and gently pull in rhythm with the mother's contractions.

When a kitten is born, the mother will tear open the sac with her teeth and clean the kitten's mouth and nose of mucous. She then licks the kitten to stimulate the circulatory and respiratory systems. The mother bites off the umbilical cord down to where it's attached to the kitten and eats both the cord and the placenta, which is expelled after each birth. Eating the placenta is common among animals and it contains hormones which help in the start-up of lactation. Even so, eating too much of the placenta can cause an upset stomach and/or diarrhea, so only let her eat one or two.

Sometimes another kitten starts coming before the mother can finish cleaning up the first one. If this happens, you should carefully break open the birth sac with your fingers. Release it from around the face and head first so the kitten doesn't suffocate. Wipe away any mucous from the mouth and nostrils with a cotton ball or swab. Gently rub the kitten with a soft warm towel to stimulate his breathing. If the mother fails to detach the umbilical cord, you can do it by tying a piece of dental floss or thread around the cord about one inch from the kitten's navel. With sterilized blunt-tipped scissors, cut the cord in front of the thread. Don't pull the cord.

During delivery, if the mother is doing everything normally, don't interfere! Some cats strongly object to human interference. A few cats even object to the very presence of a human during delivery, so be very sensitive to your cat's needs. You don't want to cause her stress because she could actually *stop* doing the procedure correctly. Before you offer assistance, like cutting the umbilical cord, be absolutely certain she's not going to do it. Make sure it does get done, though, because the kitten can get twisted up in it.

There are also some cats who don't even know what they're supposed to do after a kitten is born, so be close at hand in case the newborn kittens need your help. There is also the possibility that the mother could accidently roll over on a kitten while giving birth to another. You need to make sure the kittens stay out of the way during the delivery. It's also a good idea to have a bowl of water nearby so you can offer the mother a drink after each birth.

Make sure an afterbirth is expelled after each kitten's birth. If the mother retains one, it could cause a uterine infection, which could be fatal. After all the births, a discharge that's dark red or reddish brown in color usually indicates that all the afterbirths have been expelled. If the discharge is bright red, it could mean a hemorrhage. Any discharge that's greenish or brownish, appearing approximately 48-72 hours after delivery, means a retained kitten, afterbirth, or infection. It's sometimes a good idea to take the cat to the vet to be sure that there are no retained fetuses.

SOME DANGER SIGNS

Cats rarely have trouble during delivery, but you should keep watch for signs of trouble, and then call your vet immediately. Especially watch for the following:

1. Some cats cry out during delivery. If your cat screams in agony while trying to expel a kitten, call the vet.

2. If the mother has been straining for two hours and hasn't expelled a kitten, you need to call the vet because this may mean the kitten is too large to fit through the birth canal. It could also mean two kittens are blocking the canal. A Caesarian section may have to be performed.

3. If the mother expels a greenish, foul-smelling discharge, this may be the sign of a retained placenta, retained kitten, or an infection. Call the vet.

4. Contact your vet immediately if you see profuse bleeding from the vagina.

THE NEW FAMILY

THE NEW FAMILY

A kitten at birth weighs approximately 3-4 ounces. That weight will double in a week, triple in two weeks, and quadruple in three weeks.

Newborn kittens have closed eyes and are unable to hear. Even so, within minutes they start to crawl, their tiny hind legs pushing and their front legs paddling. They travel in search of their mother, smelling her scent and feeling the warmth from her body. They may even feel the vibrations of her purr.

When all the kittens are born, replace the soiled towels and newspapers with fresh ones. You should have a small towel-lined box nearby to keep the kittens in while you're changing the bedding. The mother may use this opportunity to go to the litter box. When she returns, she'll lay on her side to begin nursing. Make sure the kittens nurse right away so they receive the colostrum—the first milk produced by the mother. The colostrum provides immunities for the kittens against diseases because they don't have any immunities of their own yet. It's very important that they're left alone to nurse during the first thirty hours or more to be sure they get an adequate supply of colostrum. If a kitten is unable to locate a teat, you can gently place her in front of one. If she still doesn't respond, gently squeeze the mother's nipple so a drop of milk comes out. The kitten will soon start to suckle on her own.

Within a day or two, each kitten claims her own teat and suckles exclusively from that one. After delivery, an increase in mammary gland pressure causes milk ejection—at first, there's plenty of milk flowing for the newborn kittens. After a couple of days, their appetites will have grown so they'll begin to do the "milk tread" with their front paws against the mother's stomach which stimulates milk flow. (You'll even see your full grown cat "tread" when she's sitting on your lap or on a soft bed—they never seem to outgrow this kittenhood memory.) If the kittens cry constantly and don't settle down while nursing, check to be certain the mother is producing milk by gently squeezing one of her nipples. Call your vet if there's no milk, or if you feel she's not producing enough. A kitten not receiving enough milk has an abdomen that's contracted. The kitten also will cry and not show weight gain.

Newborn kittens have a body temperature of about 80°F. They huddle close to the mother and to each other for warmth. During the first six days, the kittens must be kept warm because if the environmental temperature around them drops below 85°F., they become hypothermic. They have no shivering reflex and depend upon their mother's warmth to sustain their body temperature. Keep your thermostat set at a minimum of 70°F. during the first four weeks. After two weeks, the kitten's body temperature rises to almost that of an adult, but they should still be kept warm.

Kittens should basically gain the amount they weighed at birth, weekly, until they reach five months of age. The growth rate then slows as they approach maturity. The specific rate of growth for your kittens is dependent upon the size of their parents and will vary among individuals. Females grow faster during the first month, but then the males take over. If a kitten isn't gaining weight, contact your vet. He or she will advise you on supplemental feeding. Keeping a milk replacement formula, like KMR, on hand is also a good idea so you can step right in with supplemental feeding should it be needed.

Provide the mother with as much food as she wants while she's nursing to ensure adequate milk production, and so she doesn't deplete her own body in order to feed her kittens. At first, the kittens may nurse in sessions totaling up to eight hours a day. The kittens should also eat as much as they want.

For the first four to six weeks after delivery, check the mother daily to be sure her abdomen is kept clean and the teats aren't caked with milk. With a longhaired cat, you may have to wipe her underside with a warm damp cloth to keep the hair from becoming sticky. Don't allow the hair to become matted either—this is not a time to neglect your grooming duties.

Something to watch for is a condition called "mastitis." This is an inflammation of the mother's mammary glands. The condition, due to an infection, can cause pain to the cat when the glands are touched, so she may be too sore to nurse her kittens. Her milk can also contain bacteria that could be passed to the kittens, so you should get veterinary treatment immediately. The kittens may have to be fed a milk replacement formula, available at pet supply stores. Other symptoms of mastitis may include: hard or discolored breasts, fever, listlessness, and decrease in appetite.

During the kittens' first two weeks of life, they are unable to urinate or defecate and must depend on their mother. She licks their stomachs and the genital and anal areas to stimulate digestion and elimination. She swallows the tiny amounts of waste, to be eliminated later with her own when she goes to the litter box.

Kittens remain blind for about two weeks. When their eyes open, they will be blue. Eye color will change as the kittens mature. The kittens' eyes are very sensitive to light, so keep their box out of bright light or direct sunlight. At this point, the kittens' vision is not strong yet. Once the eyes are open, there might be slight discharges from them, which is common. You should keep the eyes clean by ever so gently wiping them with a cotton ball dipped in warm water. If you don't clean them, the discharge may harden and the eyes can seal shut. Check the eyes daily for any signs of pus or swelling under the eyelids because an infection could cause blindness.

The seals on the kittens' ears open between fourteen and seventeen days. Their hearing will be sensitive, so avoid loud or sudden noises. Daily maintenance of the kittens' cardboard box is very important. Keep it clean and change the bedding daily. Make sure the towels are flat and that they fit right to the edges of the box so a kitten can't crawl under and get smothered.

WEANING KITTENS

Somewhere around the third or fourth week, the kittens cut their baby teeth. The permanent teeth come in at about six months. It's important to start weaning at this time because after the kittens have their teeth, they start to bite while nursing and this can cause pain to the mother. When weaning kittens, make the transition smooth and gradual—don't go from mother's milk straight to food. Also, abrupt weaning can cause the mother's glands to become engorged with milk. Weaning at first must be done alternately with nursing which allows the mother to gradually reduce milk production.

When the kittens are three and a half to four weeks old, you can start introducing the weaning formula. Use a commercial weaning formula made for kittens, like KMR. You can get the formula from a pet supply store or through your vet. Realize that you can't just put this formula in a dish and expect the little kittens to know what to do—you have to teach them. Put a little of the formula on your finger and let the kitten get a taste of it—put a drop on her lip. This practice teaches kittens to lap their food instead of sucking. Follow the instructions on the weaning formula for quantities and specific schedule of feeding. Once a kitten learns to lap the formula from your finger, lead her to a very shallow dish with the formula in it. Alternate these sessions with nursing sessions so the mother's glands have the opportunity to reduce the milk production. This will prevent any problems of her glands becoming engorged.

When you're sure the kittens can handle eating from a dish, you can introduce semisolid food. Blend a little canned food (the kind made especially for kittens, like Science Diet Feline Growth—or ask your vet for a recommendation) with KMR, skim milk, or water until you have a gruel of baby food consistency. Put a drop on the kitten's lip so she gets a taste of it before letting her eat from the dish. Each day, reduce the amount of liquid until you're feeding only canned food. Five meals a day is recommended. If you feed less than five, the kittens may gulp and cause stomach upsets.

Make sure you're feeding a sufficient amount of food—obesity isn't a problem in growing kittens. Your vet may prescribe a liquid vitamin/mineral supplement for your kittens. **Don't** take it upon yourself to supplement without the vet's advice. And, of course, make sure a supply of fresh water is always available, not a deep dish though, remember, you're dealing with tiny kittens. By the fifth to sixth week, the kittens should be *completely* weaned.

THE LITTER BOX

At around three weeks of age, the kittens learn to bury their own wastes. The mother takes them to the litter box for lessons. Watching a mother teach her kittens how to bury their wastes in the litter box can be one of the most comical scenes you'll witness with young kittens. Be prepared for more litter on the floor than in the box, but it's well worth the mess to watch this historic occasion. The mother leads them to the box, and there she licks their genital and anal areas to stimulate elimination. After the tiny amount is deposited, she then covers it, encouraging her kittens to imitate her.

There are always those few cats who don't follow procedure and neglect to educate their kittens. If this happens and you find yourself with an orphaned kitten who didn't get the benefit of mother's training, or if the mother skipped over these important lessons, you'll have to step in for her. Because we don't have mother's tongue, you'll have to use your finger as a substitute. First dip your finger in a cup of hot water, then put it between the kitten's hind legs and stroke from the stomach backwards, up over the genital and anal areas a couple of times. If you don't want to use your finger, a wet cotton ball will do. When the kitten has finished squatting, cover the waste using your finger—your kitten will watch and probably imitate. You can also take her front paw and gently show her how to cover. Praise and pet her, then lift the kitten out and off to more fun adventures.

For kittens, use a litter box with low sides for easy access and don't use a lid. Keep a little soiled litter in the box because the odor will induce the kittens to use it again. Don't give your kittens the run of the house until the training is complete. It's also important to keep the litter box in the same spot—don't confuse little kittens by changing its location.

THE YOUNG FAMILY

Four-week-old kittens have very soft fur and their spiky little tails stick up straight. You'll find that from this moment on, the kittens will be into EVERYTHING! Now is the time to double-check that all dangerous and poisonous substances are put away. Kitten-proofing your home is extremely important to prevent potential disasters (see chapter 4).

Kittens are remarkably fearless little creatures. They're afraid of large objects towering over them, but they more or less view other animals as playmates. The mother has to teach her young to identify possible enemies. She has a special growl which they soon learn means to scatter.

Never pick up a kitten by the scruff of the neck or by her legs. Use two hands when handling a kitten. Put one hand under the chest, support the front legs with your fingers, and support the back legs with your other hand. Teach children the proper way to pick up and handle kittens. You should also instruct children not to play too roughly with the tiny kittens and to leave them alone when they're eating or sleeping. Kittens need more sleep than adult cats so it's especially important that they get enough undisturbed rest time.

By five weeks, the kittens are playful with their brothers and sisters and differences in personalities will emerge. You should, at this time, begin a daily short grooming routine so the kittens learn to accept the ritual. This way they'll be much more tolerant when grooming takes more time as they mature.

The mother will begin her own weaning process at about six weeks by making herself less available. You will have helped her quite a bit if you began the gradual weaning process at three and a half to four weeks of age.

At six weeks, the kittens should be eating canned food. You can introduce dry meals by mixing the food with KMR, skim milk, or water. Once again, decrease the liquid each time, as you did during weaning. Buy a dry food made especially for kittens (ask your vet).

By seven weeks, you should make sure you're involving yourself with the kittens to get them used to people. Play with them several times a day—for short periods, don't wear them out. Hold the kittens gently, speak softly to them, and use gentle petting. The more love and affection you give them, the more affectionate they will become as they mature. They will also be more at ease with strangers in the house. Begin teaching your kittens through patience and kindness. Punishing leads to fearfulness, and you'll never get the results you want. For proper training methods, refer to chapter 8.

Between six to eight weeks, the kittens should be examined by the vet and receive their first vaccinations. Bring a stool sample for the vet to examine for parasites.

Kittens shouldn't be taken from their mother for adoption until they're at least eight weeks old. Before you find homes for them, make sure they've been fully vaccinated, are eating a solid diet without any problems, and are completely litter trained.

An eight-week-old kitten needs four meals a day of kitten food. When a kitten reaches three months of age, you can feed her three meals a day. At six months old, kittens can be on the two-meal-a-day schedule that full-grown cats are on, but continue to feed them the foods designed for feline *growth*. Vary a couple of brands and you'll never have a finicky eater later on.

When a cat reaches twelve months old, she's considered full grown and should no longer be eating kitten food. Start a diet of good quality, well-balanced food, varying brands and flavors.

FEEDING AN ORPHANED KITTEN

My first recommendation is to take the orphaned kitten to the vet. After examining her, your vet can best determine precisely what the kitten's immediate needs are. The vet will advise you to administer a formula such as KMR. Because a cat's milk has a higher protein content than cow's milk, you must never substitute cow's milk when feeding an orphan kitten. Feline milk has about 10 percent protein as compared to the 3 percent in cow's milk. You must buy a commercial replacement formula for orphan kittens. Most orphan feeding kits come with everything you need. If not, you can also buy an orphan feeding bottle in pet supply stores or through your vet. Don't ever use an eyedropper or spoon because there's a good chance that the kitten might inhale the liquid, which could be fatal. The hole in the nipple of the bottle should allow milk to come out slowly when the bottle is inverted.

Place the kitten on your lap and put her on her stomach. You may also want a towel on your lap. NEVER FEED A KITTEN ON HER BACK. Kittens nurse on their stomachs. Gently insert the nipple and angle the bottle so the formula can flow, but not allow air to be sucked in. Never squeeze the bottle when the nipple is in the kitten's mouth—this could be fatal. Gently pulling back on the bottle now and then will stimulate the kitten's sucking reflex. You can usually tell when the kitten's had enough by gently feeling her stomach. It should feel rounded but not distended nor bloated. The equivalent of two teaspoons per feeding is usually the right amount, but follow the specific instructions on the label of the formula. Orphaned kittens under four weeks of age need to be fed every three or four hours.

Be aware that for the first two weeks you'll have to help the kitten with digestion by gently burping her as you would a human baby. Hold her upright and rub her back, easing air bubbles out. She'll also need direct stimulation for the elimination process. Previously explained in this chapter is how to introduce a kitten to the litter box and how to stimulate urination and defecation.

An orphan kitten needs a tremendous amount of care and attention. Follow the instructions on the orphan formula as to quantities and schedule for feeding, and contact your vet with any questions or problems.

At three and a half to four weeks, put some formula on your finger to encourage your kitten to lap. Once she's learned, start blending canned food for kittens with KMR, skim milk, or water as described in the previous section on "weaning," and continue with those instructions.

SOME TIPS

■ For an orphaned kitten under six weeks, provide a waterproof heating pad, a lamp over a blanket, or towels, for warmth when sleeping. This is very important as the kitten must have enough warmth and a place to cuddle. Make sure the pad or light is not too hot, and that the kitten has the freedom to move away if she gets too warm.

■ Growing kittens need sunlight. Ordinary window glass doesn't allow the beneficial rays to get through, so you might want to consider one of the "full spectrum" lights available on the market.

■ Kittens will probably sleep after meals so avoid excessive handling, and instruct children not to play with them after the kittens have eaten.

■ Fresh water must always be available.

■ Commercial weaning formulas will have specific instructions for amounts and schedules, so be sure you read the instructions before feeding your kitten.

■ Kittens need food with extra protein for proper growth, so be sure you are feeding a food specifically formulated for their special needs.

THE PURRRFECT PATIENT

live in New York City and my vet's office is a ten minute walk from my apartment. My parents live on a farm and the nearest vet is forty-five minutes by car, when the weather's good. Knowing how to administer first aid is important for a pet owner like myself, but for pet owners like my parents it's an absolute must!

Because I'm not a veterinarian, I'm providing this chapter on first aid to familiarize you with general descriptions, symptoms, and basic procedures. There are comprehensive first-aid books available, written by veterinarians who go into specifics on every animal emergency. I strongly recommend that you make the investment in one of these books, along with a first-aid kit (described later in this chapter). Of course, these things must never take the place of seeking immediate veterinary care. For an emergency situation when there is no time to get to the vet, you should at least have him or her on the phone to guide you, if possible.

Read about first aid and learn to recognize symptoms that could indicate emergency treatment is needed. Become familiar with first-aid procedures *before* an emergency occurs.

KNOWING WHEN YOUR CAT IS SICK

With your family, you are immediately alerted to a sneeze, sniffle, change in a child's appetite, or any other possible sign of potential illness. Plus, a family member can tell you if they're not feeling well and where it hurts. Pets are at the mercy of your ability to notice anything amiss. As a pet owner, you need to be aware of your cat's everyday routine so that any change gets noticed and investigated. For instance, I am aware of how much water my cats drink. This can be important information because I'll notice if there's a marked increase or decrease in water consumption, which can be symptoms of certain diseases. I'm also familiar with my cats' litter box routines. Because I remove the solid wastes from the litter box daily, I'm able to detect any diarrhea, constipation, or other problems much sooner than the owner who only cleans out the stools once a week. Because

I feed my cats two scheduled meals daily and never leave food available, I'm able to notice changes in appetite. Not leaving food around is especially important in multicat households because it's nearly impossible to figure out who's eating and who isn't.

Also, a regular grooming schedule gives you the opportunity to examine your cat's body and detect any lumps, wounds, parasites, etc. I hold, stroke, and play with my cats everyday and am so familiar with their individual personalities that the slightest changes never go unnoticed. Now I'm not saying you have to be fanatical and start following your cat around the house all day—just be *aware*. Very often, the difference between a successful recovery and an unfortunate tragedy is an alert owner.

21 WARNING SIGNS

If you notice any of the following symptoms, it's a sign indicating something is wrong.

1. Change in appearance of coat—dull, sparse, dry

2. Change in normal behavior—cat doesn't play the way he used to, lethargic, hiding

3. Change in eating habits—increased/decreased appetite, weight gain/loss

4. Change in water consumption—increase or decrease in usual water intake

5. Vomiting—cats occasionally vomit, but be aware if there is blood in the vomit, if cat continually vomits, or if vomiting is accompanied by weakness, pain, or fever

6. Change in urination—frequent urination, straining, blood-tinged urine, inability to urinate

7. Change in stool—diarrhea, constipation, bloody or foul-smelling stool

8. Weakness

9. Pain/Limping

10. Crying—other than the vocalizing your cat normally does

11. Fever—taking your cat's temperature is described later in this chapter

12. Sneezing

13. Coughing

14. Changes in appearance of eyes—discharge, film over eyes, appearance of nictitating membrane (third eyelid), squinting, fixed pupils

15. Discharge from nose

16. Swelling on any part of the body

17. Lumps—on or below the skin surface

18. Lesions

19. Change in breathing—rapid breathing, labored breathing

20. Change in appearance of gums—swelling, pale in color, blue color

21. Bad breath

DEHYDRATION. When a cat becomes dehydrated, whether due to illness, decrease in water intake, or diarrhea, it's serious! You can test for dehydration by gently pulling up on the skin of the upper back—it should snap right back. If the skin falls back into position slowly or doesn't go back at all, then the cat is dehydrated and veterinary care is needed.

FIRST-AID KIT

Though nothing can replace immediate veterinary care, having an organized, well-stocked first-aid kit can be a life saver should "seconds" mean the difference between life and death. Familiarize all family members with first-aid procedures and keep the kit and the medical book in an agreed-upon place. In addition to the kit and the book, keep a hot water bottle, a blanket, and a flat board on hand.

You can buy equipped first-aid kits, but I find them to be lacking in several important items. The best thing to do is stock your own. You can use any kind of box, but I highly recommend a fishing tackle box with attached trays. This box keeps all the contents neatly organized and when you open the box, everything is instantly displayed so you won't have to rummage around. Keep the kit well supplied, and when you run low on something, restock right away. Be sure of expiration dates also, so you can replace unused medicine before it gets old. Every time the kit is used, it should be returned to the same place in your home, and you should also take the kit with you when traveling with your cat.

The following is a list of the contents I keep in my first-aid kit. Realize, of course, that chances are you'll never have to use a large majority of these items, but it sure is worth it to have them on hand *just in case*.

FIRST-AID KIT
LIST OF CONTENTS

1 Penlight (make sure you always have a supply of fresh batteries)

1 Rectal thermometer (in its case)

Several plastic droppers or syringes (for liquid medications)

1 Pair of tweezers (for removal of ticks and other things on skin)

1 Pair of blunt-nosed scissors

1 Pair of needle-nosed pliers (to remove objects caught in throat)

Measuring spoons

1 Plastic measuring cup

1 Ace bandage

1 Small box of cotton swabs

1 Small bag of cotton balls

Several rolls of various-sized adhesive tape

1 Box of small gauze pads

1 2-inch roll of gauze

1 3-inch roll of gauze

1 4-inch roll of gauze

Several tongue depressors

1 Tube of first-aid cream

1 Bottle of plain eyewash solution

1 Small jar of Vaseline

1 Small bottle of 3 percent hydrogen peroxide (for disinfecting wounds, also to induce vomiting. Three percent is the standard strength—this refers to 3 percent hydrogen peroxide and 97 percent water)

1 Bottle antiseptic spray (ask vet for recommendation)

1 Small bottle of rubbing alcohol

1 Small bottle of milk of magnesia (for constipation)

1 Small bottle of mineral oil (to remove tar from coat, to clean ears, and to remove ticks and ear mites)

1   Small bottle of Kaopectate (for diarrhea)
1   Small bottle of Phisoderm (for cleaning wounds)
1   Tube of plain eye ointment
Activated charcoal (for poisoning)
1   Styptic pencil (to stop minor bleeding)
1   Pressure bandage (a handkerchief will do)
Hairball remedy

ASPIRIN. Although aspirin is considered the wonder drug for humans, it is just the opposite for cats. Cats are unable to break down aspirin, so it stays in their systems a long time and can build up to toxic levels. A single aspirin is an extremely high dose and can damage a cat's liver and affect the nervous system. Aspirin may be prescribed for pain due to arthritis or after a traumatic injury when there isn't bleeding—aspirin blocks the body's blood-clotting ability. *Never* give an aspirin unless specifically prescribed. If aspirin is ever prescribed by your vet, make sure you follow the instructions precisely. Even in small amounts, aspirin can cause stomach bleeding or liver damage, and if the toxic level builds up, aspirin causes death. If your vet recommends aspirin, it will be for very short periods to prevent toxic build-up.

ACETAMINOPHEN. Acetaminophen is the name of aspirin substitutes, such as the brand Tylenol. A single dose of acetaminophen can be deadly because it prevents oxygen from traveling through the bloodstream. This drug destroys a cat's red blood cells and makes breathing extremely difficult, the gums turn blue, and the head swell. *Acetaminophen can be deadly to cats!*

ANTIBIOTICS. Antibiotics do wonderful things, but one unfortunate thing they do is disturb the normal intestinal balance, so give your cat a little plain yogurt during antibiotic therapy. This way, the acidophilus from the yogurt culture can restore the normal order of things. Otherwise, the intestines can become susceptible to a yeast infection.

TAKING YOUR CAT'S TEMPERATURE

A cat's normal temperature ranges between 101°-102.5°F. A temperature above 102.5°F. is considered a fever and the vet should be called. If the temperature is below 100°F., then the cat should also be taken to the vet because it could indicate shock or internal bleeding. Keep in mind that a cat's temperature naturally rises in the afternoon and evening, when the cat is excited, or in hot weather.

Taking your cat's temperature is not difficult at all. When doing anything to your cat, whether it be administering medicine, grooming, or taking a temperature, the key word is "relax." Don't make a big thing out of it and your cat won't either. It will also be much easier if you have an assistant.

First of all, the thermometer you need is the standard rectal one intended for humans. You'll also need some Vaseline (can also use K-Y jelly) for lubrication. Put the cat on a table or counter with his hindquarters facing you. Your assistant will gently hold the patient steady, and you should be reassuring your cat with soothing talk. Hold the end of the thermometer between your thumb and index finger and shake it so the mercury line registers below 95°F. Apply a small amount of Vaseline to the tip. Hold the cat's tail up and gently insert the thermometer into the rectum (right below the tail). About one-third of the thermometer should be inserted. If you have trouble inserting the thermometer because the cat has tensed up, just continue using gentle pressure and in no time at all he'll relax. Keep the thermometer in place for about 2-2½ minutes. Don't let go of the thermometer while it's in the cat. After a couple of minutes, remove the thermometer, wipe it off with a tissue, and take a reading. Place your cat back on the floor and don't forget to praise and pet him. Clean the thermometer and replace it in the case.

PILLING

This is without a doubt the one job that can turn cat and owner into wrestling opponents. The thought of having to give a pill to their cat has sent fear into the hearts of many owners. My advice is to stop viewing it as a dreaded battle because your cat will pick up on your anxiety before you even take the pill out of the bottle. I talk to my cats with love whenever it's time to give a pill and tell them that what I'm doing will make them feel better. You can always try hiding the pill in a piece of your cat's favorite food, but cats aren't so easily fooled. If you can get away with this method, then by all means make it easy on yourself and go for it.

PILLING POSITIONS. You can put the cat on a counter or table for pilling.

If your cat is an experienced escape artist who squirms and wriggles, you might want to put down a small window screen or rubber mat so he can dig in his claws. I prefer sitting in a chair with the cat on my lap.

THE PROCEDURE. Tilt the cat's head up slightly, not too far or he won't be able to swallow. Put the palm of your hand over the cat's head. Open his mouth by pressing with your thumb on one side and index finger on the other. Hold the pill between the thumb and index finger of your free hand, and with the middle finger, pull the lower jaw open. It may sound complicated but it's not—just practice it sometime without the pill and you'll see. Quickly pop the pill on the back of the tongue. Coating the pill with butter will make it easier to swallow. Close the mouth and let the cat swallow.

    If you hold the head up or hold the mouth tightly closed, he won't be able to swallow so be careful of this. You can also gently massage the throat in a downward motion to stimulate swallowing. Pet the cat and don't make a big deal about what just happened. If you're quick enough, he probably won't even realize what you did. Some cats are very sneaky and they hold the pill in their mouth until you're not looking, and then spit it out. To be certain the pill has been swallowed, watch if his tongue comes out to lick his lips or nose. That's a sure sign the pill has gone down the throat. If the cat coughs, it means the pill is lodged in the windpipe. Release your hold on him so he can cough it up. If it doesn't come up, then grasp the cat by the hind legs and turn him upside down to dislodge the pill.

RESTRAINING. If it's impossible to hold your cat still for pilling, then you'll have to use a restraint. An old towel is the best restraint to use. First put the towel on the arm of a chair, then bring the cat over and sit down with him on your lap. Spread the towel out on your lap under the cat. Lay the cat on his side and press his forelegs against his chest (they should face straight downward). Wrap the towel snugly around the cat, leaving only the head exposed. Quickly open his mouth and pop the pill in as described in the previous paragraph. Be fast and it will be over before he has time to complain.

ADMINISTERING LIQUID MEDICATION

First of all, you'll need a plastic dropper or syringe (without the needle). Make sure the syringe is plastic and not glass because glass can break if your cat were to bite down. Don't use a spoon because it almost always spills while you are trying to get the medication into your cat's mouth. This means you'll be giving an inexact dosage and will end up wasting a lot if you try to make up for the amount spilled. When using a spoon, you will also have to deal with the medication going all over your cat's mouth, face, and chest. With some liquids that are sticky, this makes for a big mess to clean, which stresses a cat even more.

Use one of the positions described in the section on "Pilling." Tilt the cat's head *slightly*, place the syringe in the side of the cat's mouth where the cheek pouch is, and administer the liquid in *small* amounts. Don't try to empty the entire amount in one shot because you risk inhalation of the liquid, and even if he doesn't inhale it, the medication will just dribble right out of his mouth. The safest way is to administer in small amounts, allowing the cat to swallow each time. If he's panicky or struggling too much, it's better to wait and try again later. A panicky cat could breathe in as you're squeezing the syringe and aspirate the liquid into his lungs.

Having an assistant hold the cat steady is a big help when administering medication, but the most important thing is to keep the cat calm. Use your voice to talk reassuringly and give him gentle strokes on the back of his head before attempting to medicate. For an impossible struggler, your best bet is to wrap him in a towel as described in the previous section on "Pilling." After you've administered the liquid, wipe any excess off the mouth and praise your cat for his patience.

APPLYING OINTMENT/CREAM

I find the best way to apply an ointment or cream is to sit in a chair with the cat on my lap. I first pet the cat and relax him, all the while talking soothingly. After applying the cream, I continue to hold the cat on my lap for awhile, petting him to keep him happy, to give the medication time to absorb. This reduces the amount of ointment the cat can lick off once I let him down. Sometimes the cat falls asleep on my lap, so we just stay there together and let the medication do its work without any feline interference. If licking is sabotaging the improvement of a condition, then you can ask your vet about using an "Elizabethan" collar. This collar fits around the neck and prevents the cat from licking his body.

ADMINISTERING EYE MEDICATION

Place the cat on a counter or table, or you can sit in a chair with the cat on your lap.

ADMINISTERING DROPS. First, make sure your hands are clean and thoroughly rinsed of soap. Tilt the cat's head upward and open the cat's eye by separating the upper and lower lids. Hold the dropper between your thumb and index finger. Steadying your hand on the cat's head, drop the prescribed amount into the corner of the eye. Make sure you don't touch the eye with the dropper. After the medication has gone into the eye, allow the cat to close his eyes.

ADMINISTERING OINTMENT. Of course, hands need to be clean and well rinsed of any traces of soap. Put the prescribed amount of ointment on the tip of your index finger. Tilt the cat's head upward, pull lower lid down, and wipe the medication off onto the inside of the lid. Don't touch the eye itself. Let the lid go back and when the cat closes his eye the ointment will spread.

ADMINISTERING EAR MEDICATION

Use one of the positions described in the section on "Pilling" that works best for you. With clean hands, hold the ear flap and steady the cat's head. Be gentle, because in many cases the ear will be sensitive due to irritation, and don't hold the tip of the ear, hold it at the base. Put the prescribed amount of medication in the ear, and then gently fold the ear flap down to keep it in. You don't want your cat shaking his head after you administer the medication and having it spill from the ear. If the ear isn't irritated, you can gently massage the base to distribute the medication. NOTE: If using prescription ear mite medication, *don't massage* because it's very strong and the ear is already irritated and sensitive.

If you have difficulty getting your cat to cooperate, then wrap the cat in an old towel as described in the section on "Pilling" and proceed to administer the medication.

FORCE FEEDING

Force feeding is only to be done when specifically instructed by the veterinarian. In many cases, if your cat is feeling under the weather and turns his nose up at food, it means he knows it's better for him not to eat. If your cat stops eating for more than a day or two, then you should call your vet. Cats can easily go without food for a couple of days without causing damage, so don't panic.

If you are ever instructed to force feed a cat, your vet will prescribe a specific food.

To force feed, open the cat's mouth by putting your hand over his head with your thumb on one side of his mouth and your index finger on the other side. Put a small amount of food on the index finger of your free hand (make sure your hands are clean) and pry open the cat's lower jaw with your middle finger. Quickly slide the food off your finger and onto the upper palate, just behind the front teeth. Let go of the cat's head to give him time to swallow. Wipe off any spills from the mouth, face, or coat immediately before they dry. This makes cleanup easier and is less stressful to a sick cat who definitely is not up to grooming now. Your vet will tell you how much and how often to feed. A sick cat can only handle small amounts of food, so you may only be able to feed the equivalent of a teaspoon every four hours or so.

If you are instructed to force feed liquids, be *very* careful. Never do it unless specifically instructed by your vet. Use a plastic dropper or syringe and insert it in the corner of the mouth. Gently hold your other hand over the cat's muzzle to steady his head. Tilt the head *slightly* upward (if you tilt it too far, he won't be able to swallow and could aspirate the liquid) and administer small amounts. Don't empty the entire contents in one squirt because the cat could inhale it into his lungs. Wipe any spills immediately.

STOOL SAMPLES

This is one very important way that your vet checks for internal parasites. Whenever you take your cat to the vet when he is ill, bring along a stool sample. Also, when you take your cat in for his annual exam and booster vaccinations, bring along a stool sample to be included as part of the routine checkup.

Try to bring the freshest sample possible, hopefully not older than three to four hours. If possible, try to scoop it up before your cat covers it with litter. Put the sample in a sealable plastic container or a sturdy plastic bag that seals completely. Write your name and your cat's name on a piece of masking tape and label the container.

THE HOSPITAL

THE NIGHT BEFORE SURGERY. Animals usually have to fast approximately twelve to fourteen hours before admission to the hospital for surgery. This is for scheduled surgery—with emergencies, you, of course, have no warning. Your vet will always instruct you on whether food and water must be withheld the night before.

TRANSPORTING THE CAT. If you are transporting a sick or weakened cat to the hospital, make sure he's kept warm. If your carrying case is the kind with a grill door, then you need to make sure the cat will be protected from any drafts. Tape a piece of an old towel over the grillwork to cut down on cold air. You can also do this over any other openings on the case. Make certain you put a towel on the floor of the carrying case so your cat can snuggle for warmth. If there's a chance your cat will urinate or vomit on the way to the hospital, then use a disposable diaper as bedding in the case so that it will absorb the wetness. For more information on carrying cases, see chapter 10.

PRE-OP. When you bring the cat in, he'll be put in a cage until it's time for him to be prepared for surgery. It can be a scary experience for a cat to be locked in a cage, surrounded by unfamiliar animals, smells, and sounds. To help your cat feel more secure, bring an unwashed T-shirt from home that you've recently worn, so that it has your familiar scent on it. The T-shirt will become a comforting bed for the nervous patient.

AFTER SURGERY. In most cases following surgery, your cat will stay the night at the hospital so he can be monitored to be sure of a full recovery from the anesthesia and in case complications from surgery develop. Spending the first night after surgery in the hospital is also the best way to make sure the patient stays rested. Neutering and dental surgery usually don't require an overnight stay.

    If your cat is allowed to eat regular food while in the hospital, ask the vet if it would be all right for you to bring your own from home so the cat can have what he's used to. If he has to stay in the hospital for an extended period, then it's really a good idea to provide his regular brands of cat food, provided it's okay with the vet. Also, visiting your cat during an extended hospital stay will do wonders for his spirits. Just ask your vet ahead of time if it would be allowed.

Post-op TLC. When picking up your cat from the hospital, make sure you understand all instructions regarding medications and post-op care. Bring the patient home in the carrier with a towel taped over the opening to prevent drafts.

Once your cat is home, he may still be reacting a bit to the anesthesia, so let him sleep. Following surgery, a patient needs peace, quiet, and rest. If you have other pets at home, they will be very curious about where this cat has been and will want to check out all the unfamiliar smells on him, so let your cat rest in a separate room to keep "nosey neighbors" away.

Follow your vet's advice on what to feed, how much, and how often. Administer medications at the right time and in the prescribed amounts without fail. As for sutures, check them regularly to make sure the surgical site is clean and there's no sign of swelling, bleeding, oozing, or infection. If your cat bites at his stitches (most cats just lick them), you can call your vet and he or she may advise covering the area. Don't do it unless you're instructed to because covering will slow the healing process.

In most cases, a follow-up office visit will be needed to remove sutures or just to examine the cat. Don't overlook this visit just because your cat seems healthy again.

CARING FOR A SICK CAT AT HOME

If you have a multipet household, the sick cat should be kept in a separate room. This is mainly to reduce his stress and to prevent other pets and people from disturbing him during his much needed rest. Set up a bed in the warmest part of the room, away from any drafts. Provide a small litter box with low sides for easy access, near the cat. If he has difficulty moving, you'll have to lift him in and out of the box several times each day. If he's unable to even stand, put absorbent towels down as a bedding with a disposable diaper or pad spread out on top of the towels. Change the diaper and towels, if needed, as soon as they become soiled. Also, you'll need to provide a little dish of water.

Follow the vet's advice on what the patient is to be fed and feed in small amounts. When a cat is ill, the sight of a lump of food in a dish may not appeal to him, and even if it does, he may not have the strength to get up and eat. You may have to offer bits of food on your finger. Don't force feed unless specifically advised to do so by the vet. If your vet doesn't specify a particular diet and your cat is having trouble keeping down his regular food, you can try strained-meat baby food, boiled eggs, or cottage cheese.

During an illness, your cat won't have the energy to maintain his good hygiene, so this is when he'll need your help the most. Gentle brushing and combing will prevent mats and make your cat feel better. Clean his coat of any vomitus, urine, or diarrhea. Cleaning it off right away will prevent it from hardening and becoming nearly impossible to remove later. Clean the discharges from the nose or eyes with cotton swabs. If the discharges have hardened, use a little warm water to soften them before attempting to remove. To prevent bed sores, occasionally turn the cat over onto his other side if he's unable to move.

Follow your vet's advice to the very last detail. If you're instructed to administer medication for a certain length of time, make sure you follow it through and don't skip the last couple days. When my father's dog, Poobelle, was seriously ill, she needed numerous medications, each one at a specific time of day. My father made a big poster-sized chart with all the medications listed and the times they were due. After administering one, a check was marked on the chart in the appropriate box. This method eliminated the confusion of trying to remember what was given and what wasn't. Poobelle was sick for over a month, but she received all of her medicine exactly as prescribed and recovered beautifully. If you have to administer several medications, make sure you keep track so a dose isn't forgotten or given twice.

Keep a written record of your cat's condition so you'll have all the accurate information on hand when you phone the vet with a progress report. If you are advised to regularly take your cat's temperature, record each reading. Observe and record the appearance of your cat's stool and vomitus, if there is any. This is information your vet needs to get an accurate picture of your cat's progress.

THE BIG FOUR:
STRESS, VOMITING, DIARRHEA, AND CONSTIPATION

STRESS

Stress can be the culprit behind many physical problems. Because stress puts the body's organs on full alert, it can throw things off balance.

Ongoing stress can lower the body's resistance to disease. It can also cause excessive shedding, dull coat, bald spots, and other skin disorders, to name just a few. The subject of stress is covered in chapter 8.

VOMITING

Cats vomit occasionally. If there are no other symptoms, then there's probably no need to be too concerned. Occasional vomiting could be the result of a hairball, eating too fast, food that's too cold, or anxiety. It's always a good idea to try to figure out the cause of the vomiting. Check the vomitus for any signs of hairballs, string, blood, or foreign material. Your cat needs veterinary care if there's blood in the vomitus, signs of illness, or if the vomiting continues. Persistent vomiting means something is wrong!

Internal parasites can cause vomiting, as can gastritis, disease, obstructions, or poisoning. When you take your cat to the vet, bring a sample of the vomitus, if possible. If not, at least try to describe its appearance—this can be very important. Also, try to be aware of *when* the cat vomits—immediately after eating or hours after a meal? Bring a stool sample to the vet so a parasite check can be done.

To treat vomiting, withhold all food and most water for about eighteen to twenty-four hours to give the stomach a rest. Using a plastic dropper or syringe, administer ½-1 teaspoon of Kaopectate or Pepto-Bismol (see section on "Administering Liquid Medication"). Repeat this every eight hours for the next twenty-four hours. After eighteen to twenty-four hours, if the vomiting has stopped, you can provide small amounts of bland food, like strained-meat baby food. When you're sure the cat is back to normal, he can return to his regular diet.

DIARRHEA

Diarrhea can be caused by milk, parasites, food allergies, illness, anxiety, fear, disease, or just a case of a little upset in the intestines. Making an abrupt change in the diet can also cause diarrhea, which is why you should make all changes gradually. Diarrhea that's persistent, bloody, foul-smelling, or accompanied by other symptoms is *serious* and your cat should be examined by the vet.

Mild, occasional diarrhea can be treated in the following way:

1. Withhold all food for twelve to twenty-four hours, but provide small amounts of water.

2. Administer one teaspoon of Kaopectate (see section on "Administering Liquid Medication") every eight hours, up to forty-eight hours.

3. After twelve hours, feed small amounts of bland food, such as strained-meat baby food or boiled hamburger mixed with boiled rice, every few hours.

4. If diarrhea lasts more than twenty-four hours, seek veterinary care.

CONSTIPATION

Cats may go a day without a bowel movement, so don't panic if there isn't a stool in the litter box one night. Causes of constipation include: a hairball in the intestines or other intestinal obstruction, illness, poor diet, or lack of exercise. Also, as a cat ages, the digestive system may not work as efficiently, so constipation is more common in older cats.

Severe constipation results in the stool backing up in the intestine. The cat will stop eating, become lethargic, and may vomit. In a case like that, the vet will have to give the cat an enema—*never do it yourself.* If your cat suffers from chronic constipation, no matter how good his diet is, then the vet may recommend adding a stool softener to your cat's food. I find that with the Vitality Mix, proper diet, and exercise, constipation can be prevented in most cases. For cats with repeated constipation, you MUST examine the diet and make the necessary changes. The bran in the Vitality Mix will work wonders to prevent constipation. A little raw garlic added to meals several times a week and ½-1 teaspoon olive oil once a week will help, too. Also, by grooming regularly, you greatly reduce the amount of hair your cat swallows, preventing constipation caused by hairball blockages.

If your cat is constipated, don't administer a laxative meant for humans without your vet's advice because certain ingredients are dangerous to cats, and don't use mineral oil. If constipation lasts more than one day, consult your vet. Never take it upon yourself to give an enema or stool softener. Isolated cases of constipation can be treated by administering ½-1 teaspoon milk of magnesia—but you must consult your vet first.

Remember, make the switch to a better diet!

ABOUT ENEMAS. Because cats sometimes suffer from constipation, they may at one time or another be given an enema—but enemas should only be given by the vet. If your vet ever instructs you to do it, you will be told *specifically* what to use, such as soap and water. FLEET ENEMAS OR

OTHER PHOSPHATE ENEMAS SHOULD NEVER BE USED because they can affect the heart and muscles in a potentially fatal way. Phosphate enemas can cause your cat to have convulsions and can lead to death.

SKIN DISORDERS

DERMATITIS

This is any inflammation of the outer layers of the skin. Dermatitis can be caused by allergies, external parasites, fungal infections, disease, weather, or other external irritants. Itchiness is the most common symptom, and you'll probably see your cat biting, scratching, and licking himself, which just worsens the situation. Sometimes you'll see crusts on the skin, and you may notice hair loss. It's essential that the *cause* of the dermatitis be discovered. Just medicating the cat without eliminating the irritant itself will just result in a reappearance of the skin condition.

Treatment may include antibiotics, medicated shampoo, or cortisone. My recommendation for preventing dermatitis is to keep your cat in optimal health by providing top-notch nutrition and regular grooming, reducing stress, and taking care of flea problems right away, especially if your cat is allergic to flea bites (see section on "Fleas"). Also, keeping your cat indoors will greatly reduce the chances of exposure to irritants.

Dermatitis can also be brought on by stress or anxiety. Before assuming that it's being emotionally triggered, make sure the cat is examined to rule out any physical cause. Once that's done, it's up to you to play detective and track down whatever is causing your cat this anxiety. Did you just bring a new pet home? A new baby? Perhaps you've just moved into a new house, or you got a new job that keeps you away from home more. It's up to you to find the reason and change the situation. Read the section on stress in chapter 8 to help you with your mission.

RINGWORM

Ringworm is not a worm, it's one of the most common fungal infections. Signs of ringworm are raised and crusty circular lesions. The lesions are most often found on the face and ears, but can show up anywhere on the body. There is usually hair loss with ringworm; sometimes the hairs break off and look like stubble.

Your vet can make a diagnosis by using a special ultraviolet light (hair will appear yellowish green), taking a fungal culture, or by microscopic examination of your cat's hairs. Appropriate medication is prescribed based on the severity of the infection. Ringworm is contagious to people and other pets, so be sure to wash your hands after handling your cat.

Cats in less than ideal health or under stress tend to be more susceptible to ringworm. To help prevent future infection, maintain proper nutrition for your cat and try to eliminate the cause of his stress.

DANDRUFF

Dandruff is most commonly the result of dry skin, though it can also be caused by a skin infection. Frequent bathing can cause dry skin, especially if you use a strong shampoo. Don't ever use a dandruff shampoo on your cat because it's much too harsh. How do you get rid of dandruff? The proper diet.

Almost all of the cats I come across who have dandruff are being fed low quality food, not enough fat, or their owners leave food available all the time. The lecithin in the Vitality Mix will help combat dandruff, and so will a good quality fatty acid supplement; if you haven't read the chapter on "The ABC's of Good Nutrition," then you might read it now. A regular grooming routine will also help do away with dandruff.

FELINE ACNE

Don't go running for the Clearasil, but it's true, cats can get acne. The condition, caused by bacteria, looks like whiteheads or blackheads under the chin. The bacteria comes from food left on the chin after eating because that's an easy spot for a cat to miss while grooming. Your vet may prescribe an oral antibiotic and will recommend what you should use to help keep the chin clean. Ethel developed feline acne because she's terrible at grooming herself, so I wipe her chin after meals to help her out. NOTE: Some cats develop feline acne from eating out of plastic food bowls. To be on the safe side, switch to glass or stainless steel.

RODENT ULCER

Despite the name, this is not caused by rodents. You'll notice raised, inflamed lesions usually on the head, lips, tongue, and other areas inside the mouth. The lesions are brown in color and start out small on the lips and increase in size. The condition is aggravated by licking because of the barbed tongue, and the lesions often end up being spread to the legs or abdomen. Your vet will prescribe the appropriate treatment.

STUD TAIL

This disorder mainly affects unneutered males. The sebaceous glands on the tail produce too much oil, which makes it a dirt and dust magnet, so the cat's tail becomes very dirty and greasy. Left untreated, the glands become infected and the vet will need to prescribe antibiotics.

Regular grooming will prevent stud tail. Some people don't do a good job when it comes to grooming the tail because it's usually in motion during grooming sessions. Be diligent about doing the tail and shampoo it as needed to control greasiness.

EXTERNAL PARASITES

FLEAS

These tiny little creatures can cause big trouble. Fleas are very small brown parasites that jump on unsuspecting cats or dogs and feast on their blood. What makes fighting these little devils so difficult is that they move so fast and jump high. They also multiply in alarming proportions during warm months.

Fleas lay their eggs on the cat, the eggs then drop off and nestle in the carpet, bedding, and furniture to hatch. Fleas can also survive away from the host animal and without a blood meal for a couple of months. So dealing with the fleas on your pet isn't enough. You have to be committed and declare war on all fleas, eggs, and larvae throughout your house and yard.

Aside from the uncomfortable itching that fleas cause, they also act as intermediate hosts for tapeworms. When a cat swallows fleas, as he undoubtedly does while biting and licking, he stands a good chance of additionally ending up with tapeworms. Fleas can also cause a cat to become anemic if the infestation is extremely heavy.

Some cats have allergic reactions due to flea bites which can drive them into constant biting and scratching fits. When a flea bites, it releases a small amount of saliva into the skin that contains anticoagulants which can lead cats to scratch until their skin bleeds. You may also notice rashes on the cat's skin.

To check for fleas, separate the hairs and look closely at the skin. Fleas are easiest to see where the hair is thinner. You may not see the fleas themselves—remember, they move fast—but you may spot the flea "dirt" (excrement). To be sure it's flea dirt, wet a few specks with a drop of water. If it's flea dirt, it will be a reddish brown color—that's the digested blood. To check for fleas on a cat with a dark coat, place him on a sheet of white paper and rub your fingers all through his coat. Also scratch him around the hindquarters and tail. Look for tiny black specks that drop onto the paper. Wet them with a drop of water to see if they turn reddish brown.

How do you fight fleas? Nutrition tops my list. Parasites look for acceptable hosts, which are usually weakened or less healthy animals. By keeping your cat in good shape with proper nutrition, you'll make him a less desirable target. Brewer's yeast helps repel fleas, so by making sure you include the Vitality Mix in your cat's diet, you provide a natural repellent that works from the inside. When you give your cat a treat, give him a brewer's yeast tablet instead of those commercial treat brands. In a pinch, rubbing brewer's yeast right into the fur will work also.

Raw garlic is a wonderful flea repellent because it makes the cat's blood unappealing to parasites. Crush a little garlic in your cat's meal everyday while you're fighting fleas. For cats not under siege by fleas, you can add garlic twice a week to the diet to make sure fleas don't even attempt to dine at your cat's expense. I know some people don't believe that garlic works, but I've seen it do wonders. Remember, the reason fleas are attracted to one particular animal and not another is blood chemistry. Parasites thrive on the weaker animals.

When you do actually see fleas on your cat, here's how to fight them: Fill a glass with water, then put a few drops of Avon's Skin-So-Soft Bath Oil on top. Specifically use Avon's because there's an ingredient in it that works wonders on fleas. If you can't get Skin-So-Soft, fill the glass with plain water, it will still work. Start fine-combing your cat, and after each stroke if you see a flea trapped in the comb, then dunk the entire comb in the water.

The closely spaced teeth on the comb will trap the fleas. By dunking the comb in the water, you'll drown the fleas before they even have a chance to jump away. Do this everyday. When I first got Ethel, she had fleas and I did this twice a day.

Next, have your vacuum handy and cover every inch of your house, paying very close attention to the areas your cat frequents and most especially his bed. Don't just vacuum the carpet, do the furniture, too! When you've finished, *empty the vacuum cleaner bag in the outside trash can.* Don't just dump it in the kitchen trash can because those eggs will hatch and jump right out in search of your cat again. Vacuum everyday and always empty the bag outside.

Ask your vet before using flea preparations with chemicals. He or she will know which one is best for your cat. Don't just run out and buy one because many aren't safe for cats—some are deadly.

If your vet recommends that you use a flea powder or spray, you must get one that isn't toxic to cats, and be sure to follow the instructions carefully. Use an herbal powder instead of a chemical one because it will be safest for your pet but deadly to the fleas. If you can't find an herbal powder, you can try mail-order catalogs. Ecco Bella is an excellent company that sells natural products (see Appendix). If you must use a chemical spray or fogger, be sure it contains *pyrethrins*—a "natural" insecticide derived from the pyrethrum flower (related to the chrysanthemum). Of all the chemicals, this "natural" insecticide is considered the safest. If using a spray product, don't spray your cat directly because he'll be frightened by it. First spray your fingers and then work them through your cat's coat.

Be aware that chemical flea preparations will irritate any sores on your cat and can't be used on kittens under the age of four months, so herbal preparations are really your best bet. For cats with any sores, you should always consult your vet before treating for fleas.

If your vet recommends a bath, make sure you groom your cat first. Fleas can hide in mats and tangles. When bathing, wet the head first to prevent fleas from running into the ears and mouth, and then pour lots of water over the body (for bathing instructions, see chapter 9). Use an herbal flea shampoo instead of a chemical one. If you can't find one, use a castile shampoo and mix a few drops of pennyroyal oil (found at the health food store) into it. Pennyroyal is a natural flea repellent, but don't pour the undiluted oil directly on the skin because it could irritate. After the cat is dry, you can use the herbal flea preparation or one recommended by your vet. NEVER USE MORE THAN ONE PREPARATION. Murphy's Oil Soap is an excellent flea shampoo (use the liquid, not the spray). Use ¼ cup of soap per gallon of warm water. Murphy's is safe and nontoxic to pets. Neo-Life's "Green" liquid soap is another great flea shampoo. "Green" is natural and nontoxic. Neo-Life products are sold through individual distributors (check your phone book).

If flea infestation is heavy, you may have to use a fogger in your home. Make certain that all pets are removed from the house beforehand. When buying a fogger, check the label to be sure the product is safe for pets and that it kills adult fleas, eggs, and larvae. Ask your vet for his or her recommendation.

If you allow your cat outdoors, then fleas are another reason why you should reconsider that action because as soon as he goes out in the yard, the fleas will be right back on him. If you have an indoor cat who shares his home with a dog, then you'd better not forget to check the cat if you find fleas on the dog. Ask you vet about yard sprays.

FLEA COLLARS. Flea collars emit toxic nerve gases that are absorbed into the skin and inhaled by your pet. That alone is reason enough not to use them, but there's another reason: They usually don't work. I've seen lots of cats wearing flea collars who still were infested with fleas. Outdoor cats have the added danger that these collars can get caught on branches and cause choking. Also, flea collars tend to worsen allergic conditions and can cause permanent hair loss around the neck. There are herbal flea collars available that contain pennyroyal and eucalyptus, so if you want to use a collar on your cat, at least try these instead of the chemical ones.

If you put a flea collar on your cat, make sure it's loose enough for you to fit two fingers underneath. Watch your cat *carefully* for any signs of allergic reaction. Don't allow him to get wet while he's wearing it and if you bathe him, remove the collar and don't put it on again until he's completely dry. As long as your cat wears the collar, supplement his diet with a little vitamin C everyday to help his body deal with the chemicals and gases being absorbed.

DDVP (dichlorvos) is an ingredient in several flea collars. This ingredient is absorbed into the cat's system and by continually wearing the collar, the effects are cumulative as DDVP (a suspected carcinogen) builds up in body tissues. On the label, DDVP may also be listed as vapona, 2,2 dichlorovinyl dimethyl phosphate. Try to avoid these collars.

Ultrasonic collars are an alternative to the poisonous flea collars, but

I haven't seen them work so effectively either.

Dips. As a last resort, there's always the flea dip. Never do this yourself, only the vet should dip the pet. Dips cannot be used on a cat with irritated skin or sores.

TICKS

Ticks are external parasites that firmly attach themselves to the skin and suck blood. A tick may look like a little wart on your cat's skin. As it fills with blood, the tick's body gets bloated. They're mostly found around the head, neck, ears, inside of the legs, between the toes, or in any body crevice. If your cat is shaking his head, look for ticks around the ears. If you don't see one, but your cat still shakes his head, have the vet examine him because the tick may have crawled inside the ear. Head shaking can also be a sign of ear mite infestation.

To remove a tick, cover it with a drop or two of mineral oil or rubbing alcohol. Wait a couple of minutes, and then gently pull it off with a tweezer. Be careful to grasp its head because many times the head is burrowed under the skin and if you just pull the tick off by the body, the head stays imbedded, which leads to infection. Never just pull a tick off the skin without first suffocating it with the mineral oil or rubbing alcohol. NEVER use a hot match to remove a tick due to the risk of injuring the cat. Immediately after removing the tick, kill it by immersing it in a small jar filled with rubbing alcohol. Be sure to put the cover on the jar. Then disinfect the effected area of the skin by using a cotton ball moistened with hydrogen peroxide.

Lyme disease. This is caused by a bacteria carried by the deer tick. The name "Lyme" comes from the town of Lyme, Connecticut, where the disease was first recognized.

It takes about four weeks after the bite for the disease to be detected in a blood test. Testing too early can cause a false negative.

Signs of this disease may not appear for weeks and in some cases, even years after the bite. Symptoms vary from animal to animal. There may at first be a rash in the bite area, the animal may appear to be suffering from a cold and is lethargic. Arthritis may be another symptom, becoming crippling as the disease progresses.

In the majority of cases, when diagnosed early, Lyme disease is readily treatable. If you live in an area where there have been incidences of Lyme disease, ask your vet about having your dog and outdoor cat tested during flea and tick season. If you don't allow your cat outdoors, but you have a dog, check him over regularly, paying close attention to the head, ears, armpits, and between the toes. Remember to then check your indoor cat because a tick can be carried in by the dog. Speak to your vet if you have any questions or worries because he or she is most up-to-date on the Lyme disease situation in your area.

EAR MITES

Ear mites can be found in the ear canal, where they cause inflammation and irritation. The cat may be seen shaking his head and scratching at his ears—often to the point of bleeding. He may also rub his head against objects and along the floor. Check inside your cat's ears for what looks like gritty brown-black dirt. Left untreated, ear mite infestation leads to bacterial infection.

If you notice ear mites early enough, you can probably get rid of them by using mineral oil, which won't irritate the ear. Put two or three drops of mineral oil in the ear, gently fold the ear flap down (cat will want to shake his head), and massage the base of the ear. Wait a couple of minutes and then wipe the inside of the ear with a dry cotton ball. Do this procedure faithfully everyday until all ear mites are gone.

If the ear mite infestation is bad, the ear gets inflamed, or the situation doesn't seem to be improving, then you need the vet to look at your cat. He or she will prescribe treatment. Follow the directions and administer the medication for the prescribed duration. When putting the medication in the ear, *don't massage* because these medications are very strong and will just aggravate the already irritated tissues.

INTERNAL PARASITES

TAPEWORMS

Your cat can get tapeworms by swallowing fleas, which act as hosts for fleas during their larval stage. Tapeworms attach themselves by their heads to the cat's intestines and begin feeding. They can grow very long and often segments break off and pass out with the stool. If you examine the stool right after the cat defecates, you may notice what look like moving grains of rice. You have to check the stool immediately after defecation, before the segments have a chance to burrow down into the litter. You may also find a couple of the cream-colored segments around the cat's rectum. To relieve itching, the cat may be seen dragging his hindquarters along the floor. Also, by checking the cat's bedding, you may discover some dried segments. Other symptoms can include a marked increase in appetite but without weight gain, and mild diarrhea.

Cats can also get tapeworms from eating prey that has the parasite. Any raw meat or raw fish can contain tapeworm larvae, which is why raw meat or raw fish should never be fed to your cat.

Bring a stool sample when you take your cat to the vet so a parasite check can be done.

TOXOPLASMA

Toxoplasma gondii is a single-celled parasite that lives in the cat's intestine. A cat can get it by eating raw meat, like prey, or ingesting contaminated feces. The parasite can be transmitted to humans from direct contact with an infected cat's feces. Humans can also develop toxoplasmosis from handling or eating raw meat, like steak tartare, or eating undercooked meat or unwashed vegetables prepared on the same surface used to cut raw meat.

Your cat may carry the parasite but not show any outward signs. If he does show symptoms, they might include: diarrhea, fever, loss of appetite, and enlarged lymph nodes. Cats that show no visible symptoms can still pass the parasite along to other animals by way of their feces.

CAUTION FOR PREGNANT WOMEN: Toxoplasmosis can cause birth defects. If you are pregnant or even suspect that you might be, have another family member handle litter box duties, or wear gloves. Immediate removal of solid waste from the litter box will eliminate the chance of infection because it takes forty-eight hours for the egg spores to become infective after a cat has defecated. If you are pregnant, you should avoid outdoor gardening to prevent touching contaminated soil (outdoor cats may use gardens as litter boxes) or wear gloves, and be sure to wash your hands afterward.

You and your cat can be tested to see if either of you carry the parasite. The test will also determine if you or your cat have built an immunity to it. Once exposed, an immunity is built against the organism. If you have built an immunity, then you won't have to worry about transmission. If the test indicates that your cat doesn't carry the parasite but also is *not* immune yet, then keep him indoors to reduce his chances of becoming infected. If you have not built an immunity, even if your cat has, you must still be careful about how you handle raw meat.

PREVENTING TOXOPLASMOSIS

1. Keep litter box clean and promptly remove fecal matter.

2. Wash hands immediately after handling litter box duties.

3. Don't eat raw meat and don't feed any to your cat.

4. Thoroughly clean countertops after preparing raw meat for cooking and *wash your hands.*

5. Don't prepare vegetables or salads on the same surface used to cut raw meat.

6. Wear gloves when gardening and wash your hands afterwards.

7. Don't allow children to play in sandboxes unless the boxes have covers. Outdoor cats may have used them as a litter box.

8. Don't allow your cat to catch and eat prey.

9. Control flies because they can transport egg spores from infected feces to food.

ROUNDWORMS

These internal parasites are coiled worms that range in length from two to five inches and resemble spaghetti. Your cat can ingest the eggs from contaminated soil. These eggs hatch in the small intestine, penetrate the wall, and get into the bloodstream. A cat can pass roundworms to her fetuses, so kittens can be born with them. Symptoms include: weakness, dull coat, and distended abdomen. Vomiting and diarrhea may also be symptoms. You may see a roundworm vomited up or passed through the stool. With kittens you might notice that they have tremendous appetites but remain thin with distended abdomens.

Bring a fresh stool sample with you when you take your cat to be examined. The vet will prescribe the proper medication to kill the roundworms. More than one treatment will be needed to be certain of killing any hatching worms.

To reduce your cat's chances of getting roundworms, keep him indoors so he won't come in contact with contaminated soil. If you have more than one cat, keep the litter box clean, emptying solid wastes daily.

COCCIDIA

These are single-celled parasites that infect the cat's intestinal tract. Transmission occurs by ingestion of infected feces. Young kittens are the ones who usually get infected. The cat develops a poor appetite, loses weight, and has diarrhea. He eventually becomes weak and emaciated and is at risk of dying. A stool sample check will detect coccidia, and then specific medication can be prescribed. Keeping a sanitary environment will greatly reduce the risk of spreading coccidia.

HOOKWORMS

These are small parasites that hook onto the wall of the intestine and feed on blood. Hookworms are similar in shape to roundworms but are much smaller. Hookworm infestation can occur by ingesting contaminated feces or soil, or through skin penetration. A mother can pass hookworms to her young in the womb. Symptoms include: vomiting, pale gums, emaciation, and occasional bloody diarrhea. Hookworm infestation in young or debilitated cats can cause anemia. See vet for treatment.

HEARTWORM

This internal parasite lives in the right ventricle and pulmonary artery of the heart. Heartworm is much more of a problem for dogs, but a cat can be susceptible. The parasite is spread by mosquitoes. When a mosquito bites the dog or cat, it passes the larvae into the bloodstream. The larvae find their way to the heart where they mature. Symptoms include: coughing, fatigue, and labored breathing. Early diagnosis is essential. Blood tests and X rays can be done to determine the presence of heartworm.

DISEASES AND DISORDERS

HEART DISEASE

Heart disease can happen at any age. If your cat has cardiovascular problems, be sure you follow your vet's advice on diet and exercise. Don't allow your cat to become overweight and cut out treats—mostly salty ones, like tidbits of prepared luncheon meats. Table scraps are absolutely out of the question.

Sometimes a cat is born with a heart condition. Some can be surgically corrected and some are not life-threatening.

CARDIOMYOPATHY

Cardiomyopathies are diseases of the heart muscles. Two types affect cats: dilated and hypertrophic. With dilated, the heart chambers become enlarged and aren't able to contract correctly. Symptoms are general (vomiting, appetite decrease, lethargy), so the cardiomyopathy may go unnoticed until the cat starts experiencing heart failure. Dr. Paul Pion of the University of California at Davis did a study which indicates that insufficient taurine (an essential amino acid) in the diet is connected to dilated cardiomyopathy. Since the published results of this study (*Science* magazine, August, 1987), pet food companies have fortified their products with taurine.

Hypertrophic cardiomyopathy, however, is not connected to a deficiency in taurine. With this disease, the heart muscles thicken. The heart is then unable to contract and dilate sufficiently to pump blood. By the time symptoms become obvious, the disease has progressed far along; seizures may begin and the hind legs become lame or paralyzed. Your vet can perform tests, including an ultrasound, for a diagnosis. So far the prognosis has not been good for cats with hypertrophic cardiomyopathy.

FELINE HYPERTHYROIDISM

Hyperthyroidism is when excessive amounts of the thyroid hormone are secreted. This occurs most commonly in older cats. Symptoms include: an increase in water intake, urination, and appetite. These symptoms are accompanied by a loss of weight. As hyperthyroidism progresses, there will be vomiting and diarrhea. Heart problems develop if this disease goes undiagnosed.

ARTHRITIS

Like humans, as cats age, they can suffer from stiff joints and have trouble getting out of bed in the morning, too. Aging animals commonly develop arthritis. There are things you can do to make your cat more comfortable. For instance, change to a litter box with lower sides so he can get in and out more easily. Keep your house warm and make sure your cat's favorite sleeping places are draft-free. Add vitamin C (100mg) and vitamin E (15 IU) into one meal daily to help your cat with his arthritis. Don't let him get overweight because that just puts extra stress on joints.

For a cat in pain, the vet may prescribe cortisone drugs. As far as aspirin goes, don't give it to your cat unless *specifically* advised by your vet. Aspirin can be toxic to cats (see section on "Aspirin").

HYPOGLYCEMIA

This occurs when the levels of glucose in the blood fall too low. With kittens, this can happen because of inconsistent feeding schedules, or if the intervals between feedings are too long. The body uses glucose for energy, so if the levels are too low, the cat will appear weak, dazed, and can be subject to seizures.

If you have young kittens, ask your vet about keeping a bottle of Karo syrup in the refrigerator in case of an emergency. The vet will advise you on how much to administer should it be needed to raise the glucose level. The dosage is usually about a half teaspoon.

DIABETES MELLITUS

With diabetes, the pancreas doesn't produce enough insulin to maintain normal levels of blood sugar. Insulin is the hormone that allows glucose (blood sugar) to exit the bloodstream and enter the cells. Without insulin, glucose builds up in the bloodstream and urine. The cat drinks large amounts of water and urinates more because the excessive sugar in the urine causes a loss of fluids—sugar has to be dissolved in water for elimination. Symptoms are increased water intake and increased appetite but with a loss of weight. If diabetes goes undiagnosed, the cat will get weak and eventually go into a diabetic coma.

To diagnose diabetes, the blood and urine are tested for glucose. Once the vet determines that diabetes is indeed the problem, he or she will start insulin treatment. While in the hospital, the cat's glucose level will be stabilized. The vet will then give you complete directions on how to administer insulin injections at home and you'll be provided with specific instructions on diet and maintenance. Once your cat is home, you'll have to give him daily insulin injections. Each day you'll take a urine sample (your vet will show you how) and do a simple test to determine sugar level. This monitoring is important in case a modification in the dosage is required.

As far as diet, you'll be given complete instructions on the kind of food needed and how much to feed. You have to feed the same food in the same amounts each day because insulin requirements depend on the food eaten. Never make a dietary change without your vet's approval. **Don't** add *any* supplements to your cat's food unless your vet gives you the okay to do so. Certain vitamins can lower insulin requirements or reduce the effectiveness of the insulin injections.

Your vet will provide you with directions on what to do in case of an

PREVENTING DIABETES

1. Don't allow your cat to become overweight.

2. Feed a variety of high quality food.

3. Don't leave food available.

4. Remember the Vitality Mix.

5. Don't feed your cat sweet treats meant for humans.

6. Don't feed your cat table scraps.

7. Never feed semimoist brand food (too much sugar and too many preservatives).

8. Make sure your cat gets regular exercise.

insulin overdose. You'll probably be instructed to keep a bottle of Karo syrup in the refrigerator and told how much to give in case the situation occurs. An insulin overdose can cause hypoglycemia.

PNEUMONIA

Pneumonia is an inflammation of the lungs. It can be brought on by bacteria, virus, aspiration of irritants, or parasites. Pneumonia can also be brought on if your cat inhales while you're administering liquid medication; this could easily happen if he's struggling too much. Cats are very susceptible to pneumonia caused by aspiration of mineral oil, so never use it to treat constipation.

Symptoms associated with pneumonia can include: coughing, fever, and lethargy. Immediate veterinary care is needed.

LARYNGITIS

This can be caused by a number of things: upper respiratory diseases, a foreign object trapped in the throat, irritants in the air, such as smoke, chemicals, or gases, or it can just be the result of excessive vocalization— a male loudly serenading a female for too long. Your vet may prescribe antibiotics to combat any bacterial infections. Feeding soft foods for a time may also be recommended. Providing some moisture in the air will help during the cat's recovery, so if you have a humidifier, set it up in the room your cat frequents. Keep your cat's environment clean and free of irritating dust. Avoid using aerosol room deodorizers while your cat is recovering.

FELINE ASTHMA

Dirt, dust, smoke, clay litter dust, and numerous other irritants can cause problems for a cat. Signs are wheezing, dry cough, labored breathing, and gasping. Your vet will x-ray the cat's chest and take blood tests. When you bring the cat to the vet, don't forget to take along a stool sample so a parasite check can be done.

If the cat is diagnosed as having asthma, then it will be up to you to make him as comfortable as possible. Keep the environment free of cigarette smoke and don't use aerosol sprays. Switch to a dust-free litter because that's usually the number one culprit when it comes to breathing difficulties. Check into the idea of buying an air-purifying unit. Your cat won't be the only one who will benefit from this—you'll be breathing cleaner air also. As far as medicinal care goes, the vet will prescribe treatment based on the specific case. Sometimes drugs are used to help open airways.

HAIRBALLS

The subject of hairballs is covered in chapter 9.

HALITOSIS

The most common cause of bad breath is tartar accumulation on the teeth. It can also be caused by an abscess, gum disease, or other diseases. If your cat has halitosis, have the vet do an examination.

FELINE UROLOGIC SYNDROME (FUS)

Cystitis. This is an inflammation of the bladder that can be acute or chronic. Signs include: frequent urinations in small amounts, urinating outside of the litter box, obvious straining to urinate, inability to urinate, crying during urination attempts, blood-tinged urine, strong ammonia-like odor to urine, excessive licking of the vulva or penis. Sometimes the only sign is the running back and forth to the litter box.

If you notice this or *any* of the above signs, don't walk, RUN to the vet because if left untreated, the blocked bladder swells with urine and this is *life-threatening*. While trying to urinate, the cat may cry and perhaps even scream from the pain. This is an absolute emergency and he needs to be catheterized by the vet. Treatment may include antibiotics, low magnesium food (vet may advise a prescription diet), or urine acidifiers.

While a cat is recovering from cystitis, make him comfortable by providing a nice warm bed with a soft towel. Possibly wrap a towel around a hot water bottle and put it in the corner of his favorite sleeping place. During the recovery period, have a couple litter boxes in places your cat normally frequents so he doesn't have far to go.

Urolithiasis. Urine passes from the bladder through a tube called the urethra. This tube empties into the vulva (female) or goes through the penis (male). Urinary obstructions are more common in males because the urethra is long and narrow. Contributing factors for urolithiasis are high-magnesium food, obesity, holding urine, and cystitis. Struvite crystals develop from urinary salts when the urine's pH becomes alkaline. The crystals form plugs or stones which block urine flow.

If you notice your cat straining to urinate and no urine is being passed, then there's a good chance that he has a blockage. If the obstruction isn't removed, the cat will die because toxic wastes build up and are released into the bloodstream. If you notice the following signs, it indicates an emergency situation: vomiting, depression, dehydration, and a urine-like odor to the breath. It is *urgent* that the cat get emergency medical care. Treatment includes catheterization of the urethra (a tube inserted to release the urine), medication, and based upon the severity of the condition, the cat may be hospitalized.

You really need to be aware of what's going on in your cat's litter box, especially if you own a male. Make sure you see wet litter, and if you notice

---

PREVENTING FUS

1. Feed high quality, low magnesium food. Make sure the label says "low magnesium" not just "low ash."

2. Make sure fresh water is always available. If your cat doesn't drink much water, you can put a teaspoon or two of tomato juice or plain water into each meal.

3. Include vitamin C (100mg) two or three times a week—more often if your cat is susceptible to FUS.

4. Feed two scheduled meals a day and don't leave food available. Urine becomes more alkaline after eating, so by serving scheduled meals, you will help keep the urine acidic.

5. Make sure your cat gets sufficient exercise.

6. Don't allow your cat to become overweight.

7. Reduce your cat's stress.

---

him making frequent trips in and out of the box, get to the vet. Some males have repeated blockages, so keep a very watchful eye if your cat has suffered from this problem before.

RENAL FAILURE

When the kidneys start to fail, wastes build up in the blood. Early symptoms include: increased water intake, increased appetite, vomiting, increased urination, and lethargy. With each inflammation, scarring occurs which causes degeneration of the kidneys. Eventually the kidneys stop functioning. As wastes build up, continuing symptoms also include: anemia, skin sores, emaciation, foul breath, and mouth ulcers. Untreated, the cat will lapse into a coma and die.

Treatment includes intravenous fluids and medication, including antibiotics. The vet will prescribe vitamin supplements and a special diet of less protein, but of high biological value to help with the failing kidneys.

PYOMETRA

This reproductive disorder can come on slowly. You may notice a mucous-like reddish discharge between your cat's heat cycles. With this disorder, the uterus slowly fills with pus; it usually happens in older cats. There are two forms: "open" and "closed." With open pyometra, the pus drains out of the uterus and you'll notice a foul smell. With closed pyometra, the cervix is sealed closed and the pus fills up in the uterus—you'll notice an enlarged abdomen. Pyometra may also include the following symptoms: fever, depression, excessive thirst and urination, decrease in appetite, and vomiting. An ovariohysterectomy is needed to remove the uterus.

METRITIS

This uterine infection can happen after a long heat cycle, mating, or giving birth. Symptoms include: loss of appetite, fever, depression, and can also include a foul-smelling vaginal discharge. In some cases, the cat may also neglect her young kittens. Treatment using antibiotics can be used, but removal of the uterus is usually advised.

MASTITIS

This is an inflammation of the mammary glands that can occur while a mother is nursing her kittens. It can be caused by an infection in the mammary glands. Mastitis can affect one or more of the glands. If the mother develops mastitis, she will be in pain when the glands are touched. Other signs may include: hard or discolored breasts, fever, listlessness, and decrease in appetite. You must get her to the vet immediately. Treatment usually will involve placing warm compresses on the glands. With mastitis, the mother's milk may contain bacteria that can be passed to her kittens, so depending upon what the vet says, you may have to feed them a milk replacement formula, available at pet supply stores.

CANCER

The very word is frightening, but don't let that delay you in having any lumps, bumps, or lesions that you discover on your cat checked out by the vet. Early diagnosis puts the chances of successful recovery more in your favor. Signs of cancer can include: weight loss, loss of appetite, sores that don't heal, swelling, and lumps under the skin. Remember, just because your cat may develop a lump doesn't necessarily mean it's malignant; older animals tend to develop various benign bumps. Finding out as soon as possible is the most important thing. Many animals respond very well to the various cancer treatments.

STEATITIS ("YELLOW FAT" DISEASE)

This is caused by a vitamin E deficiency and an overabundance of *unsaturated* fats. Remember, cats don't metabolize unsaturated fats very well. Steatitis is most commonly the result of a diet consisting mainly of fish, with its highly unsaturated fatty acids. Symptoms include: cat may look heavy and seem less agile, skin is painful when touched, and fever is apparent. The vet will prescribe a change in diet or vitamin E in a specific dosage, among other treatments, depending upon the individual case.

GLAUCOMA

Fluid pressure builds up within the eyeball and as it progresses, the eyeball becomes enlarged. The cat is in pain because of the constant pressure. Permanent damage will be done unless the cat gets immediate treatment. When medication doesn't help, removal of the eye will be advised.

EXCESSIVE TEARING

Tearing happens when a blockage is washed from the ducts. This is mostly a problem for peke-faced cats, such as Persians. Blocked tear ducts can also be the result of allergies, irritation, or upper respiratory infection.

CATARACTS

Cataracts make the eye look opaque and milky. They can come at any age, but are most often found in aging or diabetic cats. Your vet will discuss treatment options with you. In some cases, surgery can be performed.

INFECTIOUS DISEASES

FELINE LEUKEMIA VIRUS (FeLV)

Feline leukemia is a highly contagious blood cancer that's spread through secretions. The most common methods of transmission are by the sharing of food and water bowls and litter boxes, and also through biting and licking. This disease grows in the cells of bone marrow, depressing the immune system, and leaving the cat open for viral infection. Feline leukemia symptoms include: loss of appetite, weight loss, anemia, enlarged lymph nodes, diarrhea or constipation, lethargy, breathing difficulty, or rapid breathing.

Kittens are very susceptible to feline leukemia. Some cats can be carriers without showing symptoms themselves. This is why a new cat should be tested before exposing him to others. The disease can be detected by a blood test. Your cat can be vaccinated against feline leukemia. The vaccine is given in a series of three injections. Cats should be tested before getting vaccinated because the vaccine won't help an already infected cat, and he could go on to infect others. All cats must get an annual booster.

The feline leukemia vaccine is controversial and there are some vets who question its safety and effectiveness. I feel that cats must be protected against such a deadly disease, but if you're unsure, then discuss the situation with your vet.

If you decide against the vaccine, then you *must* keep your cat in the best of health. Keep his resistance up so he won't be as susceptible to feline leukemia by always including the Vitality Mix (those B vitamins are essential) and by using a fatty acid supplement. Add vitamin C to your cat's meal once a day (50-100mg) and a little vitamin E (15 IU) three times a week. Check with your vet about these supplements, though. Top quality food with protein of high biological value is a must! And, remember, an unvaccinated cat must NEVER NEVER be allowed outdoors, and any new cat must be tested before exposure to your current resident cats.

Cats that test positive should be isolated, kept indoors, and then retested three months later to see if the infection status has changed to negative.

FELINE PANLEUKOPENIA (FPL)

This disease, also known as feline distemper and infectious enteritis, is highly contagious. It's spread by direct contact with secretions; it can be found on food bowls, bedding, cages, and human clothing. This disease can also be spread by the fleas of an infected cat. The virus can survive in the environment for almost a year, and a cat who is an active carrier can transmit the virus for months through his urine and feces.

Feline panleukopenia is most common in kittens and the survival rate is low. Symptoms, which begin about a week after exposure, include: high fever, loss of appetite, depression, vomiting, dehydration (cat may be seen hanging over the water bowl), and abdominal pain. As the condition worsens, white blood cell production is reduced and the cat develops bloody diarrhea. The fever will fluctuate over the course of the disease and suddenly fall before death.

Treatment includes vitamins, antibiotics to prevent secondary infection, and fluid therapy to address the dehydration. Plenty of TLC is needed to keep the patient's spirits up. Diligent nursing care and support can mean the difference in the cat's will to survive. The first two days are the most critical.

Booster vaccinations are needed annually to prevent this disease.

FELINE INFECTIOUS ANEMIA

This disease is spread by a parasite, *Hemabartonella felis*, that lives on the surface of red blood cells. The body then interprets these blood cells as enemies and destroys them. Anemia develops as more and more cells are destroyed. Insects that live off blood, such as fleas, can spread this disease. Symptoms include: excessive thirst, loss of appetite, weakness, enlarged spleen, pale mucous membranes, fever, and weight loss.

With early diagnosis, the chances of recovery are good. A blood test will determine if the parasite is present. Because the number of parasites fluctuates, a few blood tests may be necessary over a period of several days for an accurate diagnosis. Treatment includes antibiotics, vitamins, and in severe cases, fluid therapy and transfusions are needed.

CHLAMYDIOSIS

This is a highly contagious upper respiratory infection that causes conjunctivitis in the eyes. Once contracted, it's easily treatable with antibiotics. To protect your cat from becoming infected with this disease, an annual vaccination is available.

If you notice your cat's eyes are red, swollen, or watery, you should have the vet do an examination to determine if it is chlamydiosis.

If your cat shows any symptoms, be sure to wash your hands after handling him, and don't rub your eyes because this infection is contagious to humans, but is also easily treated with antibiotics.

FELINE PNEUMONITIS (FPN)

This disease mostly affects the lungs, causing raspy breathing. Other symptoms can include: fever, red eyes with swollen lids, discharges from the eyes and nose, and sneezing. Treatment for pneumonitis includes antibiotics and fluid therapy.

A yearly vaccination is needed for protection from this upper respiratory disease.

FELINE RHINOTRACHEITIS (FVR)

This is the most serious of the upper respiratory diseases. For kittens, this disease is fatal. Symptoms begin with a fever, then progress to sneezing, coughing, and thickening discharges from the nose and eyes. Eye ulcers form and the eyelids become swollen. As the disease worsens, the nose becomes blocked with the thick discharge. Symptoms sometimes include ulcers inside the mouth, which make eating difficult, so the cat loses weight. Even when mouth ulcers don't develop, the cat loses his appetite because his sense of smell is blocked by the congestion.

Treatment for this disease for unvaccinated cats includes: antibiotics, intravenous fluids, nutritional support, and eye ointments. The nose and eyes have to be kept clear. In some cases, force feeding will be advised. Your vet will instruct you on what to feed and how often (see section on "Force Feeding"). Lots of TLC is needed when a cat has feline rhinotracheitis. He must be kept warm and made to feel as comfortable as possible. Severe infections can leave a cat with reoccurring colds.

The vaccine for feline rhinotracheitis is combined with the feline distemper and calicivirus vaccines in what is called the "three-in-one" vaccination. Annual boosters are needed.

FELINE CALICIVIRUS (FCV)

This disease is similar to rhinotracheitis, but the nose and eyes aren't affected as much, though there is a thick discharge. The symptoms are cold-like and can include ulcers on the nose, tongue, and roof of the mouth. As with rhinotracheitis, eating becomes difficult and the cat loses weight. It's also hard to treat the cat because the mouth is very sore.

Feline calicivirus is spread through saliva, contact with an infected cat, contaminated surroundings, or urine. The incubation period is approximately two to six days and the disease usually lasts for a couple of weeks, depending on the severity of the infection. Once a cat gets this disease, he builds an immunity to it. Treatment for calicivirus includes fluid therapy, nutritional support, and antibiotics. When treating an infected cat, you must wash your hands and change your clothes to keep from infecting others. An infected cat should also be isolated.

There is a vaccine for this disease and it's combined with feline distemper and rhinotracheitis in the "three-in-one" vaccination. An annual booster is needed.

FELINE INFECTIOUS PERITONITIS (FIP)

This disease is spread through the air or by direct contact and has a very high fatality rate. There are two forms of this disease: "wet" and "dry." Symptoms common to both include: eye and nose discharges, fever, depression, loss of appetite, and weight loss. In the effusive or "wet" form, the abdomen and chest become painfully swollen due to fluid accumulation, which causes breathing difficulty. In the noneffusive or "dry" form, lesions develop on the brain, kidneys, liver, and eyes, resulting in failing organ function. Other symptoms can include seizures and posterior lameness. Treatment includes antibiotics, fluids, and nutritional supplements.

There is no cure or vaccine yet for this disease. To reduce the risk of infecting resident cats, have any newcomer tested for FIP before introducing him. If your cat recently died from this disease, don't bring a new cat into the house for at least seven days.

RABIES

You may not think that rabies is still a health problem these days, but it is. Animals in certain areas are required to be vaccinated against this disease. Even if you live in an area that doesn't require it, you should have your cat vaccinated if he's allowed outdoors. The intramuscular vaccination is given in the leg, which may cause your cat to limp for a little while.

Rabies is fatal. Major carriers are bats, skunks, and raccoons, among other wild animals. The disease is spread through the infected animal's saliva when he bites another animal. The incubation period can be a couple of weeks or can take months. Your outdoor cat could get bitten by an infected animal, and you might not know until the symptoms start appearing.

The disease goes through phases. The initial symptom is restlessness. The cat also becomes sensitive to loud noises and/or bright light, so he'll look for a hiding place. He'll stop eating and drinking also. It's about this time that the cat starts attacking people, other pets, and any moving object, like a twig or leaf. The disease causes the muscles in the throat to become paralyzed, making it impossible to swallow, thus the cat salivates excessively. As the disease worsens, muscle coordination is lost, paralysis sets in, and death follows.

If your cat has been bitten by a wild animal or shows any of the above signs, take precautions when handling. Use a blanket to put him in his carrying case or close him in a room. Call your vet *immediately*. If you've been bitten by your infected cat, then you need to get to your own doctor immediately.

Treatment for an infected animal is painful and takes a very long time. Euthanasia is the most humane thing to do.

EMERGENCIES

HANDLING AN INJURED CAT

There are two very important things to remember when attempting to pick up an injured cat 1) you want to avoid causing further injury or stress and 2) you don't want to get injured yourself. An injured cat can become aggressive because he's terribly frightened and in pain. You don't want to get scratched or bitten.

Approach the cat calmly and quietly. When a pet is injured or sick, it's only natural that the owner will be anxious and frightened, but try to get yourself together and stay calm. The only way you'll be able to assess the severity of the injury and decide the best way to move the cat is if you're relatively calm. Reassure the cat by talking in a soothing voice, letting him know you're going to help him to feel better while you are gently stroking him on the back of the head.

When a cat has been hit by a car, had a fall, is unconscious, or is unable to move, you have to be *extremely* careful when handling him. Gently moving him onto a flat board is the best way to avoid the risk of further injury. To get him onto the board, hold the skin of the neck and the skin near the tail and slide the cat carefully. Don't bend the legs or the spine.

For a cat who is not severely injured, you can place one hand under his forelegs and the other hand under his hindquarters to provide support. Carefully scoop him up into your arms and let him rest against your chest. Never pick up a cat with one hand, by the scruff of the neck, or under the abdomen. Hold him securely to prevent him from jumping down and further injuring himself.

For an aggressive or struggling cat, wrap him in a blanket before attempting to pick him up. When there's no danger of further injury, using the carrying case to transport the cat will be the safest.

In general, you will have to use your judgement on how best to handle and transport the cat based on the specific circumstances and the type of injury involved. The most important thing is getting to the veterinary hospital for medical treatment.

ARTIFICIAL RESPIRATION

When an animal stops breathing because of an injury or illness, death will result within minutes. It's essential that you be familiar with emergency techniques such as artificial respiration and CPR. I have described below the method that was taught to me. For more comprehensive information on first aid for pets, I strongly suggest you purchase one of the many books written by veterinarians that specifically discuss all areas of first aid for animals.

ARTIFICIAL RESPIRATION

Warning signs indicating that a cat could stop breathing: labored breathing, gasping, bluish gums, and unconsciousness.

■ If the cat is wearing a collar or harness, remove it because it might be interfering with his ability to breathe.

■ Before performing artificial respiration, you need to check the mouth and nose for any object that could be causing an obstruction. With a piece of gauze, open the cat's mouth and pull the tongue outward. If you do see an object, then it has to be removed. You may need tweezers or needle-nosed pliers.

■ Clear the mouth of any mucous or excess saliva with a gauze pad. If there's vomitus in the mouth or if the cat was under water, then suspend him upside down by the hips and gently shake his body a couple of times to remove the liquid.

■ Lay the cat on his side with the body slightly higher than the head. To be sure the passageway for air is open, the head and neck should be straight.

■ Hold the cat's mouth closed by putting one hand around it. Put your mouth over his nostrils and gently exhale. Allow the air to exhale from the cat's body. Blow air in for three seconds and then release for two seconds. Repeat until you see the cat's chest rising and falling, which means he's starting to breathe again on his own.

■ Once the cat is breathing again, you must take him to the vet immediately.

CPR

When the heart stops pumping, cardiac arrest occurs. To perform CPR:

1. The cat should be placed on his side.

2. One hand goes on each side of the cat's ribs, right behind his elbows.

3. The chest should be compressed in quick motions every other second for 30 seconds-1 minute.

4. After you compress, immediately release to allow the lungs to fill with air. Don't use too much force when compressing because you could fracture a rib.

POISONING

Many common household products are poisonous to cats. Just look at the following list of some toxic products and think about how often you might have left one of them lying around or within reach of your cat.

Paint	Pills
Bleach	Shoe polish
Floor polish	Nail polish
Furniture polish	Nail polish remover
Cleanser	Cosmetics
Detergent	Hair dye

Bath oil	Shampoo
Perfume	Shaving lotion
Laxative	Suntan lotion
Aspirin	Medicine
Deodorant	Ointments/creams
Plant food	Paint remover
Turpentine	Lacquer thinner
Pesticides	Fertilizer
Weed killer	Kerosene
Antifreeze	Brake fluid

You need to go through your house, garage, and yard, looking at these places through the eyes of your cat. Products stored in your garage or basement, like paint remover, pesticides, etc., should be tightly sealed, all drips running down the side should be cleaned off, and the bottles or cans should then be locked away where your cat can't get to them. Don't just put a bottle on the shelf because a cat could accidently knock it over.

Outdoor cats have the added risk due to pest control products in gardens and yards. For example, the methaldehyde in snail and slug poisons is also highly poisonous to cats. Outdoor trash cans also pose a very dangerous risk to cats due to discarded poisons, raw meat, bones, etc.

One of the most dangerous of all poisons is ethylene glycol, which is found in antifreeze. It has a sweet taste that attracts a cat. In the winter, outdoor cats tend to go under cars for warmth and end up licking the sweet-tasting antifreeze that has leaked onto the road or driveway. If your cat has ingested antifreeze, then early treatment is essential to prevent renal failure. Symptoms of antifreeze poisoning include: depression, vomiting, and then collapse.

FIRST AID FOR POISONING. Signs of poisoning can include: vomiting (possibly bloody), pain, coughing, strange breath odor, burns around the mouth and tongue, hemorrhaging, and collapse. First of all, always have your vet's emergency number by the phone, along with the number of your local poison control center. You must NEVER try to induce vomiting until you know what kind of poison was ingested. If you're sure of the product, then follow the instructions on the label regarding poisoning. Antedotes are the same for people and pets.

If possible, call your vet or poison control center just to get verification. If you don't know what your cat swallowed or if there's no label on the product, then call your vet or poison control center. You will be instructed on whether to induce vomiting based upon your cat's symptoms. For instance, the vet will ask if there are burns around the mouth. Be ready to describe visible symptoms. Always keep chemicals in their original containers so you don't accidently give the wrong antidote because you read the wrong label.

ACID, ALKALI, PETROLEUM POISONING. Acid, alkali, or petroleum poisons burn the mouth and throat, so vomiting the poison back up would only cause further damage. Some examples of these types of poisons include: battery acid, paint thinner, floor polish, toilet bowl cleaner, kerosene, lye, and shoe polish. Signs of acid, alkali, or petroleum poisoning include: burns on the mouth and tongue, coughing, and strange odor to the breath. You need to *dilute* these poisons to slow their absorption in the body.

To Dilute:
Give two teaspoons of activated charcoal mixed with milk or water in small amounts. Watch that the cat doesn't go into shock.

Never administer anything by mouth to a cat who is having a seizure, is vomiting, or is unconscious. Rush to the nearest vet immediately. If possible, bring along the poison that was swallowed.

NONCORROSIVE POISONING. Vomiting is to be induced for noncorrosive products such as perfume, detergent, pills, or antifreeze. Signs of noncorrosive poisoning can include: vomiting, pain, convulsing, panting, and coma. Never induce vomiting when a cat is having a convulsion or is unconscious.

To Induce Vomiting:
Administer ½-1 teaspoon of 3 percent hydrogen peroxide or syrup of Ipecac. Do this every five minutes until the cat vomits. **Don't** go over three teaspoons.

When the cat has finished vomiting, give him two teaspoons of activated charcoal mixed with milk or water.

Immediately get to the vet and bring the poison that was swallowed, along with a vomitus sample. If you don't know what poison was swallowed, then it's especially important to bring a sample of the vomitus.

RODENT POISONS. Ingestion of these poisons can cause hemorrhaging. If you see your cat ingesting these, induce vomiting and rush to the vet.

POISONS ABSORBED THROUGH THE SKIN. See section on "Burns from Chemicals."

POISONING FROM PLANTS. Cats have a natural desire to eat grass. I've heard two theories as to why: Some say it's to satisfy something lacking in the diet, and others say that when a cat eats something unpleasant, he will eat grass to make himself vomit. I'm not sure what the real reason is because I know many well-fed cats who like to nibble on grass and very few of them vomit afterward. Whatever the reason, cats do like to do it.

Grass treated with weed killers and fertilizers is not good for cats, but wheat grass is. Indoor cats who don't have owners who supply a pot of wheat grass may take to nibbling on houseplants. Aside from the damage this causes your beautiful plants, it is POISONOUS to your cat. Make sure you supply a convenient pot of wheat grass for your cat so he stays away from the English Ivy.

Here is a list of some of the indoor/outdoor plants that are poisonous to cats. There are so many more—let's just say that ALL plants should be considered off-limits.

One common example is the philodendron. Yes, this popular plant that's found in just about every home is poisonous to cats. The effects are cumulative. Another example is the dieffenbachia or dumb cane. You should never have this plant in your house if you have children or pets. It causes the tongue to swell, making breathing very difficult, painful irritation of the mouth, and abdominal cramps. Other dangerous plants follow:

Amaryllis	Larkspur
Autumn Crocus	Laurel
Azalea	Lily of the Valley
Balsam Pear	Lords and Ladies
Belladonna	Marijuana
Bird of Paradise	Mistletoe
Cacti	Morning Glory
Caladium	Nettle
Calla Lily	Nutmeg
Christmas Trees	Oleander
Coral Plant	Poison Hemlock
Daffodil	Pokeweed
English Holly	Rhubarb Leaves

English Ivy	Tobacco
Glory Lily	Virginia Creeper
Honeysuckle	Water Hemlock
Hydrangea	Wisteria
Jerusalem Cherry	

If you suspect your cat has been eating a houseplant, then call your vet. Even if your cat seems fine—remember, the effects of poisoning are cumulative.

ELECTRIC SHOCK

Prevent the chance of this happening by keeping all cords hidden and secured. If you see your cat chewing on a cord, stop him immediately by shouting "NO!" or clap your hands loudly—don't grab hold of him. You may not catch your cat in the act of chewing on electrical cords, but you might notice an inflammation around his mouth. If you do see an inflammation, then check the electrical cords around your house for signs of teeth marks or damage. Even a minor burn is dangerous because pulmonary edema (see below) can result.

Never touch a cat if he's touching an exposed wire. Turn the electrical current off at the electrical switch box, then use a wooden broom stick or wooden yardstick to push the cat away from the wire. The cat may be unconscious and in shock. Keep him warm by placing a towel or blanket over him and if needed, perform artificial respiration (see page 185). Immediately get to the vet, even if the cat seems fine, because of the risk of pulmonary edema.

PULMONARY EDEMA

Pulmonary edema is the accumulation of fluid in the lungs. This can be brought on by heart disease, smoke inhalation, or electric shock. Symptoms are open mouth breathing and tending to sit or stand instead of lying down. Immediate veterinary care is needed.

BURNS

Burns can be a particular hazard for cats should they walk across stoves, stick their noses into places they shouldn't, or accidently get too close to a burner.

With *first degree* burns, the hair gets singed and the skin turns red. These burns, in most cases, heal rapidly, but they still cause pain. Apply a washcloth soaked in cold water over the area to relieve the pain. After using the cold washcloth, gently pat the area dry. Make sure the burn stays clean and dry. Keep watch in case it should blister. NEVER USE ICE because it will damage the tissues underneath. Don't ever apply butter either, no matter what you were taught in the past.

Second degree burns usually cause blistering and sometimes oozing. The skin will be very red. With this type of burn, the skin cells are destroyed. Apply a cold, water-soaked washcloth over the burn. Pat the area dry very gently—never rub. DON'T USE ICE OR BUTTER. Put sterile gauze lightly over the area, being careful not to touch any blisters, and then get to the vet.

Third degree burns are the most serious because underlying tissues are destroyed. DON'T TOUCH THE BURN OR ATTEMPT TO CLEAN IT. The cat will probably be in shock. Cover the burn with sterile gauze and rush to the veterinary hospital.

BURNS FROM CHEMICALS. Chemicals that accidently splash on the cat's body or in his eyes can result in serious injury. Fast action is essential to reduce further damage. Continually flush the exterior body with clean water. The best way to do this is to put the cat in the sink and using your hose attachment, completely rinse off the chemical. When it has been rinsed off, put sterile gauze over the burn and immediately take the cat to the veterinary hospital.

For chemicals splashed in the eyes, place the cat on his side, hold the eyelids open, and flush the eyes with water. If only one eye is affected, then tilt the cat's head back and rinse AWAY from the unaffected eye. If you know which chemical was the cause, follow instructions on the label. Use sterile gauze to cover the eyes and rush to the vet.

Be very careful when using chemicals or detergents and make sure your cat is kept safely away from the area. All chemicals should be kept tightly sealed and securely stored away.

SHOCK

Shock occurs when blood pressure falls and organs and tissues experience oxygen deprivation due to diminished circulation. Severe injury, burns, poisoning, hemorrhaging, serious illness, and heatstroke can cause a cat to go into shock. Symptoms include: weakness, collapse, unconsciousness, grayish gums, dilated pupils, rapid breathing, and coolness to the skin.

First Aid for Shock

1. Keep the cat warm by wrapping him in a blanket.

2. Wrap a hot water bottle in a towel and place it near the cat. Never put a hot water bottle next to a cat's skin.

3. Make sure the cat is breathing and the airway is clear. Administer artificial respiration, if needed, (see page 185).

4. Immediate veterinary care is needed.

CHOKING

Be very careful when it comes to such items as needles, pins, thread, yard, rubber bands, string, bones, marbles, thumbtacks, or other small objects that could get stuck in a cat's throat or cause internal damage. Never leave items such as these out where a cat could get hold of them.

When there's something caught in the cat's mouth, you may notice him pawing at his face or drooling excessively. You can probably remove the object with your fingers.

■ Open the cat's mouth and pull the tongue outward with a piece of gauze. Look down the throat with your penlight. If there's someone else in the house with you, have them hold the cat. If you're alone and the cat is struggling, then quickly wrap him in a towel.

■ If you can see the object, try to remove it with your fingers, tweezers, or needle-nosed pliers, unless it's a string, thread, or a needle.

■ If you can't see the object or you just can't reach it, lay the cat on his side and put one hand on each side of his chest, just below the rib cage. Use an inward and upward thrusting motion to try releasing the object. Check the cat's mouth to see if the object has been dislodged. If the cat has stopped breathing, then administer artificial respiration (see page 185).

CAUTION: Never try to remove a string or thread because the other end can be in the intestinal tract and to pull the string would cause it to cut the walls. Never try to remove a needle for the same reason—the thread attached may be going through the intestinal tract. JUST GET TO THE VET RIGHT AWAY! The same holds true for string or thread seen hanging from the rectum. Don't pull it, just get to the vet.

SEIZURES

Seizures are very frightening for an owner to witness because the cat goes from being normal one minute to convulsing the next. Seizures only last a couple of minutes, but they will be very long minutes for you. Seizures can result from many things, such as epilepsy, hypoglycemia, disease, a head injury, poisoning, or high body temperature. A seizure can also be brought on by a thiamine deficiency, though this is more likely in cats fed all-fish diets.

During the seizure, the cat may shake, become stiff, or lose control of his bowels, and become unconscious. Unless the cat is in danger of injuring himself, don't interfere by trying to hold him or pick him up. Place several towels *around* him (not on him) to protect him from banging into anything.

After the seizure, wipe any excess saliva or vomitus out of the mouth. Never try to do this *during* the seizure because you could get bitten. Provide reassurance and comfort to him because he'll probably be confused.

Call your vet so tests can be performed to discover the cause of the seizure. If a seizure lasts longer than a few minutes, then you need to get to the vet right away.

COUGHING

Coughing can be a symptom of hairballs, choking, illness, or disease. Look in the mouth and throat to see if anything is caught in there (if so, see section on "Choking.") Never give your cat cough suppressants meant for humans.

Coughing caused by illness or disease will have accompanying symptoms. Seek veterinary care to determine the cause.

HEATSTROKE

This can happen in a matter of minutes if a cat or any animal is left in a parked car. Even leaving the windows cracked doesn't provide enough ventilation. A car parked in the shade will still turn into an oven in minutes. It only takes a short time before damage is done to an animal's nervous system, heart, and brain. Unfortunately, many animals die this way due to the unawareness of owners. Heatstroke can happen to an animal in any confined warm area without sufficient ventilation.

Signs of heatstroke are rectal temperature over 105°F., panting, drooling or foaming, bluish gums, anxiety, weakness, or collapse.

First Aid for Heatstroke

1. Put the cat in the sink and rinse him with cold water. If you can't get to a sink, then wrap the cat in a cold wet towel.

2. Use an ice pack on the head.

3. Take the cat's rectal temperature every ten minutes. Stop the cooling procedure when the temperature reaches 103°F. You must be careful because if the temperature goes too low, the cat is in danger of hypothermia.

4. Provide cool water for him to drink, but don't force him.

5. If the cat is unconscious, you must take him to the vet.

HYPOTHERMIA

This occurs when there is a sudden fall in body temperature. Causes include: exposure to cold, drugs, severe illness, or shock. A rectal temperature of below 100°F. indicates hypothermia. Signs include depression and anxiety. When you touch the cat, he may also feel cold.

First Aid for Hypothermia

1. Cover the cat right away with a blanket.

2. Fill a hot water bottle with WARM water and wrap it in a towel before putting it next to the cat. The rewarming must be slow to avoid shock.

3. If you can't get the cat's temperature back to normal within forty-five minutes, or if he's in shock, get immediate medical attention.

FROSTBITE

This is caused when exposure to cold destroys tissues. The ear tips, tail, and feet are the places usually affected. A sign of frostbite is the skin will first look pale, but then will become red, swollen, and hot; the skin will also be painful if touched. Sometimes the outer layers of the skin peel. Frostbitten areas later become more susceptible to cold.

To Treat:
Immerse the area in *lukewarm* water for approximately fifteen minutes. Never submerge the head.

Afterward, very gently pat the cat dry. DON'T RUB AND DON'T USE A HAIR DRYER! Soothe the area by applying a little bit of Vaseline. Wrap the cat in a blanket and get to the vet.

WOUNDS

There are two types of wounds: closed and open. A closed wound is when the skin isn't broken, such as a bruise. It can range from a minor injury that affects only the tissues below the skin to a serious injury with potential internal bleeding. If ever in doubt about the seriousness of a bruise, you should consult your vet.

With open wounds you need to:

■ Clean with mild soap and water, and then apply 3 percent hydrogen peroxide.

■ Control bleeding by applying pressure with a sterile gauze pad.

■ Gently bandage the wound and get to the vet.

If bleeding is profuse, then don't clean the wound, just apply pressure. If the injury is to a limb, then hold up the limb to reduce the blood flow. Rush to the vet because stitches may be required.

Puncture wounds can heal on the surface, trapping bacteria underneath (see section on "Abscesses"). Clean these wounds with mild soap and water, and then flush the area with 3 percent hydrogen peroxide. Clip the hairs around the wound for easier monitoring, and bandage lightly. Clean and redress the wound each day. Get to the vet at the first sign of swelling, infection, or if the wound doesn't seem to be healing right.

WHEN AND HOW TO APPLY A TOURNIQUET. A tourniquet is only to be used when the wound is on the lower section of the leg and only as a LAST RESORT to control life-threatening bleeding. Irreversible damage and the loss of the leg can result from the use of a tourniquet.

Make a tourniquet by tying a piece of cloth or gauze around the leg, a couple inches above the wound. When tying the tourniquet, don't make a knot because you want to be able to remove it very rapidly, so I suggest you tie a bow.

It is crucial that you rush to the nearest vet immediately to prevent permanent damage to the limb. If you are quite a distance from the nearest veterinary hospital, be sure to loosen the tourniquet every 25 minutes to allow blood to flow to the limb.

HEAD INJURIES

If there's bleeding, use gentle pressure. Don't clean the wound because you risk getting particles of dirt in the brain. Just get your cat to the vet as fast as you can, but move him very gently.

INJURIES TO THE EYE

The most common causes of eye injuries are scratches from another cat's claws (this can happen during innocent play, so keep all cat's claws trimmed), foreign particles or irritants, or scrapes from branches.

Signs indicating eye injury:

- appearance of the nictitating membrane
- redness
- inflammation or swelling of the eyelid
- fixed pupils
- abnormal eye movements
- loss of hair on eyelids
- tearing
- discharges or bleeding
- squinting
- sensitivity to light or touch
- rubbing of the eye with paw
- milky look to the eye

REMOVING A PARTICLE FROM THE EYE. To remove a particle from the eye, gently pull down on the lower lid and raise the upper lid to locate the foreign material. *Dampen* the tip of a tissue first, and then touch it to the particle— it will stick to the tissue. Never use a dry tissue. When you're unable to remove a particle from the eye with a dampened tissue, then use a sterile eyewash solution to flush it out. If a sharp object is embedded in the eye, you musn't attempt to remove it. Just put a *loose* bandage over the eye to keep the cat from pawing, and rush to the vet.

EYE INJURIES. If there's bleeding, place a sterile gauze pad over the eye. Wrap a strip of gauze around the head to hold the pad in place and tape the end of the gauze to itself. Get immediate veterinary treatment.

DISLODGED EYEBALL. This can be caused by a sharp blow to the head. Keep the eye lubricated with plain eye ointment. If you have none, then use lukewarm water. Immediately get to the vet.

CORNEA ULCERATION. One of the causes of cornea ulcerations can be a result of a fight with another animal. Once this happens, the cat is in pain— he'll paw at his eye and keep the eyelid partially closed. The eye may also be tearing quite a bit. This condition can worsen rapidly, so don't delay in seeking veterinary care.

APPEARANCE OF THE NICTITATING MEMBRANE. The third eyelid (the nictitating membrane) is located in the lower inside corner of each eye. This membrane usually is visible when the eye has been irritated or injured. Certain diseases, such as feline leukemia, also can cause it to unfold. If you see the membrane remaining in the unfolded position, seek veterinary attention.

BITES FROM ANIMALS

During a fight, there's a chance your cat could be bitten by a dog or another cat. On the skin surface these bites may look like small punctures that quickly heal. In some cases, you may not even notice the bite because it's hidden by the coat. Unfortunately, what usually happens is that when the wound heals, it traps the infection underneath and an abscess forms (see the section on "Abscesses" below).

Check your cat regularly for bite wounds. If you see one, look over the rest of the body because there might be more. Clean all bites with mild soap and water, and then flush with a 3 percent hydrogen peroxide solution. Do this a couple times a day for the first few days. Snip the hairs away from the wound for easier monitoring. If it seems that the wound isn't healing, or at the first indication of infection or swelling, get veterinary treatment. For large bites, you should take the cat to the vet right away.

ABSCESSES

An abscess forms as a result of skin sealing over a wound and bacteria getting trapped under the surface. Your cat may stroll home after a fight and you won't notice anything because most often, the fur hides the wound. Within twenty-four hours, a fever develops, the cat seems depressed and doesn't want to eat. The site of the wound starts getting swollen and becomes painful. Usually, by the time you notice the bite, your cat won't let you even touch it. Your vet is the only one who can treat this. He or she will clip the hairs and clean the area—the cat will be under anesthesia. The abscess is opened, drained, and the area is then flushed with an antibiotic solution. You'll be advised on maintenance of the area because a space will be left where the abscess was, and you have to prevent the space from becoming filled with fluid.

The easiest way to deal with the problem of an abscess is to *prevent* it. Keep your cat indoors or, at the very least, have him neutered so he won't have the tendency to roam and encounter other males. Since a female can develop an abscess after a violent mating, having her spayed and keeping her indoors will prevent that danger.

INSECT STINGS

This usually happens on the head, around the mouth and the nose. Remove the stinger, if you can see it, with tweezers. Clean the area with mild soap and water, then use 3 percent hydrogen peroxide to disinfect. To relieve the itching, you can apply a thin paste of baking soda mixed with water. If there's swelling, apply a cold compress. In most cases, there are no complications from insect stings, but if your cat doesn't seem quite right or has trouble breathing, get to the vet immediately.

FRACTURES

You may notice your outdoor cat coming home with a limp or holding one leg in the air—this could mean there's a fracture. With fractures you shouldn't try to clean the wound, just gently put a cloth around the leg to prevent further injury. After the leg has been wrapped, you can try to apply a splint, but never attempt it if your cat is struggling because you'll worsen the situation.

If you do apply a splint by using the tongue depressors from your first-aid kit, make sure the ends go passed the fracture (tape each end). Fractures high on the leg shouldn't be splinted. The best advice is don't waste time trying to splint a fracture, just get your cat to the vet immediately.

THE SENIOR CITIZEN

Like humans, cats don't all age at the same rate. Some are more fortunate than others. Look at the chart in chapter 3 and you'll see how a cat ages in terms of human years. It's not 1 year equals 7 human years as we've so often heard about dogs. Your cat has reached middle age at about six years old and at ten years, she's into old age.

As with humans, the body starts functioning less effectively as a cat ages. Some changes that occur with age are:

- decreased sight
- decreased hearing
- decreased sense of smell
- decreased kidney function
- decreased absorption in the intestines
- decreased thyroid function
- decreased liver function
- decreased activity
- decreased cardiovascular output
- decreased metabolism
- decreased salivary secretion
- decreased sensitivity to thirst
- decreased pancreatic function
- degeneration of teeth and gums
- loss of muscle tone
- appearance of gray hairs, usually around the face
- thinning coat
- incontinence

CARING FOR THE OLDER CAT

■ Keep up-to-date on vaccination boosters. Your cat needs them now that her immune system is not as strong.

■ When a cat loses her sight and/or hearing with age, it happens gradually enough so she learns to adjust. With loss of sight, as long as you keep the furniture the way it's always been, she'll have very little trouble getting around. Keep her food, water, litter box, scratching post, and bed in the places she's familiar with.

■ Reduce your older cat's exposure to stress because you know how it makes animals more susceptible to disease. Older cats have more difficulty warding off disease as it is.

■ As your cat ages, she may become less careful with grooming. Brush her daily so she doesn't have to work as hard at it. This will also stimulate her sluggish oil glands. Now more than ever, use grooming time to check for lumps, warts, or anything out of the ordinary that should be examined by your vet.

■ Keep your cat's nails trimmed because she probably will be using her scratching post less often.

■ Maintain good oral health. Clean the teeth and examine the gums on a regular basis to make sure they stay healthy. Have your cat's teeth checked every time you visit the vet.

■ Continue to play with your cat, but don't expect her to do the gymnastics she was so famous for in her youth. You may have to be satisfied with her batting at the peacock feather as you wave it in front of her. Remember, don't overexert your older cat—she needs plenty of rest.

■ Provide sunlight for your aging companion to be sure she's getting a good supply of vitamin D. Imagine how good it must feel for an older cat to be able to curl up and sleep in the sun. Regular glass windows don't allow the beneficial rays to get through, so you might want to check into the possibility of installing plastic windows (they're sold in hardware stores and allow the rays to penetrate) or using a "full spectrum" light.

■ Keep your older cat warm in the winter and cool in the summer. Make sure her bed is away from drafts in the winter.

■ If your cat has always like elevated places, but is no longer able to jump up to them, make a step so she can get to those favorite spots, like the bed or a sunny window.

■ Be understanding about accidents. You may have to provide more than one litter box now to make it easier on your cat.

■ Don't bathe your cat if it's going to cause her stress. If she likes baths, then you can continue them but be extra careful about drafts. When bathing is too stressful, then do the best you can with a washcloth.

FEEDING THE OLDER CAT

As always, please stay away from poor quality foods and don't feed your cat baby food either. Continue the high quality diet, but feed small meals more often (three times a day) since it's probably difficult for her to digest large amounts of food now. To combat dry skin, be sure you're including the fatty acid supplement. The B vitamins (in the brewer's yeast) in the Vitality Mix are very important now, as is the bran for sluggish digestion. The calcium in the Mix will help prevent brittle bones.

Depending upon your particular cat's condition, your vet may prescribe a specific diet. If so, be sure to follow it faithfully. For instance, if your cat is diabetic, the vet will prescribe a specific diet and you musn't feed anything else because the amount of insulin needed will depend on what was eaten. Your vet may also prescribe a vitamin/mineral supplement now.

Be certain your cat is drinking water. Since a cat's sensitivity to thirst decreases as she gets older, to prevent dehydration you need to be aware of your cat's water intake. If you don't think she's drinking enough, you can add tomato juice or water to meals. Also, notice if she's excessively thirsty (a common sign of diabetes) and report any changes to your vet.

When a cat's sense of smell starts failing, she very often loses her desire to eat. If this happens, try sprinkling a few of her favorite morsels on top— maybe a little cooked fish, but not tuna. You can also put a little garlic in the food to arouse her appetite.

A decrease in appetite can also be caused by dental problems such as calculus, loss of teeth, or peridontal disease. Check and clean your cat's teeth regularly, and make sure the vet checks them every time you bring her in for a visit.

Since your cat is less active now that she's older, she will require less food. Don't allow your cat to become overweight because you're feeding her the same amount of food as when she was a lively three year old.

Continue your good practice of regularly weighing your cat and keep her at an ideal weight. Obesity at this age is extremely dangerous.

COMMON ILLNESSES THAT APPEAR WITH AGE

■ Kidney failure is one of the most common causes of death in older cats. Have your cat examined more than once a year (every six months) is my recommendation, so your vet can test her kidney function. For more on renal failure, refer to chapter 13.

■ Arthritis can appear in older cats, more so in overweight cats, but is more common in dogs. Your vet will prescribe treatment to help make your cat more comfortable. Don't give your cat aspirin unless specifically told to do so by your vet!

■ Cancer is another common disease that can affect older cats. Aged animals very often develop lumps. Many of these lumps are benign, but they should always be checked by a vet. For more on cancer, see chapter 13.

■ Hyperthyroidism may show up as a loss of weight. Weigh your cat on a regular basis. Any significant weight loss should be reported to your vet (see chapter 13 for more on this disease).

■ Diabetes can develop in older cats, though it's more likely to occur when a cat is also overweight. This disease is covered in chapter 13.

■ Constipation, though not a disease, is a common ailment of older cats. Keep the diet of high quality food and continue adding the Vitality Mix and the fatty acid supplement. If constipation continues to be a problem, your vet may prescribe a stool softener or laxative. **Don't** administer a stool softener without a vet's advice. Another way to help reduce the chances of constipation is to keep up the daily grooming, which cuts down on the amount of hair your cat will swallow. A hairball remedy may have to be administered in certain cases, even with your diligent grooming. Just be sure to add a little vitamin E into the food on those days.

After the love and devotion that your cat has shown you all these years, she deserves that extra TLC at this time in her life. She may not be able to bound up the stairs with the energy she used to, and she may no longer show any interest in the birds outside her window, but she's still the same wonderful companion and she's earned this retirement. Enjoy these years together.

SAYING GOODBYE

EUTHANASIA

This is a decision you may have to make someday. It's truly the most painful decision for an owner, and if you're dealing with this crisis right now, my heart goes out to you.

Euthanasia should only be performed when an animal is suffering in a way that can't be relieved and the quality of his life has deteriorated. Putting him to sleep is then the humane thing to do. Owners who want a pet euthanatized because they no longer want him, or because they can't train the animal are luckily not accommodated by most vets.

Performed by injecting an anesthetic overdose, euthanasia takes only seconds and the animal feels no pain. If you're there for the procedure, try to be calm so your pet doesn't pick up on your nervousness and get upset himself. Try your hardest to make it peaceful for him.

I know that there's always guilt associated with the decision to euthanatize a pet, but if you've discussed the situation thoroughly with your vet and you both feel that it's the best thing for your cat, then try to take comfort in the fact that you love your pet too much to let him continue to suffer.

DEALING WITH THE LOSS OF YOUR CAT

Losing a pet can be as difficult as losing any other family member. Unfortunately, society isn't always sympathetic enough when it comes to the grief you feel over your pet. You aren't offered days off from work or sent sympathy cards, and most people don't know how to give the kind of support you need at this time. My best advice, and I'm speaking from much personal experience, is to be open about your grief. Don't be embarrassed about the pain you feel over losing your beloved pet. Allow yourself the right to grieve for this cat who gave you years of love and companionship. He was a member of your family and he deserves to be mourned. If someone hands you the line about it being "only a cat," just realize that it's probably their own fear of emotions causing them to say that.

Talk about your grief—don't hold it in. There are sympathetic ears out there who are willing to listen. Any pet owner will be understanding of your pain.

There are pet loss support programs available to help owners cope with the death of a pet. Some of the larger animal hospitals have grief counselors on staff. There are also counselors available by telephone through some of the veterinary universities. Check the Appendix.

Be very sensitive when it comes to dealing with children. Discuss what happened to the cat honestly and openly. Don't talk in vague terms or try to cover it up with lines like "Fluffy went away." Not letting children know all the facts could leave them feeling guilty or responsible for what happened. With your children, plan a small memorial for your cat. Involving children in the decision making may help the grieving.

As for the subject of getting another pet, my advice is to trust your heart to know when the time is right. Don't run out and "replace" your pet—he doesn't deserve that after all the years of love. Besides, "replacing" a pet never works—the newcomer is a completely different animal and you'll end up causing frustration to yourself and to him.

With time, the pain becomes more bearable and you'll be able to look back on the years you had with your cat with loving and warm memories.

PROVIDING FOR YOUR CAT IN THE EVENT OF YOUR DEATH

Have you ever thought about what would happen to your cat in the event of your death? So many of us are used to thinking of a pet's life naturally being shorter than our own.

When you're preparing your will, include your wishes for your cat's future welfare. If you've already done your will, set up a codicil. Take the time now to find a suitable adoptive parent for your cat. Make sure they fully understand what would be involved. It's wise to have a "backup" adoptive parent, too.

Set up the codicil to your will so that the adoptive parent would be able to take your cat right away and not have to wait until the formal reading of the will. The sooner the cat gets into his new home, the better.

Once you've taken care of the legal aspect of making sure your cat would be provided for, you should take the time to ensure his emotional welfare is looked after also. Sit down and write about your cat. Tell all about his likes and dislikes. What are his favorite foods and how does he like them prepared? What are his favorite games? What kind of treats does he like and when does he expect them? Any litter preference? This information, along with his medical history records, the name of his vet, and any other facts you want to include will be VERY important should he ever have to be placed with the adoptive parent. Being put in a strange home without you will be traumatic enough—just imagine being there without *any* of the things he's used to. Providing this information will make the transition easier for both the cat and his adoptive parent.

BREEDS
IN BRIEF

The following are descriptions of the different cat breeds. In addition to the general physical descriptions, I've included some nutritional suggestions that might benefit a specific breed. As you know, any dietary alterations or supplementation should first be discussed with your vet.

Since my descriptions are very general, if you are considering getting one particular breed, I suggest you find more specific information. There are books available that cover individual breeds in depth. If possible, talk to friends who own the breed you're interested in and talk to local breeders and ask as many questions as you need. Most veterinarians are willing to answer any questions that can help you decide which cat is right for you.

Another recommendation is to find out when and where a cat show is in your area and spend a day looking at all the different breeds. Whenever I go, I find that owners and breeders who are showing their cats are more than happy to give me lots of information about their breeds.

ABYSSINIAN

The Aby is a medium-sized cat with a graceful and muscular body. The ticked coat can be red, ruddy, or blue. The head has a wedge shape with large ears. The tail is long and tapered at the end. Because the Aby is a shorthaired cat, it doesn't take much work to maintain the beautiful coat.

These cats are highly intelligent, very athletic, and extremely affectionate. If you're thinking about getting an Abyssinian, make sure you have enough room for her to run around. Abys are very active and aren't happy when confined to small spaces.

The Abyssinian breed is generally very healthy, but these cats are susceptible to gingivitis—look for inflamed gums. This is where a well-balanced diet is essential. Feeding a low magnesium, excellent quality dry food, two or three times a week might be helpful in reducing tartar accumulation.

AMERICAN SHORTHAIR

This is a medium- to large-sized, shorthaired cat with heavy shoulders and muscular legs. The large head has full cheeks. This is your classic sturdy cat. There are thirty-four colors and patterns that are recognized for this breed: white, black, cream, red, blue, in solids, or in any pattern combination—also, tortoiseshell and calico. Tabby, is of course, the classic.

These are hardy cats and the only potential health problem is obesity. Don't overfeed this cat and especially forbid table scrap stealing.

AMERICAN WIREHAIR

This cat looks like an American Shorthair but with a wiry, springy coat. Even the hairs in the ears, between the toes, and the whiskers are crimped. There are thirty-four colors and patterns for these coarse-haired cats. The coat can be easily damaged by grooming, so be very careful. A poor diet will cause breakage of the hairs, so providing this cat with top-notch nutrition is a must. The American Wirehair will reward you for your care with her good natured personality and lots of affection.

BALINESE AND JAVANESE

These cats look like a Siamese with long hair. The body is svelte and graceful, with a fine, silky coat. The wedge-shaped head has almond-shaped eyes and large pointed ears. Balinese colors are seal point, chocolate point, blue point, and lilac point. Javanese colors are red, tortie, and lynx point patterns. The mask, ear, leg, feet, and tail color contrasts with the body color.

As for personality, these cats are affectionate, highly intelligent, and good natured. Be advised though, they're vocal and very inquisitive. If you like a cat who will stick her nose into everything you're doing, then these are the cats for you. Provide this cat with lots to occupy her time, like a good sturdy scratching post, room to run, a sunny window with lots of activity, and interesting toys.

Because these are longhaired cats, you'll have to be consistent with the daily grooming.

Make sure you add the Vitality Mix to replace the B vitamins that might get used up from all that energy. Vitamin C from daily tomato juice is also a big help.

BIRMAN

This is a stocky cat with a long body. The head is round, with full cheeks and a Roman nose. The nearly round eyes are always blue. This longhaired cat has a silky coat with a heavy ruff around the neck and a long bushy tail. The Birman is known for the white gloves on her paws. Colors are seal point, chocolate point, blue point, and lilac point. The beautiful fur doesn't mat but still requires regular grooming to remove dead hairs and reduce shedding. Supplying adequate fatty acids in the diet will keep this a fit feline with fabulous fur.

The Birman is intelligent and playful. She has a quiet voice and is good with children. This is a cat who loves people and will be a gracious host to your guests.

BOMBAY

This medium-sized cat has a short, satiny, jet black coat. The fur has no other markings, but you'll find the contrast between her black coat and beautiful gold to deep copper eyes breathtaking. The eyes are set wide apart on a full face, with round ears that tip forward slightly. The male Bombay is usually larger than the female.

Companionship is what this cat likes and you'll find her to be a quiet and intelligent pet. Just groom the beautiful coat a couple times a week to keep it glossy, and you'll have a happy cat.

BRITISH SHORTHAIR

This is a medium- to large-sized cat with a powerful, compact body. The large head has full cheeks, medium-sized ears, and round eyes. The nose has a slight dip. The coat is dense, resilient, and firm to the touch. There are eighteen recognized colors and patterns in solid shades of black, blue, cream, red, and white with tabby, tortoiseshell, and calico patterns. The eye color is either gold or copper.

These cats are placid and gentle and sleeping is their favorite thing to do. To maintain muscle tone and prevent your British Shorthair from turning flabby, I suggest you make sure that the diet consists of excellent quality food. Since this cat is placid, don't make the mistake of overfeeding. The fiber in the Vitality Mix is appropriate to give to this cat because she will be satisfied and the fiber will do intestinal cleansing.

BURMESE

The Burmese is a medium-sized, shorthaired cat. The body is compact and muscular with a round head. The full face has rounded to almond-shaped eyes in gold or yellow. The ears are medium-sized with rounded tips and are set wide apart. The glossy coat comes in rich sable brown, champagne, blue, and platinum. Grooming is easy to maintain the gloss of the coat.

This athletic cat will do somersaults and tricks to amuse you. I promise you'll never be bored with a Burmese.

A generally healthy breed, kittens can be prone to respiratory diseases. The Vitality Mix is an extra booster for good health. Vitamin C a couple times a week is a good addition in this cat's diet. Keep this athlete fit by providing food with top quality protein.

CHARTREUX

These large shorthaired cats have a soft, plush blue coat in various shades. Eye color varies from gold to copper. The Chartreux has a broad head, full cheeks, and a short nose with a slight break. Male cats are usually larger than females. These are friendly cats who are good with children and other pets. They love to lounge on sunny windowsills and watch the world go by. These well-behaved cats can be groomed easily. Brush at least two times a week to keep the coat shiny and to remove loose hairs.

The health record of these cats is excellent. Be sure you don't allow your Chartreux to become overweight. A liquid fatty acid supplement added to food daily will help keep the coat shiny.

COLORPOINT SHORTHAIR

The difference between this cat and a Siamese is that each hair of the Colorpoint's coat is tipped with another color. Colors of the Colorpoint Shorthair are cream point, red point, blue-cream point, lilac-cream point, cream-lynx point, chocolate-lynx point, seal-lynx point, lilac-lynx point, blue-lynx point, red-lynx point, tortie-lynx point, blue-cream lynx point, lilac-cream lynx point, seal-tortie lynx point, seal-tortie point, and chocolate-tortie point.

This cat is of medium size with a long, lithe, muscular body. The head is wedge-shaped with slanted blue eyes and a long nose with no break. The tail is long, thin, and tapered at the end. Maintaining the lithe shape of this cat means high quality protein. Fiber is important, too, so don't forget the Vitality Mix and the vegetables.

These cats are very intelligent and outgoing. Like the Siamese, the Colorpoint has a lot to say and says it in a loud voice. She can also be demanding, but is always very loving.

CORNISH REX

This is a small- to medium-sized cat with a tight wavy coat that lies close to the body. The small narrow head has a Roman nose, large ears that stand erect, and oval eyes that slant upward. Gold is the most common eye color.

The wavy coat on this cat—even the whiskers are crinkled—is delicate and has no outer guard hairs. You must keep these cats warm. The Rex is not the cat for you if you have a drafty house, or if you keep your thermostats lower. This is not an outdoor cat. To protect the coat, do only occasional grooming with a very soft brush. Because of her lack of guard hairs, the Cornish Rex might be a good choice if you're allergic to cat hair. You'll love her playfulness. The Cornish Rex is talkative and loves to position herself right in your lap whenever you're sitting.

These cats have higher metabolisms. Their temperature is one degree higher than other breeds. Don't let your Cornish Rex overeat because they have big appetites. Good quality protein is needed for these cats' energy requirements to keep warm. The daily fatty acid supplement is essential. The Vitality Mix which is rich in B vitamins is important to maintain that energy.

CYMRIC

This large tailless cat is basically a longhaired Manx. The Cymric has a silky coat that comes in a variety of colors and patterns. The muscular hindquarters of this cat are higher than the front legs. The taillessness can be connected with defects, so be sure the cat stands and walks properly. Watch for any weakness in the hindquarters.

The Cymric is quiet, intelligent, and very loyal to her owner. These cats are also good with children and other pets.

Daily grooming is necessary to prevent matting and to remove dead hairs. You may want to give a hairball medication twice a week. If you do, add a little vitamin E to the food that day. Remember, the mineral oil-based medication for hairballs robs the body of vitamin E.

Treat this cat to a tablespoon of yogurt now and then.

DEVON REX

This is a medium-sized cat whose coat is wavy and fuzzy. The coat is longer and less curly than the Cornish Rex. The Devon Rex has a slender body and is not arched like the Cornish Rex. The face is wedge-shaped and you'll find crinkled whiskers.

The coat comes in a wide variety of colors and patterns. Groom very carefully. Don't overbrush! And, like the Cornish Rex, you must keep this cat warm. She has a higher body temperature than other cats.

The Devon Rex is a talkative cat, though not as much as the Cornish Rex or the Siamese. They love to climb and are very good with people—though **not** a choice for multicat households.

Top notch protein with good quality fat is needed for the high metabolism of the Devon Rex, so provide professional food and a daily fatty acid supplement.

EGYPTIAN MAU

The spotted coat pattern is the distinctive characteristic of this medium-sized cat. The coat colors can be bronze, silver, or smoke. The texture is silky and dense. The forehead has the characteristic "M" mark and frown lines between the ears, continuing down the back of the slightly wedge-shaped head. The lines turn into spots on the spine. The tail is dark tipped. The shoulders bear markings of spots and stripes, with heavily barred front legs. The almond-shaped eyes are light green ("gooseberry green") or amber. Both eyes and cheeks have mascara lines. Keeping the Mau's coat in tip-top shape requires grooming about twice a week to remove dead hairs.

Some Maus are more tolerant of being handled than others. Basically a reserved and quiet cat, some can be unpredictable. **Not** a breed recommended for children. The B vitamins in the Vitality Mix and brewer's yeast tablets may be a help with the unpredictability of this breed's behavior. By the way, "Mau" means "cat" in Egyptian.

EXOTIC SHORTHAIR

Exotic Shorthairs are a hybrid of the Persian and the American Shorthair. These medium- to large-sized cats look like a shorthaired Persian. The Exotic Shorthair has a massive round head, rounded ears, large round eyes, and a short nose with a deep break. The legs are short and so is the tail, though it's in proportion to the body. The dense, medium-length coat comes in a vast array of colors and patterns. These cats are easy to groom—just routine brushing to remove dead hairs. The Exotic Shorthair is great for people who love Persians, but don't have the time or desire to do the daily grooming.

These cats are quiet, gentle, and good natured. They love to make themselves comfortable, curling up in a favorite spot. They're also good with children.

Watch for the same breathing difficulties that Persians have. They can be prone to tearing eyes and sinus problems. Be sure your cat isn't breathing through her mouth or making snorting sounds.

To help ward off any infections associated with the sinuses, keep up the routine of adding the tomato juice to supply extra vitamin C (see chapter 7). Also, you might crush a 100mg vitamin C tablet in the food two or three times a week. The daily fatty acid supplement is important to help maintain that lush coat.

HAVANA BROWN

The dark, rich brown coat is what you'll notice about this beautiful cat. They're medium-sized cats (males are usually larger than females) with a graceful body and long legs. The rectangular muzzle has a distinct stop at the eyes and a break on either side of the whisker pads. The Havana Brown has a strong chin, large erect ears that tilt forward, and bright green eyes.

Normal grooming will remove the dead hairs from the coat, and you can rub with a chamois cloth to bring out the shine.

This very hardy cat loves people and other cats. She can frequently be seen grooming her roommates. Though somewhat vocal, the Havana Brown has no problem amusing herself. Place an open paper bag on the floor and watch the fun she'll have.

To maintain the glossy coat, add the daily fatty acid supplement to the food.

HIMALAYAN AND KASHMIR

This breed was developed by crossing a Persian with a Siamese. These longhaired cats have a Persian-type cobby body. The large head has a short snub nose with a break, full cheeks, and large round blue eyes. The small ears are round and tilted forward. The tail is full and short but in proportion to body length. The coat forms a ruff around the neck.

Himalayans have point patterns in seal point, blue point, chocolate point, lilac point, flame (red) point, cream point, tortie-point, blue-cream point, blue-lynx point, and seal-lynx point. The Kashmirs have solid colors of chocolate or lilac with no points. Daily grooming is necessary to prevent tangles.

Himalayans and Kashmirs have a tendency toward malformed tear ducts so their eyes may tear. Some cats may also be susceptible to respiratory infections.

These cats are intelligent, gentle, and affectionate. If you already have a pet in your household, you'll find these cats get along just fine with other animals. If you like to hear purring, these cats make a louder sound than Persians, but, of course, not as loud as the Siamese.

Make sure you encourage plenty of exercise so your cat doesn't become overweight. The fatty acid supplement will help prevent a dry coat. Give a hairball remedy twice a week between meals—put vitamin E in the food on those days.

JAPANESE BOBTAIL

You guessed it, the bobbed tail is the distinctive characteristic of this medium- to large-sized cat. The tail is held erect and may form a corkscrew or have kinks. The fur on the tail is thick and grows in all directions—similar to a rabbit's tail. The body of the Japanese Bobtail is muscular with tall hind legs that are angled so the cat looks level. The triangular head has high cheekbones with an obvious whisker break. The eyes are slanted and the large ears face upright.

The preferred color of the Japanese Bobtail is tricolored. The Japanese believe that to be good luck. Twenty-three color combinations are recognized: basically, patches of white, black, and red-orange (calico), bicolors of white and black or white and red, and solid colors of white, red, or black. Also included are tortoiseshell patterns with cream, black, and red.

These cats are affectionate and love being right in the thick of things, but you must be *very careful* of their tails. The sensitive tail is easily injured. Manipulation of it can cause **severe** pain and permanent damage. Once injured, the cat will always be fearful. This breed is **not** recommended for children.

Another thing about these cats—they love water, so don't be surprised if your Japanese Bobtail tries to take a swim in your bathtub.

KORAT

This is a medium-sized cat with a semicobby body. The glossy coat is silver-blue tipped with silver (the more silver, the better), lying close to the body. The head is heart-shaped with the eyebrow ridges forming the upper curves of the heart and the sides of the face curving to the chin, forming the heart's bottom. The large eyes are slanted, though they look round when open. Eye color is green and green-gold. Ears are flared at the base and rounded at the tips.

The Korat is a very intelligent, lively cat. They are protective of family members and suspicious of strangers. Korats are not especially vocal, but are extremely alert. They have been known to alert the family of an emergency.

Regular brushing (twice a week) will help maintain the glossy coat, and encourage the cat to exercise to keep the muscles toned. A high quality diet is essential to keep this cat from becoming flabby. Twice a week crush a 100mg tablet of vitamin C into the meal.

MAINE COON

This is a L-A-R-G-E cat (somewhere between twelve and nineteen pounds). The shaggy coat comes in all colors and patterns. The medium-sized head has a squarish muzzle and large, wide-set eyes. The large tufted ears are set high on the head. The large paws are tufted and the long tail has lots of flowing fur.

The Maine Coons are successful hunters and are very rugged. They can endure harsh climate changes, and yet they're so good natured and have sweet, small voices.

Even though this is a longhaired cat, the fur doesn't mat easily, so brushing two or three times a week will probably be all that's necessary to remove the dead hair and reduce shedding. Dental maintenance is a must. Check for tartar accumulation and watch that gums stay healthy.

This is a hardy cat, though kinked tails sometimes appear. To keep your Maine Coon healthy, don't let her get fat. She's already big enough. Feed top quality food, alternating brands. For good dental health include low magnesium dry food in the diet two or three times a week.

MALAYAN

The Malayan is different from the Burmese in color only. Malayan colors are champagne, blue, and platinum; Burmese are sable brown. This medium-sized cat has a compact body, good muscle tone, and strong shoulders. Like the Burmese, you'll find the Malayan has a surprising weight for her size. Eye color is gold. The glossy coat lies close to the body and is easy to groom. After a gentle brushing, rub with a chamois to bring out the shine.

This assertive cat is the boss of the house. She's very lively, and there will never be a dull moment in your home if you own a Malayan.

Don't let this cat get fat. To keep the good muscle tone, you have to provide a well-balanced diet with good quality protein. The Vitality Mix, which is rich in B complex, and the vitamin C in the tomato juice help ward off potential respiratory problems. A vitamin C tablet (100mg) every now and then might be a good idea also.

MANX

Taillessness is the distinctive characteristic of this medium-sized cat. The body is firm, muscular, and deceptively heavy. The Manx really is a round-looking cat with a round head and full face. Adding to the roundness are a thick neck and a short back that arches from the shoulder to rump. This is unique in Manx cats.

Some Manx cats have tiny tails. The ones with the longest are called "tailies," the shortest are called "stumpies," and the tailless are called "rumpies." The lack of a tail is really a spinal defect and it can come with some special problems. Make sure the cat can stand, walk, and run normally, and has no weakness in the hindquarters.

The fur has a cottony undercoat with a glossy, hard-textured topcoat. The coat comes in all colors and patterns, and a twice weekly brushing will keep it in good condition. The daily fatty acid supplement and a well-balanced diet will keep the coat glossy and maintain the body's muscle tone.

A one-on-one relationship is the Manx cat's specialty. They are great companions for single people. They're affectionate, loyal, and have a soft voice. Oh, yes, they are also devilish!

NORWEGIAN FOREST CAT

These cats are able to endure the harsh Norwegian climate because their coat is water-resistant. The long fur has an undercoat and outer oily guard hairs. The Norwegian Forest Cat is medium to large in size with a relatively long body and a full chest. The muscular hind legs are higher than the front legs, and the tail is long and flowing.

Intelligent, alert, and loving, these cats hate to be alone. Your Norwegian Forest Cat will always be within petting distance.

The beautiful coat on these cats can come in all colors and combinations. Since the coat is water-resistant, you shouldn't bathe this cat because you'll remove the oil. Grooming is easy because despite the length, the coat doesn't mat or tangle. Just groom two or three times a week to remove dead hairs. In addition to making the coat look better, it will greatly reduce the amount of hairs you find on your sofa. Brushing also distributes the oil evenly over the coat. Grooming is most important when the Norwegian Forest Cat is shedding her winter coat. Give this cat a hairball remedy twice a week. Don't forget the vitamin E on those days.

OCICAT

The beautiful thing about these cats is that they have a feral appearance. They look wild with the spotted pattern coat. The coat consists of dark spots on a lighter background; Ocicats come in eight colors. The texture is satiny and it lies close to the body. This cat's long muscular body is very athletic. Females are medium in size while males are larger (twelve to fifteen pounds). They have a modified oval head and almond-shaped eyes that are angled downward toward the nose.

Despite their feral appearance, Ocicats are very gentle and friendly. These warm, good-natured animals are very good with children. Being a relative of the Siamese, they are also somewhat vocal.

This is a very healthy breed. The B vitamins in the Vitality Mix will help calm any Siamese nervousness in them.

ORIENTAL SHORTHAIR

Except for the color, this medium-sized cat resembles the Siamese. The Oriental Shorthair comes in numerous colors and patterns; many are unique to the breed. Like the Siamese, this cat has a long lean body and a long pointed tail. The wedge-shaped head has almond-shaped eyes and a straight nose. The coat is short and hard and very easy to groom.

These chatty cats are intelligent, loyal, and very affectionate. They can be a little high-strung, so make sure you're putting the Vitality Mix into every meal—the B vitamins are needed by energetic cats. When you give treats, use brewer's yeast tablets because they, too, will help alleviate some of the nervousness.

The Oriental Shorthairs are generally very healthy, but some cats can be prone to upper respiratory illnesses.

PERSIAN

These elegant cats are medium- to large-sized, with large round heads. The small, round-tipped ears are set far apart, low on the head, and tilt forward. The snub nose has a deep break. The round eyes are very large and give the Persian a sweet expression. The cobby body sits low on the short thick legs. The tail is short but in proportion to the body.

The beautiful long hair on these cats comes in more than fifty colors and patterns. The ears and toes are tufted, the tail is very full, and the ruff between the front legs is full. Daily grooming is absolutely essential to prevent tangles and mats. An occasional bath may also be necessary to remove excess oil from the coat. Also, because the snub nose puts pressure on the tear ducts, you'll find that your Persian's eyes run. Clean the eyes at least once a day with a damp cotton ball or swab.

Some white cats are born deaf. They usually have blue eyes or are odd-eyed (being deaf on the blue-eyed side). Deaf cats should never be allowed outdoors.

Persians are quiet, affectionate, and are not as active as other cats. You musn't let your Persian get fat. FUS (see page 175) is more likely to occur in inactive cats, so be sure you're feeding high quality food, the Vitality Mix, and the tomato juice.

Persians need hairball medication twice a week, with the addition of vitamin E in the food on those days.

RAGDOLL

This relative of the Persian and Birman is very large and heavy. The Ragdoll has a modified wedge-shaped head and a nose with a slight break. The large oval eyes are blue in color. The chest on this cat is broad and the hindquarters are high. The medium to long coat comes in three coat patterns: colorpointed, mitted, and bicolored. The colors can be seal point, blue point, chocolate point, and lilac point. The coat doesn't mat, but regular grooming is needed to remove dead hair and keep the fur looking its best.

Ragdolls are good natured, love people, and talk only when they're upset. Their two favorite things are sleeping and eating.

This cat will eat and eat and eat, so don't leave food available during the day and watch that she doesn't become overweight. Table scraps are out of the question. A hairball remedy should be given twice a week. Mix a little vitamin E in the food on those days.

RUSSIAN BLUE

The plush double coat of blue is the important characteristic of this cat. The short silky coat is bright blue with the guard hairs tipped, giving the coat a silvery sheen. Other physical characteristics include a muscular, graceful body and a wedge-shaped head. The face is broad across the eyes and the top of the skull is long and flat. The eyes are a vivid green. The large ears are wide at the bottom and moderately pointed at the tips.

The coat on the Russian Blue doesn't lie flat. When grooming, brush backward, then brush in the right direction. You don't want to flatten the coat.

These observant, gentle cats are easy to train. Females are extremely quiet, but males can be temperamental if handled too much. These cats are also affectionate and very devoted to their owners.

The Russian Blues are very healthy, but because they're relatively reserved, don't let them become obese. The fatty acid supplement will help keep the plush coat looking magnificent. You may need to give a hairball remedy to your Russian Blue once a week. If so, add a little vitamin E in the meal.

SCOTTISH FOLD

The distinctive ears fold forward and down on these medium-sized cats. The head is round with prominent cheeks and whisker pads. Males can have a jowly appearance. The eyes are round and the nose is short with no break—just a slight dip. Body shape is round. The coat is short, dense, and easy to groom. Twenty-three colors and patterns are available.

This breed is affectionate and quiet. The Scottish Fold is good natured and gets along with other pets.

Think very carefully before deciding to get a Scottish Fold. The ears need special care and can be a potential problem. This may not be the cat for first time owners. Regular ear maintenance is needed to prevent infection and ear mites. Once a week, gently clean ears with a cotton swab dipped in a mild hydrogen peroxide solution. White cats may be deaf. Check to make sure there is no lack of mobility due to the short legs of this cat. The tail should be flexible. Thick inflexible legs or tail indicate fusion of the spinal column.

Top quality nutrition is important to the Scottish Fold. The brewer's yeast in the Vitality Mix and garlic will help guard against ear mites. Vitamin C twice a week and the daily dose of vitamin C in the tomato juice will help keep your cat in top form.

At the first sign of ear mites (tiny black specks) or any other problems, take your cat to the vet immediately.

SIAMESE

The Siamese has a long body that sits on tall slim legs; the hind legs are slightly taller than the front. The head is long and wedge-shaped. The almond-shaped eyes slant toward the nose. Eye color is vivid blue. The profile of this cat's head is straight with no dip in the nose or whisker break. The ears are large and pointed. The long tapered tail is whiplike and should not be kinked. The short tight coat has a light body color with darker points on the mask, ears, feet, and tail. Point colors are seal, chocolate, lilac, or blue. The coat is very easy to groom.

Let me start by telling you that I spend much of my day trying to figure out ways to outsmart my cat, Albert (who is only one-half Siamese), and I have yet to succeed. Siamese cats know everything! You can't keep any secrets from them and, believe me, they don't keep any secrets from you. Your Siamese will tell you exactly what's on her mind. If you're ten seconds late with dinner, you'll hear about it. The Siamese is extremely intelligent and fearless. She can be sweet one minute and demanding the next. I warn you though, if you don't want a talkative cat, don't consider getting a Siamese. Many people find their voice annoying.

Adult Siamese cats are very healthy. There is some susceptibility to upper respiratory disease in young cats.

These athletic cats need those B vitamins in the Vitality Mix. Vitamin C (100mg) twice a week is also a good idea. This lean animal needs a top notch diet providing the highest quality protein. Adding some fresh vegetables, like grated carrot, will also help with intestinal cleansing.

SINGAPURA

This sociable cat has a small muscular body. The head is round with a broad muzzle and a blunt nose. The ears are large and slightly pointed. Eye color can be hazel, yellow, or green. The Singapura's coat is tight and silky, in an ivory color with dark brown ticking.

These cats have delightful personalities. You'll discover them to be playful, devoted, and quiet. They're very sociable and are comfortable when there are strangers in the house.

SNOWSHOE

A medium- to large-sized cat, the Snowshoe has a solid muscular body. The head is a modified wedge, with large ears that are wide at the base but pointed at the tips. The blue eyes are oval in shape. The tail tapers toward the end. The glossy coat is medium length and close-lying. The color is a lightly shaded body color with Siamese-like points on the mask, ears, legs, and tail. The face has a white "V" pattern. The chest, chin, and muzzle are white. Front paws are white tipped and the hind legs are white up to the hock. Grooming once or twice a week will keep the coat glossy and remove dead hairs.

This cat is quiet and alert. Your Snowshoe will be very devoted to you and follow you everywhere.

Don't let this cat get fat. The Snowshoe should feel muscular and firm. To keep the muscles toned, provide excellent nutrition, the Vitality Mix, and set aside some playtime each day.

SOMALI

A medium-sized cat, the Somali is really a longhaired Abyssinian. Somali colors are ruddy, red, or blue. The fur is longer on the ruff and breeches and the tapered tail is a thick brush. Head shape is a slightly rounded wedge with large tufted ears that are slightly pointed. The almond-shaped ears are large and expressive. Eye color is gold or green. The back is slightly arched with a rounded rib cage.

Despite the fact that this is a longhaired cat, the coat on the Somali doesn't easily tangle. Daily grooming will reduce shedding and hairballs. Use a natural bristle brush and be gentle so you don't break the fine fur.

The Somali is an affectionate cat who loves company. Make sure you have lots of room because this is an active cat who dislikes confinement. The B complex vitamins in the brewer's yeast will help calm your Somali if she gets too revved up.

SPHYNX

The Sphynx is virtually hairless. The other distinctive characteristic is the wrinkled skin. In the winter, the Sphynx does get a very fine down. The body type is similar to the Rex. The ears are large and the eyes are very expressive.

The body temperature of the Sphynx is several degrees higher than other breeds. You must always protect this cat from the cold. Buy a sweater or T-shirt for your Sphynx. This is a cat who doesn't store fat, so she must eat more often—feed her four times a day. Obesity isn't a problem for the Sphynx. High quality protein and a fatty acid supplement are a must.

Grooming involves an occasional wipe with a warm damp sponge to remove dander and excess oil. If skin becomes rough and dry, massage gently with vitamin E oil.

As you could guess, the Sphynx loves warm body contact. This is an affectionate, sensitive cat who purrs often.

TIFFANY

This is the longhaired version of the Burmese. The difference is its silky, medium-long coat. The color of this cat is sable with gold eyes. The hair tends to mat on the tail and hindquarters, so daily grooming is needed.

The Tiffany is soft-voiced, playful, and devoted. This is a cat who will follow you from room to room.

Like the Burmese, this cat depends on high quality protein food. Hairball medication may be needed once or twice a week. Add vitamin E to the food on those days.

TONKINESE

The Tonkinese is a cross between a Siamese and a Burmese. This is a medium-sized cat (males are larger than females) with a solid, muscular build. Hind legs are slightly longer than the front. The head is a modified wedge with high cheekbones. The almond-shaped eyes are slightly rounded at the bottom and blue-green in color. The glossy coat is close-lying and comes in five colors. The point colors that dilute into body color are natural mink, honey mink, champagne mink, platinum mink, and blue mink. To keep the coat looking its best, groom with a rubber brush, then use a chamois cloth to enhance gloss.

These are chatty cats who love to climb, so nothing is safe around your house. I recommend that you provide this cat with a sturdy place to climb. Purchase or build a cat tree. If you can't find a sturdy enough one in your local pet store, you can order them through the mail. Check *Cat Fancy or Cats* magazine.

The Tonkinese is a healthy breed, though kittens are susceptible to upper respiratory diseases. Like the Siamese and Burmese, high quality protein food is essential for these cats. Fiber is also important, so don't forget the Vitality Mix and the fresh vegetables.

TURKISH ANGORA

Small- to medium-sized, the Turkish Angora has a graceful, firm body with higher hind legs. The fine, silky coat is medium long with a ruff around the neck, a full brush tail, and tufted ears. Solid colors are white, black, cream, blue, and red. Classic and mackerel tabby patterns are in brown, silver, cream, red, and blue. Other patterns are tortoiseshell, calico, dilute calico, blue cream, blue smoke, and bicolor. Blue-eyed white cats are often deaf. Odd-eyed cats may be deaf on the blue-eyed side.

The coat on the Turkish Angora is not as thick as the Persian's but requires frequent grooming. You should also regularly check the teeth for tartar accumulation.

These cats are intelligent, playful, and good-natured. Turkish Angoras also like water. They are devoted to their owners and are best for single pet households.

Hairball medication twice a week is recommended—vitamin E goes in the food on those days.

A NOTE ON COLORS

Solid color means each hair is one overall shade from the root to the tip.

Shaded or **tipped** has a light undercoat with a darker color on the tips of the hairs. The coat appears to be one overall color, but if you part the hair you'll see the light undercoat.

Point colors refer to the mask, ears, legs, feet, and tail, which are known as the points, that are a dark color, contrasting with the lighter body color. The mask is the whole face but not over the top of the head.

Particolor coats have two or more distinct colors. This includes the popular tortoiseshell (black with large red and cream patches) and calico (tortoiseshell and white).

Tabby has complex patterns (usually stripes) in two or more colors.

CAT SHOWS

At one time or another, just about every cat owner toys with the idea of entering their cat in a show. Across the country there are numerous shows each year, from the small fun ones to the large and prestigious competitions.

Cat shows offer a spectator the opportunity to conveniently see all the different breeds of cats. They also offer cat owners the opportunity to compare notes on specific breeds. These shows are very important to the professional breeder, as a winning cat can mean bigger business.

There is, unfortunately, a very big negative that goes along with cat shows, and that is the *danger* they pose to cats. While care is taken to ensure that only healthy animals are entered, there are many cats who develop upper respiratory infections after the show. Sometimes the infection is mild, but there are cases where it becomes severe. A cat returning from a show where he has contracted an upper respiratory infection can end up infecting other cats at home or in the cattery. These infections can be fatal. So if you are intent on showing your cat, keep him in his cage while at the show, and don't allow spectators or other cat owners to pet or handle him.

My personal feeling on cat shows is that unless you're a professional breeder and your business growth depends on whether you have Grand Champions in your cattery, then I suggest you not expose your pet to these dangers. Cats must endure a large amount of stress during these shows which makes them more susceptible to disease.

IF YOU DECIDE TO SHOW YOUR CAT

Before you plunge into the idea of showing your cat, I suggest you first go to a show as a spectator. It will be much easier on you and your cat if you're familiar with what will be expected of you beforehand. To find out when and where the nearest show will be held, check *Cat Fancy* or *Cats* magazine. They carry the on-going calendar.

CAT REGISTRY ORGANIZATIONS

There are many cat shows and the guidelines and classifications vary among the different organizations. First, register your cat with one of the registry organizations. In the Appendix, you will find a list of the most popular registries—write to them for information.

ENTERING YOUR CAT

Check your *Cat Fancy* or *Cats* magazine for upcoming shows. The name, address, and phone number of the entry clerk will be listed. About eight weeks before the show, write or call and request show information and an entry form. Also state that you're new at this, because some organizations supply additional information for novices. The information flyer you'll receive along with your entry form will provide show location, all fees, who will be judging, and everything else you'll need to know.

When you receive your entry form, read it over very carefully and be sure you fill it in correctly. There will be a space for cage requirements (you rent these). You can request a single (24" x 24" x 24") or a double (24" x 24" x 48"). There is also a space on the form where you write in which classification you're entering your cat. Be sure you read all the show rules correctly so you don't make a mistake on any item.

Mail the completed entry form with the fee and you'll get written confirmation from the show secretary. Hold onto this because you'll need it when you check in at the show.

Cats can compete in three major categories. Here is a brief explanation of the Cat Fanciers' Association classes.

CHAMPIONSHIP:

OPEN CLASS
For registered cats who are eight months or older on the opening day of the show, who haven't yet completed the requirements for Championship. After winning the required number of ribbons, the cat qualifies for confirmation as a Champion.

CHAMPION CLASS
For recognized Champions who are not Grand Champions yet. A cat must receive 200 points to qualify as a Grand Champion.

GRAND CHAMPION CLASS
For cats that have received enough wins or points by beating other Champions.

KITTEN

Kittens must be over four months and under eight months on the first day of the show.

HOUSEHOLD PET

Open to domestic cats or kittens of unknown or mixed ancestry. Cats over eight months old must be neutered or spayed. Declawed cats aren't eligible. Judging is based on beauty, coloring, grooming, disposition during handling, and overall condition.

PROVISIONAL BREED

For breeds where the CFA has provisionally accepted the standard but are not yet recognized for Championship classes.

AOV CLASS (ANY OTHER VARIETY)

Refers to pedigree kittens or cats entitled to Championship, but who don't conform to standard because of some physical feature.

PREMIERSHIP:

OPEN

For cats over eight months who are neutered or spayed and who have not yet completed Premiership.

PREMIER

Recognized Premiers (must be neutered or spayed) but not yet Grand Premiers. Seventy-five points are required to compete as a Grand Premier.

GRAND PREMIER

Neutered or spayed cats who have enough wins or points from beating other Premiers.

PREPARING FOR THE SHOW

■ All cats must be vaccinated, clean, healthy, and free of parasites, such as fleas, ear mites, and fungus.

■ Since your cat will have to be caged during the show, make sure in advance that he's comfortable with this. A cat who is not used to being confined like that will end up displaying his worst behavior at the show and you'll both end up being nervous wrecks.

■ Meticulous grooming should begin about a month prior to the show.

■ Make drapes for the cage to allow privacy and to prevent hissing by neighboring cats. Draping three sides of the cage will greatly reduce the amount of stress on your cat. Also, use a towel to line the bottom of the cage.

■ Disposable litter boxes are usually provided by the show, but you may wish to buy your own "cage size" pan just in case.

■ Most shows make cat food available to the competitors, but I urge you to bring your own. While under stress, your cat needs the food he's used to. Don't forget that you'll also need food and water bowls, a can opener, a spoon, and a small plastic garbage bag.

THE DAY OF THE SHOW

Plan to be there at least an hour before judging begins so you can check in and get settled. Before leaving for the show, make sure you've packed everything you'll need, such as food and feeding supplies, grooming tools, some toys, paper towels, a small garbage bag, your entry confirmation, the drapes for the cage, a couple of towels, and a nontoxic disinfectant in case you want to disinfect the cage. You can ask your vet for a recommendation on which disinfectant to use.

Your cat should be transported in his carrier, which should be labeled with your name and address.

When you arrive at the show, check in with the secretary. Your cat will be assigned a number which will correspond with the number on his cage. His number will be called over the loudspeaker when it's time for him to go to the judging ring. Find out when your cat is due to be judged so you'll have enough time to prepare him. Before you put him in the cage, use the nontoxic disinfectant and then arrange the towel, drapes, litter box, and water bowl. When you hear his number called, proceed to the judging ring and put him in the cage there. The judge will put him on the table in front of the spectators' chairs and proceed to evaluate him. This is where a cat show is fascinating as you watch the judge's expert eyes and hands go over every inch of the cat.

While you're at the show, politely discourage people from touching your cat with, of course, the exception of the judges. Some people put little signs on the cages that say "Please Don't Touch."

APPENDIX

The addresses and phone numbers in this Appendix are current as of June, 1990.

SOURCES FOR ADDITIONAL INFORMATION

ASPCA (American Society for the Prevention of Cruelty to Animals)
441 East 92nd Street
New York, NY 10128
(212-831-6006)

For information on low-cost spay/neuter programs and general animal welfare education.

American Veterinary Medical Association
930 North Meacham Road
Schaumburg, IL 60196
(312-605-8070)

Will help you locate a vet in your area and can provide information on vets who specialize.

Feline Health Center Cornell University College of Veterinary Medicine
Ithaca, NY 14853
(607-253-3414)

Publishes newsletters for the public and for vets. Has a hotline number where a vet answers questions on feline health. Hotline number is (607) 253-3934.

University of California at Davis School of Veterinary Medicine
Davis, CA 95616

Has a Pet Loss Support Hotline to help owners deal with the death of a pet. Hotline number is (916) 752-4200. Hours: 5:30-9:30 P.M., Monday-Friday.

University of Pennsylvania School of Veterinary Medicine
Philadelphia, PA 19104

By making a donation to the small animal clinic, you can become a subscriber to their informative newsletter. They also hold an annual Feline Symposium each spring. Write for Symposium information or call (215) 898-8862.

Colorado State University
School of Veterinary Medicine
Ft. Collins, CO 80523
(303-221-4535)

*Their program is called
CHANGES: Support for Pets and
People, which provides pet loss
counseling for CSU clients. There is
also educational material available
for the general public.*

University of Georgia
School of Veterinary Medicine
Athens, GA 30602

*There is a Toxicology Hotline open
8:00 A.M.-5:00 P.M. on weekdays.
Hotline number is (404) 542-6751.*

College of Veterinary
Medicine
Kansas State University
Manhattan, KS 66506
(913-532-5700)

*Phone consultations are available
weekdays from 8:00 A.M.-5:00 P.M.*

Cat Fanciers' Association
1309 Allaire Avenue
Ocean, NJ 07712

For information on breeds.

CAT PUBLICATIONS

Cat Fancy Magazine
P.O. Box 6050
Mission Viejo, CA 92690

Cats Magazine
P.O. Box 37
Port Orange, FL 32029

CAT EQUIPMENT

Petdoors U.S.A.
4523 30th Street, W.
Bradenton, FL 34207

pet doors

Hobar Mfg., Inc.
Route 56 at King Street
Leicester, MA 01524

*attachable carpeted window
shelf, grooming table*

Booda Products
439 S. Detroit Street
Los Angeles, CA 90036

litter box

The Felix Company
3623 Fremont Avenue N.
Seattle, WA 98103

scratching posts

Galkie Company
P.O. Box 20
Harrogate, TN 37752
(615-869-8138)

Kitty Tease toy

Ecco Bella
6 Provost Square
Suite 602
Caldwell, NJ 07006
(201-226-5799)

natural herbal products

Neo-Life Company of America
P.O. Box 5012
Fremont, CA 94537-5012

ionizer, "Green" liquid soap

MAIL-ORDER COMPANIES
Write or call for catalogs.

Master Animal Care
411 Seventh Avenue
Two Harbors, MN 55616-0007
(800-346-0749)

Drs. Foster & Smith, Inc.
509 Shepard Street
P.O. Box 100
Rhinelander, WI 54501
(715-369-3305)

Care-A-Lot Pet Supply Warehouse
1617 Diamond Springs Road
Virginia Beach, VA 23455
(800-343-7680)

CAT FOOD MANUFACTURERS

Alpo Pet Food, Inc.
Lehigh Valley, PA 18001-2187
(800-366-6033)

Alpo Cat Food

Carnation Company
5045 Wilshire Blvd.
Los Angeles, CA 90036
(213-932-6000)

*Chef's Blend, Bright Eyes, Fancy
Feast, Friskies Buffet, Fish Ahoy,
Tidbits, Fresh Catch, Perform*

Hill's Pet Products, Inc.
P.O. Box 148
Topeka, KS 66601
(800-445-5777)

*Science Diet Feline Maintenance,
Feline Growth, Feline Maintenance
Light, special prescription formulas*

The Iam's Company
7520 Poe Avenue
Dayton, OH 45414
(800-525-4267)

*Iams Cat Food, Iams Kitten Food,
Iams Less Active*

Kal Kan Foods, Inc.
Vernon, CA 90058
(800-525-5273)

Kal Kan, Sheba, Whiskas

Ralston Purina Co.
Checkerboard Square
St. Louis, MO 63164
(800-345-5678)

Purina, Pro Plan, Tender Vittles,
Happy Cat, Thrive, Cat Chow,
Kitten Chow, Meow Mix, Alley
Cat, Special Dinners, Smart Cat,
Kit 'n Kaboodle, Select

Pet Specialities, Inc.
Consumer Affairs
P.O. Drawer 287
Nashville, TN 37202
(800-722-3261)

ANF Tami Cat Formula
ANF Tami Kitten Formula

Star-Kist Foods, Inc.
Heinz Pet Products
180 East Ocean Blvd.
Long Beach, CA 90802
(213-590-7900)

9-Lives, Amore, Tender Meals,
Kozy Kitten, Kitten Dinners

Triumph Pet Industries
P.O. Box 100
Hillburne, NY 10931
(914-357-6666)

Triumph, Hi-Tor

Veterinary Nutritional
Associates, Inc.
229 Wall Street
Huntington, NY 11743
(516-427-7479)

Cornucopia

Wysong Medical Corporation
1880 North Eastman
Midland, MI 48640
(517-631-0009)

Feline Vitality

Bumble Bee Seafoods, Inc.
P.O. Box 23508
San Diego, CA 92123
(619-560-0404)

Figaro Tuna

Tyrrell's Inc.
P.O. Box 31126
Seattle, WA 98103
(206-632-4472)

Tyrrell's

Lick Your Chops, Inc.
50 Water Street
Norwalk, CT 06854
(203-854-5001)

Lick Your Chops

Old Mother Hubbard
Pet Food Co.,Inc.
P.O. Box 1719
Lowell, MA 01853-2411
(617-454-8083)

Old Mother Hubbard

Natures Recipe
1050 N. Batavia
Orange, CA 92613
(714-639-1134)

Optimum Feline Diet

Pet Guard, Inc.
P.O. Box 728
Orange Park, FL 32073
(904-264-8500)

Premium

Health Valley Foods
700 Union Street
Montebello, CA 90640
(213-724-2211)

Health Valley

Edward Lowe Industries, Inc.
21752 Allegheny Road
Cassopolis, MI 49031
(616-445-3886)

Perfect Menu

Nutro Products Inc.
445 Wilson Way
City of Industry, CA 91744
(818-968-0532)

Max Cat

Natural Life Pet Products, Inc.
P.O. Box 476
Maple Plain, MN 55359
(612-479-2280)

Feline Formula

Beecham Laboratories
501 Fifth Street
Bristol, TN 37620

Pet Tabs-Feline, FaVor
vitamin/mineral supplements

BenePet Care Products
P.O. Box 8111
St. Joseph, MO 64508

Felo-Pet
vitamin/mineral supplement

Norden Laboratories
601 West Cornhusker Hwy.
Lincoln, NE 68521

Felobits, ProBalance
vitamin/mineral supplements

Pet Food Institute
1101 Connecticut Avenue, N.W.
Washington, DC 20036

pet food labeling guidelines,
AAFCO testing protocols

Charles P. Frank
Georgia Dept. of Agriculture
Capital Square
Atlanta, GA 30334
(404-656-3637)

Official Publication of AAFCO
($20.00)

CAT I.D. TAGS

Boulder Brass Works
5421 Western Avenue
Boulder, CO 80301

**Merion Station Mail Order
Co. Inc.**
Box 6
Merion Station, PA 19066

Pet Tag Company
5695 Xenon Way
P.O. Box 668
Arvada, CO 80001

St. James & Son
Box 15626
San Diego, CA 92115
(800-345-8911)

Vet Tag Supply
P.O. Box 301
Merion Station, PA 19066

CAT REGISTRY ORGANIZATIONS

**The American Cat
Association, Inc.**
8101 Katherine Avenue
Panorama City, CA 91402

**American Cat Fanciers'
Association, Inc.**
P.O. Box 203
Point Lookout, MO 65726

Cat Fanciers' Association, Inc.
1309 Allaire Avenue
Ocean, NJ 07712

Cat Fanciers' Federation, Inc.
9509 Montgomery Road
Cincinnati, OH 45242

**TICA — The International
Cat Association**
P.O. Box 2988
Harlingen, TX 78551

United Cat Federation
5510 Ptolemy Way
Mira Loma, CA 91752

PET SHIPPING COMPANIES

ARIZONA

Canine Country Club
2332 East Washington Avenue
Phoenix, AZ 85034
(602-244-8171)

CALIFORNIA

A Dog's World
2869 Ridgeway Drive
National City, CA 92050
(619-267-2577)

Jet Pets
9014 Pershing Drive
Los Angeles International
Airport
Playa Del Rey, CA 90291
(213-823-8901)

Pet Express, Inc.
P.O. Box 881390
San Francisco, CA 94188
(415-822-7111)

COLORADO

Pegasus Pet Shipping Service
P.O. Box 1302
Arvada, CO 80212
(303-431-4951)

CONNECTICUT

Canine Carriers
5 Brook Street
P.O. Box 3271
Darien, CT 06820
(800-243-9105)
(203-655-7295)

FLORIDA

Air Animal Inc.
4120 W. Cypress Street
Tampa, FL 33607-2358
(813-879-3210)

Jet Pet International
Country Squire Kennel
7855 S.W. 94th Street
Miami, FL 33156
(305-251-3238)

ILLINOIS

Air Pet Transport
7560 Central Avenue
River Forest, IL 60305
(312-366-7080)

Pet Express, Inc.
2071 Irving Park Road
Hanover Park, IL 60103
(312-289-3900)

MASSACHUSETTS

Holiday Kennels, Inc.
1014 Pearl Street
Brockton, MA 02401
(508-583-8555)

MICHIGAN

May-Will Kennel
6792 Rochester Road
Troy, MI 48098
(313-879-0530)

MISSOURI

KCI Pet Services
13720 N. Nevada Street
P.O. Box 20705
Kansas City, MO 64195
(816-464-2325)

Kennelwood Village
2008 Kratky Road
St. Louis, MO 63114
(314-429-2100)

NEW YORK

**Pet Travel Agency at
Emerald Acres Pet Motel**
R.D. 5, Box 281A
Mariaville Road
Schenectady, NY 12306
(518-355-1749)

World Wide Pet Transport
13-14 College Point Blvd.
College Point, NY 11356
(718-539-5543)

NORTH CAROLINA

**Charlotte Transpets
Paws Inn Kennel**
5420 George Street
Charlotte, NC 28208
(704-399-1609)

OHIO

Charmac's
11798 Hamilton Avenue
Cincinnati, OH 45231
(513-825-0840)

PENNSYLVANIA

The Funny Farm
211 Echo Road
Carlisle, PA 17013
(717-249-5512)

Frame's Kennels
1119 Haverford Road
Ridley Park, PA 19078
(215-521-1123)

**Parkway Kennels
Parkway West Pet Care
Center**
R.D. #5, Box 90
Gringo-Clinton Road
Coraopolis, PA 15108
(412-774-2727 or
412-262-2727)

TEXAS

Animal Care Center
6321 Bissonnet Street
Houston, TX 77074
(713-774-2595)

**Pet Mobile/Animal Port
Houston**
P.O. Box 60564 AMF
Houston, TX 77205
(713-821-2244)

WASHINGTON

Atwood's Pet Transport
2040 S. 142nd Street
Seattle, WA 98168
(206-241-0880)

WISCONSIN

Animal Motel
13175 W. Silver Spring Road
P.O. Box 228
Butler, WI 53007-0228
(414-781-5200)

Golrusk Pet Care Center
1991 Allouez Avenue
Green Bay, WI 54311
(414-468-7956)

INDEX